# COUNTRY MATTERS

Signed by the Author

# Country
# Matters

## A COUNTRYSIDE COMPANION
74 tips, tales and talking points

## MEG CLOTHIER AND
## JONNY CLOTHIER

PROFILE BOOKS

First published in Great Britain in 2023 by
PROFILE BOOKS LTD
29 Cloth Fair
London ECIA 7JQ
*www.profilebooks.com*

A CIP catalogue record for this book is available from the British Library.

ISBN 978 1 78816 869 4
eISBN 978 1 78283 881 4

Designed in Gill Sans, Garamond Premier Pro and 1820 Modern
by James Alexander at Jade Design
Printed and bound in Great Britain by Clays Ltd, Elcograf S.p.A.

For Jane (Moo, JB, Mamoo, Wolf),
the *genius loci*

# CONTENTS

...........................

# Contents

# WELCOME

........................

Jonny has spent his life in the country; Meg has spent her life in books. Between us, father and daughter, we reckoned we had the wherewithal – head-in-the-clouds theorising grounded by down-to-earth knowledge – to write a book. And so we did, and here it is. A book all about the countryside. Jonny's old friend, Meg's new love.

But what, exactly, have we written?

Back in the 1950s, the philosopher Isaiah Berlin wrote a very appealing essay, in which he says you can divide people (and their books) into hedgehogs, who know one big thing, and foxes, who know many things – things which might appear disparate, unrelated, perhaps even contradictory. In the flesh, we're probably keener on hedgehogs than we are on foxes, but nevertheless, there's no doubt that the book in your hands has serious fox energy. We have, you see, followed our noses, whether they led us to frolic in the chicken coop, to slink around the standing stones at dusk, or to go to ground deep in a patch of ancient woodland.

For, of course, the countryside means different things to different people. It can be where you work long, hard hours, or where you escape, to dream, to play. It can be a backwater from which you ache to run away – or your happy place, where you wish you could always be.

It can feel timeless, unchanging, perfect. That honeysuckle, those bluebells. Bleat of lambs, sweet kiss of cider at the cricket, sharp bite of cold water in the dark pool on the high moor; it's all true. But, as you probably know, it can also feel damaged, diminished, even doomed. Blighted habitats, decimated wildlife. Boarded-up pubs, cancelled bus routes. Clear-felled hillsides and rivers full of chickenshit. That, sadly, is true as well.

And, for every person who lives in the countryside, in every house, every farm, every village, there is a *different* countryside, a *different* way of doing things. But just because people do things differently, it doesn't mean that they don't like each other, that they don't get along. The market gardener doesn't scowl at the whipper-in when they pass on the back lanes. Silos, after all, are for silage, not people.

Fundamentally, though, we wrote this book because we wanted to explore how all these differences came about. We wanted to show you why the land (the woods, the fields, the meadows, the moors, the gardens, the footpaths) is the way it is, and why its people (the farmers, the walkers, the hunters, the poachers, the ravers, the druids) are the way they are. We also wanted to shine a little bit of light on the mistakes that have been made in the past, and share a few ideas about how we might do better in the future.

This book, then, attempts to herd all these disparate ideas together, even when they threaten to scatter and bolt. After all, haven't we all got our share of contradictions?

We, for example, have sent hundreds of lambs to market, but we no longer eat meat. We don't much care for hunting, but we've broken bread with plenty of people who do. We've shot birds, but we've eaten what we've killed. And although we've planted up acres of old sheep pasture with oak and beech, with lime and cherry, we still mow our lawn like clockwork.

This book isn't going to exhort you to think this, to do that. We've not, if we're honest, written it to educate you, but rather to entertain you, and perhaps, occasionally, to enlighten you. It's a map, really, to do with as you will. There's no route you have to follow.

One last word about place. We live in one particular patch of the countryside: Somerset, on the southern slopes of the Quantock Hills. This means (because this book is neither comprehensive nor conclusive) that our references skew west (not east), south (not north) and English (not Welsh, Scottish or northern Irish).

And so, whoever you are, wherever you are – hello, welcome. Dig in. Plough through, start to finish, like a mole on a mission, or hop gaily about like a robin.

If you only need a few moments diversion, why not nibble some cheese (page 134) or confront a cow (page 53)? Or, if you've time to spare, you could take a deep dive into farming, past, present and future (pages 25, 60 and 338), or consider the rights and wrongs of grand houses and their gardens (pages 220 and 247). If you're feeling practical, you could knock up some jam (page 239) or fashion your own crop circle (page 309). We've also nailed how to make children enjoy long walks; that holiest of grails (page 55). And, when you've had enough of us, we've borrowed some poems and prose: John Agard's 'Caribbean Eye over Yorkshire' (page 231) contains multitudes. Look closely at the trees (pages 93 and 103), but don't forget to enjoy the woods as well (page 82).

# THE SOIL

..........................

*After dinner they met again, to speak not of Byron but of manure.*
E. M. Forster, *The Longest Journey* (1907)

If you're pondering a patch of land, whether you're walking through it or living on top of it, the first question you should ask yourself is this: I wonder what the soil's like?

Soil can be good or bad. Healthy or unhealthy. It can drain easily or clog horribly. It can husband rainwater or spill it heedlessly downhill. Is it acid or alkaline? The child of granite? – of chalk? – or the leavings of a slow and winding river? You need to know whether it's pale and unforgiving sand, or beautiful black loam, rioting with worms. You need to know the answers.

Soil is a mixture of air and water, of minerals and organic matter that has taken thousands of years to come into being. It's alive (sort of), in that it plays host to a cornucopia of creatures, from bacteria and mycelial networks of fungi to millipedes and colonies of ants. Not to mention rabbits, moles – and, in a way, us.

And it's one of those very important, very everyday things, about which we're still peculiarly ignorant. But, of course, our lives, all lives, depend on it: a truth we've always known. *Adamah*, after all, is Hebrew for *earth*. From the earth Adam came, and back to the earth he, and all the rest of us, must return. The soil is so much more than something to stamp off our boots at the end of the day: it is a massive recycling centre beneath our feet, where stuff we no longer want is turned into stuff we desperately need. No surprise, then, that we sometimes become dangerously attached to it.

We have the power to change the soil. Depending on how we treat it, what we put into it, what we take out of it, it can get better or worse. But soil can also change us. As Robert Pogue Harrison, a beguiling thinker about the natural world, reminds us in *Gardens: An Essay on the Human Condition* (2008), what holds true for the soil, 'that you must give it more than you take away', also holds true for nations, institutions, marriage, friendship, education – in short for human culture as a whole.

But what happens if it *is* all take? In that case, we find ourselves like the writer Jacquetta Hawkes in *A Land* (1951), lying in her London garden, staring up at the sky, pondering the clapped-out soil beneath her back. 'The humus, formed by the accumulations first of forest and then of meadow land, must once have been fertile enough, but nearly a century in a back garden has exhausted it.' Her plants flower no more, and struggle even to make a decent show of leaves.

How, though, do you know what sort of soil you're starting with?*

..........

* For a quick answer, visit www.landis.org.uk/soilscapes or look up Agricultural Land Classification maps. You'll see the countryside in a whole new way.

## 1. LOOK

Go for a wander. See what you can see. Here are some encouraging signs:
- Flat or gently sloping land
- Strong healthy trees and hedges
- Rich, green pasture, lots of white clover
- Strong healthy weeds (nettles, ragwort, thistles, docks)
- Deep soil, reddish or dark brown
- Views nice enough: you can imagine Jane Austen taking a wholesome turn

And some less encouraging ones:
- Steeper hills and valleys
- Straggly hedges, gothic trees
- Thin grass, full of heartbreakingly beautiful flowers
- Sedges, mosses, heathers, gorses
- Thin soil, white or grey
- Views *stunning*: you can imagine Emily Brontë running up that hill

## 2. TOUCH

Get a little closer. Rub the soil between your fingertips and see what happens if you try to turn it into a ball. You'll soon have a pretty good idea which of four main types you've got:

**Rough, gritty, grainy; won't make a ball → sand**
+ Warms up quickly in the spring.
− Dries out fast. Nutrient levels low.
**Sticky, claggy, plasticine-y; great balls → clay**
+ Holds on to nutrients.
− Heavy. Drains slowly. Compacts easily. Bakes rock hard in heatwaves.
**Silky, squishy; slimy balls → silt**
+ More fertile than sand. Easier to work than clay.
− Drains slowly. Compacts easily.
**Nice and earthy; adequate balls → loam**
+ Goldilocks soil. A mixture of clay, sand and silt. Drains well, but not too well. Warms up fast, but doesn't dry out. Holds on to nutrients and organic matter. Do a little dance.
− Absent the rule of law, people will try to steal it from you. Stash AK-47s in your septic tank.

3. MEASURE
Buy a cheap pH-testing kit. They're about a tenner. Remember, they won't work if the ground's dry, so water slightly if droughty.

**pH 3.0–5.0 → very acid**
Bacteria are sluggish so organic matter doesn't rot down and release nutrients. Nutrients dissolve quickly and are washed away. Holds water. Think moorland.
**pH 5.1–6.0 → acid**
Excellent for ericaceous or lime-hating plants such as rhododendrons, camellias, heathers and blueberries.
**pH 6.1–7.0 → moderately acid**
Jackpot. Most plants will grow. Bacteria and earthworms happy. Organic matter rots. Plants get nutrients.

## pH 7.1–8.0 → alkaline

Drains fast, low in nutrients. Great for brassicas, grape-vines, wild flowers. Think chalk downs or limestone cliffs.

### HOW DO YOU LOOK AFTER IT?

In the wild, plants and animals die *in situ* and decompose, meaning that what was once bracken or a badger, is broken down into nutrients for another generation of bracken or badgers to enjoy. In farms and gardens, on the other hand, we grow a lot of identical things on one patch of soil, which we then take away and eat, meaning that what was once beans or beef ends up in sewers or septic tanks or grave-yards – not back in the soil.

Plants need to extract three macronutrients (plus some micronutrients, but we'll leave those to the pros) from the soil: nitrogen (N), phosphorus (P) and potassium (K).* If your soil is to prosper, you need to replicate decomposi-tion by adding easy-to-absorb plant or animal matter, in the form of compost or manure. There is, of course, a very popular third option: synthetic NPK, or fertiliser.

And so, whether you're a smallholder hitching your muck-spreader to your tractor, a grow-your-own gardener shovelling compost, a regenerative farmer sowing green manure, or an agri-business finance officer wincing at the price of fertiliser, you're all in the same boat. You're trying to keep your soil's nutrient tank topped up. If you run it down, if you ask your soil to run on empty, you'll soon find it sputters to a halt.

..........
* The K is derived from the Arabic word *al-qaliy*, meaning burnt ashes, which is also the origin of the word *alkali*. Wood ash, soaked in water, is called *potash*, which is a source of potassium and the source of the word *potassium*.

## I. ANIMALS

For a long time, the most efficient way to add NPK to your soil was via poo – which is, after all, nothing more or less than a concentrated sludge of nutrients, neatly broken down by an animal's digestive system, ready to be incorporated into the soil.

**Animal poo, direct.** Bring your sheep down from the hills (or turn out your cows or chickens), and let them graze either the stubble from your previous arable crop or the fodder crop (clover-rich grass; turnips) you planted specially for them. Your animals will poo everywhere, and your soil will be all the better for it.

**Animal poo, indirect.** Guano from remote sea cliffs was once the king of this category; the fate of several islands was made and broken by the bird-poo-rush. Today, though, you can buy lots of other types of poo, processed, plastic wrapped, ready to use. Or you can simply round up cow slurry, horse-muck or chicken-shit, whether from your own animals or somebody else's, and spread it on your fields or in your garden. Remember, you need to give it time to bed in.

**Human poo.** People used to spread night soil on their fields, but we've got wise to the drawbacks: pathogens. Plus, we're more squeamish now. Farmers do still use human poo after it's been carefully treated. In fact, figuring out how to process our waste to reuse in a palatable form is an interesting challenge for the future.*

**And it doesn't have to be poo.** Other waste bits of animals work as well. Blood meal, bone meal, wormery juice. Bracken or straw that's been used for animal bedding. It's all good.

..........

* Think how gross meaty dog poo is compared to grassy rabbit poo. Is there a market in vegan poo? One to ponder.

## 2. PLANTS

Composting is the most virtuous of circles, and it's easy to do at home. You take your mowings and rakings, your prunings and peelings, the courgettes which marrowed in September, the pumpkins which leered in October, and you shove the whole lot on to a compost heap. Zero miles, zero plastic, zero pillaging of peat bogs. Here's a quick how-to.

1. Assign an out-of-the-way corner of your garden.
2. Use pallets, slatted wood, rails, wire netting, whatever you think will work, to create four compartments, sized according to the space available and/or the scale of your ambition. Not too small, though, or the bacteria get cold, and cold bacteria are lazy bacteria. Two for compost (one current, one rotting), two for leaf mould (ditto). Don't cover them: they're aerobic digesters, and need air, light and rain.
3. Fill, remembering to keep it vegan and gluten-free. No fish fingers, fusilli, Babybel, eggshells, etc., or you'll get rats. Max 20 per cent lawn clippings, or it goes soggy. Chop up big leaves (gunnera, rhubarb). Don't add any stems past their first birthday: too woody.* And beware weeds. Perennials with a tap-root or annuals with a seedhead mustn't go in: your compost's temperature is unlikely to get high enough to disarm them. You can turn your heap every now and then, a bit like stirring a Christmas pudding. Fun, but not essential.
4. A mat of wet leaves can annihilate a handsome lawn in days. Grit your teeth and pick the bastards up. Every last one of them. No mercy. Choose a misty-mellow-fruits

..........

* The serious composter will have two additional bays for stalkier stuff that'll take longer to break down, e.g. asparagus forest, raspberry canes, fruit-tree prunings.

sort of morning, arm yourself with a rake (cheap metal is better than rustic wood), a pair of plywood boards for scooping and a nice big garden bag. No plane leaves – they layer up like filo pastry and don't rot.

5. And finally, deploy. Both compost and leaf mould are usually ready after just over a year, so what you cut down and rake up in the autumn will be ready the spring after next. You get to feel like a god, adding an inch of goodness to your beds, a process which would otherwise take centuries.

### 3. CHEMICALS

Most farmers (and plenty of gardeners) buy their nutrients from big firms. These synthetic fertilisers give the soil precisely calibrated quantities of NPK, but they fail to provide the organic ballast which the soil also needs. It is, in fact, as we're learning, a bit like eating a grab-bag of M&M's and a multivitamin and calling it lunch.

## TOWN MICE, COUNTRY MICE

*I'm not soppy about the 'country'. I was brought up a damn sight too near to it for that.*
George Orwell, *Coming Up for Air* (1939)

Officially, we ceased to be a rural nation in 1851, when the census first reported that more of us lived in towns and cities than in the countryside. And it was a change that came *fast*. In 1801, two-thirds of people in England and

Wales lived rurally. A hundred years later only a fifth did.* Today, if you exclude little country towns, and only count people who live in villages, hamlets and farms, that number falls well below 10 per cent. And, barring a monster catastrophe, it looks set to stay that way.

But, long after the reality vanished, the rural ideal lives on, so much so that you can find yourself at a village fete in a London square which hasn't been a village for centuries. Maybe it's not surprising: 1851 is only three decent lifetimes ago. A mature beech tree. A not-very-old oak. Nothing.

We have a name for the generation of artists and writers who lived through those decades, who watched a rural country becoming an urban one: the Romantics. They gave us a language, verbal and visual, to capture the countryside, marking a huge break with their cultural fathers and grandfathers, bewigged sophisticates – wits, fops, satirists, rakes – who were disinclined to get moony over daffodils.

Let's start in the 1790s. There was war in Europe. Prices were rising. People couldn't afford to heat their homes. The government was freaking out with draconian laws. People felt they couldn't speak freely. A young man, with no job, not much money, on a police watchlist, rocked up in a village on the Quantocks, where he entertained a stream of visitors, with strange habits, strange clothes, strange ideas. The locals weren't sure about him. His wife looked frisky – a democratic hoyden. But he, Samuel Coleridge, and his friend William Wordsworth were determined, as Adam Nicolson writes in his excellent account, *The Making of Poetry* (2019), to get away from it all, away 'from cities; from politics; from gentlemanliness and propriety; from the expected; towards nature'.

..........

* Rurally, according to these statistics, means anywhere with a population of less than 2,500.

In one long year, they wrote an extraordinary collection of poems, whose legacy was to send their (rich) contemporaries hurrying away from their country estates, their London townhouses, to explore the fells and fields of Britain. (And where else were they to go, what with the French fleet imposing a cross-Channel travel ban?) This generation cultivated a mystical attachment to place, a passion for combining the wild and walks and words, and their Romanticism still affects how we relate to the countryside today.*

But even as the Romantics were falling in love with the countryside, the wheels of industrialisation were spinning faster and faster. It's hard for us today, now that the engine has gone into reverse, to remember what a devastating rupture it was, and how radically the countryside was transformed.

The sense of upheaval, as we moved from country to town, writes Jacquetta Hawkes in *A Land*, was comparable to the Roman and Norman invasions, especially in the north of England and the south of Wales.

> As mills, factories, foundries and kilns multiplied, the little streets of the workers' houses spread their lines over hills that belonged to wild birds and mountain sheep, and up valleys where there was nothing busier than a rushing beck. Without intention or understanding the greater part of the people of Britain found themselves living in towns, uprooted, and in a strange, unstable environment. The growths of brick and stone [...] might coalesce one with another in urban areas so large that it was difficult for the inhabitants to set foot on grass or naked earth.

..........

* Romantics weren't necessarily romantic, as Sara(h) Coleridge (her husband preferred her name without the *h*) had plenty of time to reflect while she looked after the babies.

Here's the writer and commentator J. B. Priestley, bearing witness in his *English Journey* (1934) to what industrialisation had done:

> It had blackened fields, poisoned rivers, ravaged the earth, and sown filth and ugliness with a lavish hand. You cannot make omelettes without breaking eggs, and you cannot become rich by selling the world your coal and iron and cotton goods and chemicals without some dirt and disorder.

But there were, he said, on balance, 'too many eggshells and too few omelettes', which made him both angry and ashamed. 'What right had we to go strutting about, talking of our greatness, when all the time we were living on the proceeds of these muck-heaps?'

The culmination – of anger and of shame – was the abomination of the Aberfan disaster. One Friday morning in 1966, just after school had started, an avalanche of coal slurry buried 28 adults and 116 children in the Welsh village of Aberfan. It wasn't only a tragedy for every single person involved: it was also a moment of national mourning, a horrific indictment of shoddy industrial practices, of a cavalier attitude to people's safety.

But for a long time, the stories we told ourselves about industrialisation were ones of national pride. Britain was the workshop of the world. We were rich and powerful and able to swank about, assuring ourselves and everyone else that we were happy and glorious. To question that narrative was – unpatriotic, unBritish?

In the midst of industrialisation, it was possible to look to the future, to believe the grime could be transformed into a brave new world. Cue, at the dawn of the twentieth century, a fascination with the bright white lights of progress, socialism, modernism: those were the rallying cries, the big international movements, the big ideas crossing borders, zipping along telegraph lines, railway tracks, even flight paths, everything fast, straight, sleek, modern.

Against such shiny, steely hopes for the future, the countryside could seem like very shabby old hat: 'Personally, I cannot understand how anybody manages to exist in the country, if anybody who is anybody does,' is up-town Gwendolen's snub to Cecily the rube in *The Importance of Being Earnest* (1895). Oscar Wilde, here, is simply depicting her as a modern woman, as well as a total cow. For as the town moved faster and faster (so many people, so many ideas) the country seemed ever slower and duller in comparison, and it became harder to integrate the two. Pick a side. Are you Ernest in town – or Jack in the country?

Some people thought we could have the best of both worlds. Take William Morris, whose prints curtain both country cottages and grand houses to this day. 'I want the town to be impregnated with the beauty of the country,' he wrote, 'and the country with the intelligence and vivid life of the town.' But Morris, in *News from Nowhere* (1890), is consciously constructing a utopia, a golden-glow future where everyone is preternaturally handsome and wears beautiful home-forged accessories and floats up the Thames on barges to go harvesting. (It is impossible to read that vision today without expecting the scene to morph into a slavering *Wicker-Man*-style blood cult.)

Others, though, mounted a more obstinate resistance to the twentieth century, cultivating a sentimental attachment to the English countryside which endures to this day.

In counterpoint to the go-faster stripes of modernism, came a desire for stillness, slowness, connection, which could manifest in something as benign as an interest in church murals, or quaint village plays and quirky local guidebooks, or quixotic campaigns to save historic buildings. When the world is spinning too fast, we sometimes rush to embrace the local, the specific; to know one place and to know it well; the difficult corner, the bend where it floods, the gate where the branches are too low.

For some, this attachment provoked an intense nostalgia, a longing for a lost youth, a lost world – a world erased by the double blow of two world wars. After the first, the poet Siegfried Sassoon dreams of one perfect village cricket game: 'I cannot think of it now without a sense of heartache, as if it contained something which I have never quite been able to discover.' After the second, Evelyn Waugh's Charles Ryder dreams of lying on a sheep-cropped knoll under a clump of elms, eating strawberries and drinking wine, drugged into stillness by the beauty of England and Sebastian Flyte, the boy from Brideshead.*

Or the countryside simply offered salvation – liberation from the unending pep and punch of city life. Here's a put-upon 'spinster' in Sylvia Townsend Warner's *Lolly Willowes* (1926), falling into a reverie over plums and greengages: 'She forgot that she was in London, she forgot the whole of her London life. She seemed to be standing alone in a darkening orchard, her feet in the grass, her arms stretched up to the pattern of leaves and fruits ...'

But that impulse, the search for answers amongst the leaves, could darken. The countryside could come to mean more, much more, than a place for sweet repose. Laura (called Lolly by her selfish family) leaves town, becomes

..........

* Jez Butterworth's noughties play *Jerusalem* takes the piss out of wallowing in the past. Two friends, not half so posh and pretty as Charles and Sebastian, hark back to the good old days when the local country fair wasn't *shit on toast*. Says Ginger: 'When I was a boy there was this big fucking farmer, right, and you paid ten pence to take a run up and hoof him in the bollocks. If you brung him to his knees, you won a pound.' *Simple*, agrees Lee, *pure*.

a witch, and sits with a devil in the dark beneath the trees. But hers is a personal and particular quest. For others, the longing for connection with the land, with the soil, became a political movement, which released other devils; devils which were – and are – all too real.

It could start off innocently enough. You could join an organisation such as Kibbo Kift (founded 1920; think Boy Scouts for Tolkien fans): camp out in the country; sew cowls and jerkins; make tools from coppiced wood. Carry staves. Create initiation rites. Some people might think you were a bit weird – but harmless enough? Unfortunately, this was a place from which some (but, of course, by no means all) people turned very hard right.

Take one Kift member, Rolf Gardiner. He was a Morris dancing revivalist. An organic farming pioneer and founding member of the Soil Association. He also joined a group called English Mistery, which talked a lot about vigour and instinct and 'national breeds' which, with grim inevitability, led to him meeting up with the Nazi agriculture minister, Richard Walther Darré, an advocate of *blood-and-soil* ideology. That was the problem: how to love the soil, without getting mixed up with the blood?

Melissa Harrison's 2018 novel, *All Among the Barley*, is an excellent dramatisation of this cultural moment. Smiling Constance, a Londoner, is visiting a village to research the Old Ways. She tells us she's sick of drawing-room conversations, of dressing for dinner, of everyone rushing off to the theatre, talking nonsense about modern art. We're suckered in, gently, until her truer colours are revealed: she is trying to inveigle the locals into joining a proto-fascist society, riddled with the sorts of unpleasant yet seductive ideas that once made some people say Hitler and Mussolini knew a thing or two.

This, as Harrison discusses in her historical note, reflected a very particular interwar atmosphere: 'a murky broth of nationalism, anti-Semitism, nativism, protectionism, anti-immigration sentiment, economic autarky, secessionism, militarism, anti-Europeanism, rural revivalism, nature worship, organicism, landscape mysticism and distrust of big business – particularly international finance'.

You can find many of these elements in spades in the work of D. H. Lawrence, who rhapsodised the countryside while excoriating what industrialisation had done. In *Lady Chatterley's Lover* (1928), smuts settle across the Christmas roses, like 'black manna from the skies of doom'. The big house is 'full of the stench of this sulphurous combustion of the earth's excrement' (i.e. it smells of coal; his language often reads like self-parody). And this destruction of beauty, of purity, provokes in him, or his literary avatars, a ferocious longing for something older, something better. In *England, My England* (1922), he writes:

> His heart went back to the savage old spirit of the place: the desire for old gods, old, lost passions, the passion of the cold-blooded darting snakes that hissed and shot away from him, the mystery of blood sacrifices, all the lost intense sensations of the primeval people of the place, whose passions seethed in the air still, from those long days before the Romans came.

His admirers liked his outspokenness, his disavowal of Victorian prudery, his muscularity, his earthiness, but the philosopher Bertrand Russell, who had once admired him too, called it right. Lawrence, he wrote in his autobiography, developed 'the whole philosophy of fascism before the politicians thought of it'. The feted novelist, Russell was dismayed to discover, 'had no real wish to make the world better, but only to indulge in eloquent soliloquy about how bad it was'.

This, therefore, was the danger, the fraught place. How to celebrate the countryside, its people and its past, without excluding the realities of the present, the people of the future? It was – and is – a fine balance.

By the time the Second World War came, we'd wised up to the dangers of blood-and-soil rhetoric, and the country-side became simply a down-to-earth resource, somewhere to grow food, a safe haven away from Nazi bombs. Over the course of the war, a million children were evacuated: some were miserable; others adored the new world into which they were thrown. You can find audio recordings of men and women, now long dead, who remember the war years as the happiest of their lives, and these shared experiences have nurtured our sense of the countryside as a cherished site of childhood innocence.

After the war, some of those children, now with children of their own, went back to the land, dreaming of self-suf-ficiency, of an authentic life, re-inventing themselves far away from Abbey Road and Carnaby Street, back when it was still just about possible to find a tumbledown cottage for a song. (Near a stone circle and a magic mushroom patch if a more psychedelic take on crofting was your vibe.)

But those men and women were the exceptions. In the last forty years of the twentieth century, while the UK's urban population grew by more than a third, the rural population actually *shrank* by 4 per cent, with the average age climbing ever higher and higher.* Why? There simply

..........

* Our village primary school, by way of illustration, shut its doors in the late sixties, becoming a base for outward-bound residential trips for children from the city. The village's overall population, by contrast, has remained more or less the same.

weren't the jobs any more. Thanks to mechanisation, farmers needed fewer and fewer people to grow crops and raise livestock – two things which they were starting to do with devastating efficiency.

And so, with disposable incomes rising, the country-side assumed a new role. It was a place to get your kicks (whether that meant raving all night or hiking all day); an emotional and physical hinterland serving the needs of the town; the town which (it turned out) had increasingly strong ideas of what the countryside was, what it was for. But, safe to say, not everyone in the countryside liked this proprietorial attitude.

Take this, from James Rebanks's *A Shepherd's Life* (2015). He's remembering a particular assembly, a particular visiting speaker, at his school in the Lake District in the 1980s:

> I listened, getting more and more aggravated, as I realised that curiously she knew, and claimed to love, our land. But she talked about it, and thought of it, in terms that were completely alien to my family and me. She loved a 'wild' landscape, full of mountains, lakes, leisure and adventure, lightly peopled with folk I had never met.

Those folk – the long-dead poets, the walkers who will walk no more – were seen as more real, more vital, than ordinary, everyday people like him, or that's how it felt. And this tendency is one we shouldn't ignore, the tendency of the town to think the countryside is getting it all wrong. Perhaps you recognise the tune?

*We* are wholesome, outdoorsy, in touch with nature.
*They* are insular, inward-looking, hostile to strangers.
*We* are rewilding, digitally detoxing, wild swimming, forest bathing.

*They* are white, old, conservative, Conservative, Brexity, beastly to animals.
*We* are sipping locally brewed cider, playing our guitars under the harvest moon.
*They* are gunning their quad bikes, necking pesticide and red diesel cocktails.

But that, of course, is not to say that the countryman or woman mightn't have their own long list of barely rational prejudices. Please enjoy (as we did) Sarah Langford's funny and very familiar list in *Rooted* (2022) of all the things her uncle, a (stereo)typical traditional farmer, most dislikes: the BBC, *Countryfile*, *Farming Today*, George Monbiot, Chris Packham, Greta Thunberg, vegetarians, local villagers, land agents, government agents, the Met Office, the National Farmers' Union, *Lambing Live*, the new landlords of the local pub, use of 'eco-', 'enviro-', 'green', 'natural' or 'sustainable', any products containing those words, Natural England, the National Trust, the Right to Roam, regenerative farming, non-farming critics of farming, walkers who get in the way of his spraying schedule.

Farmers like him don't tend to write books; he mightn't like this one much. Farms like his don't have inviting websites and enticing farm shops; but they're part of the countryside, too. And when something needs fixing in a village, it can be traditional farmers like him who step right up. Paul Kingsnorth, environmental activist turned writer, warns in his book *Real England* (2008) that we don't want to be left with a 'twee dead countryside packaged as a rural idyll and sold to bankers and retired civil servants'.

This sense, whoever we are, whatever our politics, whether we live in town or country, that things are going wrong, that something is slipping through our fingers, has always run strong. For the countryside, far from being a timeless idyll, a bastion of tradition, has *always* been changing. Some change is sudden and shattering. Some is insidious and slow. Invasions and plagues, enclosure and mechanisation, urbanisation and gentrification. The loss of horses and elms – of ice and snow.

Raymond Williams, the perceptive critic who lived through the turbulent middle years of the twentieth century, reminds us in *The Country and the City* (1973) that there's always been a *back in the day*. In my mother's time, in her mother's time. Back when Thomas Hardy was alive, back when George Eliot still wrote. When John Clare walked, when William Cobbett rode, back and back we go. Where do we stop? Everything was fine before William the Conqueror, before the Romans, before the Bronze Age migrants. Back and back we go – to the Garden of Eden. For, unavoidably, one of the props of our collective consciousness is that long-ago expulsion, that we had paradise, and we messed it up.

And that's why we care so much: we want to get it right this time.

# TOPONYMY, OR WHAT'S IN A NAME

Our place-names are a pile-up of the languages spoken by the different peoples who've migrated here over the last three thousand years, starting with Cornish, Welsh, Gaelic and Irish (the Celtic family), followed by a layer of Latin, a large wedge of Old English, a dollop of Old Norse and a sprinkling of Norman French.

| LANGUAGE | ROOT | MEANING | EXAMPLE |
|---|---|---|---|
| **Cornish** | tre- | settlement | Tregony |
| | pol- | pond, lake | Polzeath |
| | pen- | hill, headland | Penzance |
| **Welsh** | aber- | river mouth | Abergavenny |
| | avon- | river | Avonmouth |
| **Gaelic** | ben- | peak | Ben Nevis |
| | glen- | valley | Glen Coe |
| **Latin** | -castra | camp | Lancaster |
| | strata- | road | Stratford |
| | -colonia | settlement | Lincoln |
| **Old English** | -combe | valley | Crowcombe |
| | -hurst | (woody) hillock | Chislehurst |
| | -worth | homestead | Kenilworth |
| | -bourne | brook | Redbourne |
| | -mere | lake | Haslemere |
| | -bury | town | Glastonbury |
| | -ing | people of | Reading |
| **Old Norse** | -by | settlement | Whitby |
| | -thorpe | hamlet | Cleethorpes |
| | -ness | headland | Orford Ness |
| | -thwaite | clearing | Braithwaite |
| | -wick | bay | Lerwick |
| | -holm | island | Holmfirth |
| **Norman French** | Pierpoint | name to show ownership: 'mine', says M. de Pierpoint | Hurstpierpoint |
| | beau- | lovely | Beaulieu |

# FARMING: PAST

......................................

*I am the giant of giant-castle, and have eat up all my neighbours.*
Thomas Coke, 1st Earl of Leicester (anecdotally)

If Lords & Ladies PLC had briefed a team of management consultants to come up with an exciting new strategy for the agricultural sector of early modern England, the opening slide would have been disarmingly titled, 'Enclosure: cost benefits and efficiency gains'. The executive summary would have promised an end to the raggedy, mulish, moth-eaten, lackadaisical, we've-always-done-it-this-way system of open-field farming, and trumpeted a new era of integration, consolidation, rationalisation, systematisation – plus big fat profits.

### ARE WE TALKING ABOUT ALL OF ENGLAND?
No. Not all. Picture the north and the west. Picture the moors and uplands. Picture narrow lanes and sunken paths and little woods and lumpy hills. Those parts of the country, to generalise massively, weren't traditionally open fields. Now picture the big central belt, from Yorkshire down to Dorset, especially the Midlands and Northamptonshire. That was. It's a big area, accounting for much of England's prime arable land.

### SO WHAT WAS OPEN-FIELD FARMING EXACTLY?
The system, says the land historian Oliver Rackham, was one of *rococo complexity*. But, very roughly, you'd have a parish, with a village as its focal point, and around the village, you'd have two or three very large fields, plus

chunks of woodland, meadow, pasture and heath, known as the *commons*.

The fields, though, would look strange to our eyes: no hedges, no fences, no walls. Instead, each field was divided up into long, thin strips or *selion*s, and the villagers, including the landowner, would each farm a number of strips around the district. Naturally, the landowner had by far the largest share (called his *demesne*), and he didn't actually have to farm it himself: the villagers did that, often for free, in lieu of rent for their strips. An individual's strips weren't all in one place, which was a bit of a pain, but it did mean that nobody hogged the best soil. And on each field, which was basically a collection of lots and lots of strips, everyone grew the same thing, according to the crop rotation which everyone had agreed, teaming up to work collectively on big days in the farming calendar, e.g. at harvest time.

People got together to decide these rules, to re-allocate strips (it's *his* turn to have the boggy bottom), and to pass judgement on people who didn't play ball (*his* weeds are seeding in *my* strip). Finally, all the villagers could use specific non-field parts of the parish for grazing animals, cutting hay, gathering brush-wood or (if we buy into the idea of Merrie England) generally larking about.

In many places, this system pre-dated the Norman Conquest. When William the Conqueror took over, he parcelled England up between his barons but the losers, by and large, were the old ruling class; the ordinary people carried on living and farming as they'd always done – but it was a *custom*, not a *right*.

CROP ROTATION: REMIND ME?

If you the plant the same stuff in the same place year after year the soil gets knackered, so it's a good idea both to vary your crops (different crops have different needs), and to give your fields time to recuperate as often as you can. This practice also minimises the build-up of pests and pathogens e.g. if a particular fungus loves wheat, but there's no wheat around for two seasons, hopefully the fungus will give up. It also spreads risk: if one crop fails, you've got something else to fall back on.

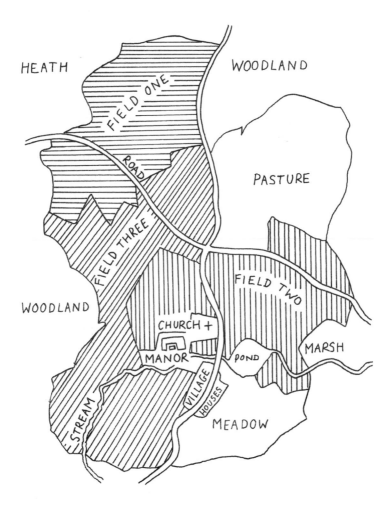

Before enclosure, people used the *three-field system*.

**Field one.** Wheat or rye.

**Field two.** Oats or legumes, e.g. peas or beans.

**Field three.** Leave fallow i.e. plant nothing, but let your animals graze stubble and weeds, knowing that their poo will prime the soil for next year's arable.

The following year, everything moved up a spot, so peas and beans on field one, nothing on field two, arable on field three.

After enclosure, people largely turned to the 'Norfolk' *four-field system*, pioneered by an East Anglian viscount who everyone now remembers as Turnip Townshend, such was his enthusiasm for root crops. This system did a better job of nourishing your soil *and* nourishing your livestock.

**Field one.** Wheat or rye.

**Field two.** A root crop (turnips!) for your livestock.

**Field three.** Barley or oats, under-sown with a grass forage crop (or *ley*), some proportion of which might be leguminous, e.g. clover.

**Field four.** Your livestock graze last year's grass and clover, which are much more filling than stubble and weeds.

## WHY DID THE SYSTEM NEED TO CHANGE?

You don't need to be an agronomist to see that it was, in many ways, a fantastically inefficient system. Think of all the time people spent humping tools from one strip to another. Think of the land left fallow, the gaps between strips. And if everyone swapped strips every few years, the average peasant wasn't going to look after the land properly, were they? They weren't going to really get the best out of it, really put it to work, really leverage it, really maximise its full potential. And, come to think of it, weren't the peasants grazing too many of their measly animals on the commons? Wouldn't it be better if the land was run by clever well-bred people, people with *vision*, with deep pockets, people who—?

You get the idea.

## ENCLOSURE, ROUND ONE, VERY ROUGHLY 1350–1650

During this period, wool was more profitable than wheat, and there was absolutely nothing to stop greedy and/or ambitious landowners evicting people so they could make more money.

It was enough of a *cause célèbre* for Thomas More, the great Tudor lawyer-philosopher-statesman (or the sanctimonious obsessive if you prefer Hilary Mantel's *Wolf Hall*), to attack sheep-mania in his satire, *Utopia* (1516). The nobility, the gentry and even the clergy, he said, despite already living an easy life, resolved to do harm instead of good. 'They stop the course of agriculture, destroying houses and towns, reserving only the churches, and enclose grounds that they may lodge their sheep in them.'

Sheep and profits, first. People and centuries of custom, second.

The kings and queens, however, were annoyed about people being kicked off the land, believing – rightly – that it would lead to vagrancy and unrest, which they would have to deal with. Parliament therefore passed a number of laws, including limits on flock size and a poll tax on sheep (a sort of reverse subsidy), as well as straightforward legislation, known as the Tillage Acts, which ordered the landowners to *stop*.

## ENCLOSURE, ROUND TWO, ROUGHLY 1700–1850

Enclosure had ticked along quietly in some places, usually by deals done on the ground, but if we skip ahead to the end of the seventeenth century, we find that parliament is now pro-enclosure, and enclosure itself is no longer about get-rich-quick sheep schemes, but is part of a revolution of agricultural improvement. You will perhaps find some of the rhetoric familiar.

Back then, nobody talked about idle work-shy unproductive benefits scroungers, but they did talk about idle work-shy unproductive peasants who eked out an idle work-shy unproductive living from their strips of land, plus what benefit they could scrounge from the *wastes* (marginal land that wasn't part of the open-field system), from the woods and heaths – from the commons.

Enclosure, ratified by some 4,000 acts of parliament (a parliament which was overwhelmingly made up of and voted in by rich men who owned land), put an end to that forever. Technically, it was all above board, with compensation for the villagers, in either land or cash. But what to do with a tiny pot of money? How to ditch, fence and hedge your tiny plot of land as the new laws demanded? And how to make that plot pay when you no longer had access to the commons? How to even begin to compete with the lord of the manor? Answer: sell him your tiny patch and become a wage labourer.

And it was this *huge* transformation that created today's familiar quilt of quadrilateral fields; that scenery which looks so effortlessly English, but is in fact only a few hundred years old.

## CLEARANCES, ROUGHLY 1750–1850

The Highland Clearances are an equally grim piece of Scottish history, involving the eviction of farmers from *runrig* land (a similar system of open fields and shared pasture) in favour of bigger sheep farms, which brought a better return than crops on less fertile land. The displaced people could set up as crofters (very small smallholders), but would realistically have to work in other industries (fishing, quarrying) to make ends meet. Soon, there was neither enough land nor enough work, and to avoid starvation many people were forced to emigrate, often to the United States, Canada, Australia and New Zealand.

WHY DOES ENCLOSURE MATTER SO MUCH?
It dismantled a way of life which, if definitely not luxurious, had the advantage of community, familiarity and autonomy. Life pre-enclosure obviously wasn't Edenic, but access to the commons gave you, as Raymond Williams put it in his *The Country and the City*, 'protection against the exposure of total hire'. Yes, it was still pretty feudal. Yes, you had to work the lord's land. Yes, you had to submit to collective rules. But you could also exploit the commons, giving you a side hustle, a margin, whatever you want to call it, the commons gave you resources, which meant that a portion of your income, your living, was under *your* control. You weren't part of the labour market – nor the consumer market either. That, maybe, was the difference between a hard life and an unbearable one. And that was taken away.

The poet John Clare expressed with unforgettable clarity what enclosure meant to the people who lived through it. 'Inclosure', he wrote, 'came and trampled on the grave/ Of labours rights and left the poor a slave.' Clare was an anomaly, a man who wrote about the countryside, while actually having worked the land, and his poems briefly made him the toast of the town. But he died in an asylum in 1864, unable to make a living as either a poet or a farm labourer, while the world he described in such detail, with such attention and care, and with such a keen sense of loss, is now the heartland of agri-business in Northamptonshire.

This mistrust of what some call progress and others call

rupture unites voices across England's class barriers. Mary Russell Mitford, an acquaintance of Jane Austen and a relative of the aristocratic Russells, was an un-revolutionary (if very astute) diarist. In the 1820s and 1830s, fallen on lean times, she published an incredibly successful collection of sketches called *Our Village*. In them, she writes: 'We have the good fortune to live in an unenclosed parish, and may thank the wise obstinacy of two or three sturdy farmers, and the unpopularity of a ranting madcap lord of the manor, for preserving the delicious green patches, the islets of wilderness amidst cultivation, which form, perhaps, the secular beauty of English scenery.' We wonder whether those green patches are still there today.

In Tudor times, England's rulers feared the blowback of enclosure: they didn't want hungry and resentful people roaming the countryside. Come the eighteenth century, they had a solution: hungry and resentful people could find work in the growing towns and cities of the industrial revolution. And that's why, for a long time, the enclosures were filed under *necessary evil*: you couldn't make an economic powerhouse without breaking a few eggs. Without the enclosures, we wouldn't have had factories, exports, trade, colonies, wealth, progress, modernity, the whole Rule Britannia package.

For many years, the establishment saw this as the country's almost divinely mandated destiny, but others experienced it as a loss. The poet Edward Thomas, writing a little over a century ago, said we were robbed of 'the small intelligible England of Elizabeth and given the word Imperialism instead'.

# Common-land rights

Common land was never a free-for-all. It remained private property, owned by somebody, historically the lord of the manor, who would originally have been granted his estate by the king, or one of his vassals. But it was land, whether woods, pasture, heath or marsh, over which you might have had certain rights, whether assigned to you as an individual (rights *in gross*) or to the house you lived in (rights *appurtenant*).

In 1600, as much as 30 per cent of England was common land. Three centuries years later, after the enclosures, that figure was down to 5 per cent.

The few common-land rights that exist today are protected by law; in the past they were administered by the manorial courts. The details (e.g. how many animals you could graze, for how many days) could be modified to make sure no resource was exhausted.

You might, then, have had a right:

of **animals ferae naturae**: You could hunt wild animals.

of **estovers**: You could collect wood (brush-wood, not whole trees), reeds, heather or bracken. This could be *ploughbote* (for mending carts, ploughs and other tools); *firebote* (for fuel); *hedgebote* or *heybote* (for mending fences and gates); *housebote* (for mending houses).

of **marl**: You could extract lime-rich clay to condition your soil.

of **pannage**: Your pigs could feed in wooded areas.

of **pasture**: You could graze your livestock; which exact animals (sheep, horses, cattle, goats, pigs or poultry) would be specified.

of **piscary**: You could fish from ponds and streams.

of **turbary**: You could dig turf or peat for fuel.

# THE MORES

...............................

## by John Clare

Far spread the moorey ground a level scene
Bespread with rush and one eternal green
That never felt the rage of blundering plough*
Though centurys wreathed springs blossoms on its brow
Still meeting plains that stretched them far away
In uncheckt shadows of green brown and grey
Unbounded freedom ruled the wandering scene
Nor fence of ownership crept in between
To hide the prospect of the following eye
Its only bondage was the circling sky
One mighty flat undwarfed by bush and tree
Spread its faint shadow of immensity
And lost itself which seemed to eke its bounds
In the blue mist the horizons edge surrounds
Now this sweet vision of my boyish hours
Free as spring clouds and wild as summer flowers
Is faded all – a hope that blossomed free
And hath been once no more shall ever be
Inclosure came and trampled on the grave
Of labours rights and left the poor a slave
And memorys pride ere want to wealth did bow
Is both the shadow and the substance now
The sheep and cows were free to range as then

..........

* Clare, here, is very ahead of his time. Some farmers now see ploughing as
inherently problematic: it disrupts bacterial and microbial activity, butchers
worms, and makes the soil far more vulnerable to erosion.

Where change might prompt nor felt the bonds of men
Cows went and came with evening morn and night
To the wild pasture as their common right
And sheep unfolded with the rising sun
Heard the swains shout and felt their freedom won
Tracked the red fallow field and heath and plain
Then met the brook and drank and roamed again
The brook that dribbled on as clear as glass
Beneath the roots they hid among the grass
While the glad shepherd traced their tracks along
Free as the lark and happy as her song
But now alls fled and flats of many a dye
That seemed to lengthen with the following eye
Moors loosing from the sight far smooth and blea
Where swopt the plover in its pleasure free
Are vanished now with commons wild and gay
As poets visions of lifes early day
Mulberry bushes where the boy would run
To fill his hands with fruit are grubbed and done
And hedgrow briars – flower lovers overjoyed
Came and got flower pots – these are all destroyed
And sky bound mores in mangled garbs are left
Like mighty giants of their limbs bereft
Fence now meets fence in owners little bounds
Of field and meadow large as garden grounds
In little parcels little minds to please
With men and flocks imprisoned ill at ease
Each little path that led its pleasant way
As sweet as morning leading night astray
Where little flowers bloomed round a varied host
That travel felt delighted to be lost
Nor grudged the steps that he had taen as vain
When right roads traced his journeys end again –
Nay on a broken tree hed sit awhile

To see the mores and fields and meadows smile
Sometimes with cowslaps smothered – then all white
With daiseys – then the summers splendid sight
Of cornfields crimson oer the 'headach' bloomd
Like splendid armys for the battle plumed
He gazed upon them with wild fancys eye
As fallen landscapes from an evening sky
These paths are stopt – the rude philistines thrall
Is laid upon them and destroyed them all
Each little tyrant with his little sign
Shows where man claims earth glows no more divine
But paths to freedom and to childhood dear
A board sticks up to notice 'no road here'
And on the tree with ivy overhung
The hated sign by vulgar taste is hung
As tho the very birds should learn to know
When they go there they must no further go
Thus with the poor scared freedom bade goodbye
And much the[y] feel it in the smothered sigh
And birds and trees and flowers without a name
All sighed when lawless laws enclosure came
And dreams of plunder in such rebel schemes
Have found too truly that they were but dreams

## What is – or was – a heath?

There's such a thing as mountain or maritime heath where it's too high or northerly or salty for trees to grow. Such places (e.g. on Shetland, Orkney or the Outer Hebrides) are our version of tundra. We don't have much of it, but that's down to our climate, latitude and altitude, and not (especially) because we've wrecked it.

There is also man-made heath, often found on poor-ish soil in lower, drier areas, where our predecessors felled the trees, but neither ploughed the land, nor grazed it intensively. Heaths felt wild compared with cultivated fields, although they weren't necessarily high or remote, but because landowners couldn't see anything very constructive going on – people were courting! playing cricket! – heaths got a reputation for being dangerous and desolate, the haunt of highwaymen and ne'er-do-wells.

What's happened to them?

Many were ploughed after the enclosures. Some were swallowed up by the growth of town and cities; some reverted to woodland; some both: e.g. Hampstead Heath. Others were earmarked for nuclear power stations, prisons, reservoirs, military training grounds, the sort of thing you could park on whatever you'd decided to call 'unproductive wasteland'. A few scraps remain, and people are trying to retain, to manage, to encourage their special ecological features, but it feels, frankly, like an uphill struggle.

# An encomium to the goat

The *ne plus ultra* of heath animals, tough and genial: to know goats is to love them. Don't believe us. Believe the great reforming farmer and journalist, William Cobbett. Here he is, hymning their qualities in his classic handbook, *A Cottage Economy* (1822).

**They'll eat anything.** 'Nothing,' says Cobbett, 'is so hardy; nothing is so little nice as to its food.' Mouldy bread or biscuit; fusty hay and almost rotten straw; furze-bushes, heath-thistles; this book (when you've read it): 'they will make a hearty meal on paper, brown or white, printed on or not printed on, and give milk all the while!'

**They don't get sick.** 'When sea voyages are so stormy as to kill geese, ducks, fowls, and almost pigs, the goats are well and lively; and when a dog of no kind can keep the deck for a minute, a goat will skip about upon it as bold as brass.'

**They don't wander.** 'They come in regularly in the evening, and if called, they come like dogs.'

**They're not scaredy-cats.** 'The sheep is frightened at everything, and especially at the least sound of a dog. A goat, on the contrary, will face a dog, and if he be not a big and courageous one, beat him off.'

But now ... the bad.

**They'll eat anything.** They can destroy trees as quickly as any squirrel, and if you let them in your vegetable patch, you will no longer have a vegetable patch.

# GOOD FENCES MAKE GOOD NEIGHBOURS: THE HEDGE

A generation or two ago, you could get a grant to grub out hedges, perhaps dating back to enclosure, in pursuit of bigger – and therefore more efficient and more productive – fields. Thousands upon thousands of miles of hedgerows: gone. Try that now, and you'd be a) a pariah and b) liable for a big fat fine. Instead, the government is paying farmers *to put the hedgerows back.*

Hedges, we now realise, aren't just green walls. They're ecological power-houses: food for insects (including crop pollinators and pest predators), nesting for birds, shelter for little mammals and reptiles, shade for sheep, black-berries for us. Plus, they can help control soil erosion and run-off. And, obviously, they store more carbon than wire.

But you need to look after them. A hedge is always trying to become not-a-hedge. Left to its own devices, it will seek the sky, becoming straggly at the top, gappy at the bottom, no longer lush and dense, but a row of spindly trees.

Managing a hedge tends to involve a tractor with a blade giving it a brutal flat-top once a year, which is efficient, stops it growing out, but is overkill. You can mostly get away with trimming them every two or three years, but every decade or two, you'll need to do a major hands-on overhaul, which is called *laying.*

IF YOU'RE STARTING FROM SCRATCH:

1. If you're eligible for farm subsidies, you (currently) get £22.97 per metre if your new hedge is beneficial, e.g. you're putting back old hedgerows or joining up bits of

woodland. If you're not eligible, there are other grants out there for big-ish hedges, e.g. from the Woodland Trust.

2. Look around and see which shrubs and trees are prominent in local hedgerows. Common species to plant are hawthorn, blackthorn, hazel, field maple, spindle, wayfaring tree, wild service tree, dogwood and guelder rose. Add wild roses and honeysuckle for scent. Plant saplings in two parallel rows, 12–18 inches apart, staggered so everything overlaps.

3. In year one, control anything that might out-compete your little shrubs and trees, including brambles. Once your hedge is thriving, encourage blackberry-bearing brambles to join in.

IF YOU'RE RESTORING AN OLD OR UNLOVED HEDGE:

1. In the deep mid-winter, when plants are dormant, gather your hedge-laying kit. You need: a well-honed billhook, a light chainsaw, a lump-hammer or small sledge-hammer, stakes (preferably locally coppiced hazel), a ball of biodegradable bailer twine. Wear robust boots, thick gloves, sturdy trousers. Blackthorn is *vicious*.

2. Start by removing all the bits of wire and pallets that have been shoved into the hedge over the years to plug the gaps. If you're a hedge purist, you could also eliminate any elder, but that might upset local foragers.

3. Check to see whether any saplings look especially promising. If so, mark them for preservation: they can be allowed to grow into beautiful shade-trees. Hot cows and roosting bats will thank you.

4. Hammer stakes into the ground inside the hedge at sensible intervals. Every couple of metres or so will do.

5. Peer inside your hedge. You will see a mixture of single

stems and *stools* (multiple stems, one base). You need to decide which of these stems you're going to lay, and which you're going to remove. Don't be too tentative. Pick winners and cut out the surplus: if you don't cut enough out, the stools won't get enough light, and the hedge won't regenerate.

6. At this point, a passer-by will inevitably ask you what the bloody hell you think you're doing destroying a hedge. Enlighten them, politely.

7. Cut into the first stem you're planning on laying. Your cut has to be deep enough for you to be able to hinge it, but not so deep that you cut off the sap. It'll die eventually, but you want it to live long enough for new stems to grow around it. Bend the stem, which is now called a *pleacher*, to somewhere between horizontal and 45° (styles vary across the country) and tie it in to a stake. Repeat along your hedge.

8. Getting this right takes years of practice.

# WALKING

..................

*Solvitur ambulando* – or *you'll be right as rain after a walk*
Everyone from St Augustine to your mum

From where we live, in the middle of a one-pub, no-shop village, there's a circular walk that takes about an hour.

You head up the road and turn left through the lychgate by the war memorial. The way climbs a little, passing a fifteenth-century church and a Georgian manor house, before leading you on to a grassy walk with a deliciously overgrown walled garden on your right and several acres of parkland on your left, where sheep or bullocks graze between stag-headed oaks. A wooden fence marks the end of pasture and the boundary of a cricket pitch (the club's been going since 1820), which you leave behind as the path takes you through a gate into agricultural land.

Depending on where the farmer's at in his rotation, you might meet wheat, maize or turnips, and you're also likely to see pheasants about, because there's a little shoot up on the hillside. The slope steepens into dips, delves and boggy patches, hopeless for crops, and so, after a few hundred yards, you're amongst sheep again. You pop out through a gap in the hedge on to a rough road, a dead end leading to an old farmhouse, now a holiday let (sleeps sixteen; £2,500 for the weekend).

Now you head straight uphill, through woodland, with gates barring the way to a piece of commercial plantation. It's a stiff climb, but at the top, the land opens out into heathland, gorse, heather, bracken, plus the occasional Bronze Age barrow, all open access. You'll almost definitely meet wild ponies, and your dog will let you know if there are deer about.* A sharp right, and you stride along the top, drinking in the view, before diving down a steep narrow lane – a mud bath in winter – which'll take you home, past the pub (currently closed).

That's a lot of work and play, of business and pleasure, of history and geography, packed into one, by tourist-board standards, unremarkable loop. You can trace the route, following green or pink lines depending on the scale of your Ordnance Survey map, which takes in official footpaths,

..........

* Not so long ago, you'd have seen strips of deerskin hanging on the fences, a warning sign to the dead animal's relatives not to stray off the hills and on to the fields.

bridleway, byway and a section of a special long-distance cross-county route.

These paths weave in and out of land that is, as Rebecca Solnit puts it in her excellent history of walking, *Wanderlust* (1999), both 'utilitarian and aesthetic'. They are, she says, a very distinctive part of our countryside, and help create a particular sense of 'cohabitation', a very English compromise between the needs of some people to husband the land, and the needs of other people to pass through it; the veins that make the countryside feel whole, not atomised.

Often, we can divine a path's original purpose: the high dry road to market, the short cut up to the village from an outlying hamlet, the parson's route to church. Some of these paths are lovingly tended, even landscaped. Others only exist because a handful of locals walk them week in week out with their dogs – but every step keeps down the nettles, letting those who come after know that, yes, this is the right way.

For there is, undoubtedly, great comfort to be taken from knowing we are on the right track. 'Good-bye!' Gandalf calls after Bilbo and the dwarves as they plunge into Mirkwood. 'Be good, take care of yourselves – and DON'T LEAVE THE PATH.' If only they'd listened. It's the same in Susan Cooper's frost-bit tale, *The Dark is Rising*, which is deeply rooted in English folklore: the gathering forces of evil can't touch Will, our gifted young hero, so long as he doesn't leave the Old Way, 'trodden by the Old Ones for some three thousand years'.

But the pleasure we take in finding our way – the rusted marker on a stile, the scuffed grass leading across a field – is a reminder that we cross the land under sufferance, that even if we won't get strung up by giant spiders, trouble can still await us if we stray. And in parts of the countryside that aren't criss-crossed by welcoming lines on the map, we can quickly become confined, caught between the hum of roads and the impasse of private property. In such places, we can find ourselves butting up against what Kenneth Grahame (in an essay collection called *Pagan Papers*, not in *The Wind in the Willows*) called 'the stony stare of the boundary god' which confronts us 'at the end of every green ride and rabbit-run'.*

Nowadays, though, the paths are very often empty. If we met two people on our loop, we'd call it a busy morning. But once upon a time, the countryside would have bustled with walkers, with men, women and children going to work or to school, with tradesmen buying and selling, with lovers courting (or *walking out*), with the community going about its business.

But who now really walks long distances for anything other than pleasure? Very few people. The wanderer Laurie Lee, in his memoir *As I Walked Out One Midsummer Morning*, likened the men he met on the road in the hard years of the 1930s to somnambulists, to a broken army. And you do still occasionally pass them, dishevelled men striding down the country A-roads, taking up a whole lane, defying the drivers to run them down. But, largely, such walking out of need has passed beyond our experience.

No, when we walk today, we are, whether we know it or not, latter-day Romantics, walker-adventurers, if only for an hour or two. For the Romantics took the quotidian act of walking, and turned it into a spiritual endeavour, abetted by the tingle of starlight, the intoxicant of friendship – and

..........

* If you want to save on maps, follow Edward Thomas's advice in *The South Country* (1909). If he had a few days to walk, he let himself be guided by 'the hills or the sun or a stream'. If he only had one day, he walked 'in a rough circle, trusting, by taking a series of turnings to the left or a series to the right, to take much beauty by surprise and to return at last to my starting point'.

the 'divine luxury' of 'just, subtle, and mighty' opium.* At full moon, you can still find Coleridge's heirs settled on the long red hump of the Quantocks, their backs against the trig points, drinking in the ineffable.

But if the Romantics gave us the idea that walking was good for the soul, the Victorians, their cheeks heartily flushed, told us it boosted our moral fibre as well.** Victorian man of letters Leslie Stephen (father to Virginia Woolf; herself a flâneuse, rather than a walker) wrote in *Studies of a Biographer* that if only Lord Byron hadn't been so (literally) lame, he might have walked off his unwholesome humours and his morbid affectation and his perverse misanthropy. His advice has, of course, an irritating grain of truth: while it might not cure all ills, walking does make you feel better.

And it has another surprising benefit: solace for the agnostic. Once default Christianity started to waver amongst the intelligentsia, a passion for the outdoors presented itself as an alternative. 'Love of Nature', writes Jan Marsh in *Back to the Land* (1982), 'helped many late Victorians to dispense with God gradually, as it were, without losing their sense of immanent divinity.' The Sunday walk, in other words, could either complement the Sunday trip to church – or replace it altogether.

Walking, then, could improve you both inside and out, could make you feel (Leslie Stephen again) like 'a felicitous blend of poet and saint', something which was increasingly treasured by people who worked long hard hours in

..........

* Thomas De Quincey, pushing his favourite tipple, in *Confessions of an English Opium-Eater* (1821).
** You can discern traces of this in the teenage rite-of-passage that is the Duke of Edinburgh expedition. Walking for UCAS points? Coleridge would not have approved.

town. On his *English Journey*, J. B. Priestley reflects how a 'sharp walk of less than an hour' from the end of a Bradford tramline would bring you to the bare heights of the Pennines, the pure sky, the heather and ling. Recalling his own boyhood, he remembers how working men thought nothing of tramping thirty or forty miles every Sunday, sustained by a farmhouse 7d. tea.

> You caught the fever when you were quite young, and it never left you. However small and dark your office or warehouse was, somewhere inside your head the high moors were glowing, the curlews were crying, and there blew a wind as salt as if it came straight from the middle of the Atlantic.

Priestley loved these old-fashioned, lonely-as-a-cloud walkers, but he is somewhat less sure about the more collective, more political sort of walking that was on the rise in the 1930s. He thought people should walk in twos and threes, none of this setting off in bands of twenty or thirty. It worried him: 'They almost looked German.' Their 'semi-military, semi-athletic' air, he said, suggested 'the spirit of the lesser and priggish Wordsworth rather than the old magician who had inspired us'.

But it's easy to understand why young, working-class people chose to walk the uplands together. They weren't aping the Hitler Youth, far from it: they were part of a hiking craze, fuelled by higher real wages and cheaper travel. Yet this craze fell foul of some landowners who didn't like people on 'their' moors. As a police officer said at the time: 'We don't like hill walkers in Derbyshire. They are not welcome.' This led the more militant walkers to organise annual access rallies in the Peak District at Winnats Pass, as well as a now famous mass trespass at Kinder Scout, high on the Dark Peak.

After the Second World War, the radical Labour government, sympathetic to their demands, brought in the National Parks and Access to the Countryside Act. It's easy now to downplay its impact, to point out the barriers which still remained, but nevertheless it was the first big win (similar bills had been voted down for years) for the principle that people should, within reason, be able to enjoy the countryside in which they lived.

For it's a piquant quirk of the English language that two different concepts – 1) crossing a moral boundary and 2) crossing a physical boundary – are squished together inside one word: *trespass*. In other languages, when you ask God to forgive your sins, you don't use the same word that landowners hammer on gates.* This is probably why, when we trespass in England, we feel so keenly that we're doing wrong, that we're *sinning* – as anyone who has taken a wrong turn in a pheasant wood and found themselves trying to hide themselves and a bumptious dog from a gamekeeper will readily tell you.

The Countryside and Rights of Way Act of 2000, another piece of Labour legislation, unlocked more of the countryside (roughly 6,700 square miles of 'mountain, moor, heath and down'), but landowners fought hard against it, saying that they'd open up access voluntarily, that they needed to be recompensed, that new age travellers would exploit the rules, disturb wildlife and destroy crops. No such horrors came to pass, but even so, legislation is tightening up. Trespass isn't (despite what the signs say) a criminal offence, but you could find yourself accused of aggravated trespass. As Nick Hayes explains in *The Book*

..........
* In old French, *trespasser* did mean both *to cross over* and *to violate*, hence our usage. In modern French, however, *trépasser* has evolved, and now means *to die,* a one-way walk into the arms of the heavenly gamekeeper.

*of Trespass* (2020), 'if you are doing something that is not illegal (photography, dancing, playing the flute), while doing something that is not criminal (trespassing) you can be automatically arrested, and liable to six months in prison and a level-four fine'.

What campaigners are asking for today isn't land redistribution, isn't an end to private property, but for something that is already law in Scotland and in many parts of Europe: namely the right to walk, eat and sleep where you want, so long as you keep clear of houses, gardens and agricultural land and don't behave like an idiot. 'Without this,' says Hayes, 'we are treating the natural world like a museum, isolated exhibits of a culture long gone, something to be observed behind a red rope.'

If you track back through the decades you can find surprising advocates for this right to roam. Leslie Stephen, our eminent Victorian, advocated a judicious combination of footpaths and 'a little trespassing'. But he, of course, could stray with confidence, knowing that if he was challenged he could fall back on being a man of a certain class, with the right look, the right voice, the right beard. For it is, unarguably, easier for some people to walk off the beaten track than others.

'What's that coming over the hill? A white, middle-class Englishman! A Lone Enraptured Male! From Cambridge!'* That's the poet Kathleen Jamie, in a review of a (very good) book about our wildernesses, making this point robustly.

If you want a painfully well-written account of how it feels to be perceived as *different* in the British countryside, we'd steer you towards V. S. Naipaul's stunning piece of autofiction, *The Enigma of Arrival* (1987), which probes,

..........

* Declaration of interest: Meg is married to so very exactly one of these.

with lancet-like prose, how his narrator, a Trinidadian of Indian descent, experiences the downlands.

> After all my time in England I still had that nervousness in a new place, that rawness of response, still felt myself to be in the other man's country, felt my strangeness, my solitude. And every excursion into a new part of the country – what for others might have been an adventure – was for me like tearing at an old scab.

Other writers have explored how women and girls (and indeed non-masculine men) might experience a similar nervousness when walking alone. In *Gossip from the Forest* (2012), Sara Maitland examines the unease that snatches at her in out-of-the-way places: 'the sorts of things that create this sort of fear are strongly connected, for me, with masculinity'. As our ancestors might have stiffened at the print of wolf or bear, so certain proofs today – rifle shots; broken bottles, empty beer cans; wrecked bothies; the growl of quads and dirt bikes – put her on her guard. This fear can fade with age, but for every woman gamely eating up the miles, there's another for whom a solitary walk across an overgrown stretch of heath isn't remotely inviting.

And how much harder is it if you are both a woman and a person of colour? In *I Belong Here* (2021), Anita Sethi walks the Pennine Way, the backbone of Britain, after experiencing a vicious hate crime on a train in the north of England. Floored by anxiety and flashbacks, she decides not to stop travelling alone, but instead to seek hope on the heights. Up there, colour discrimination seems so ridiculous, she says. 'Can you imagine a blade of grass having low self-esteem, being made to hate its colour or shape? Despite being so literally trodden upon, it is so sure of itself, so confident in its skin. *Be more like grass growing*, I think.'

Yes, says Sethi, walking does have the power to quieten our minds, to soothe our hearts, but it also, she reminds us, has the power to unsettle: to make us see the world anew, to reconsider our place within it.

The freedom to walk – never mind the poetry, never mind the politics, just to walk (and, what's more, if you enjoy it, to walk alone) – is one of the greatest joys, the greatest privileges there is. If you doubt this, just think how it feels when old age or ill-health or foot-and-mouth or Covid close the countryside to us. Let's treasure this freedom, let's not squander it, and let's make sure it's a joy and a privilege in which as many people as possible can share.

# COW BINGO

.........................

This pint-sized guide should allow you to appear superficially knowledgeable about four distinguished cows you might run into, whether you're walking up hill or down dale.

**The Hereford.** The big swinging dick of the beef market. Bulls weigh in at nearly a tonne. Deep red coat. White face and white trimmings around its tummy, legs, feet and tail. A Herefordshire native, it has found its way all over the world, delivering fine steaks however rough the conditions.

**The Holstein Friesian.** The big swinging udder of the dairy market. Usually black and white. Originally from the Dutch-German corner of northwest Europe, they've largely displaced our old Ayrshires and Dairy Shorthorns. The best time to see them is early spring, when they're first turned out on to fresh pasture, skipping and jumping for joy. One cow can produce around 7,500 litres of milk a year, and can keep it up for 3–4 years.

**The Jersey.** Our Lady of clotted cream. The Channel Islands are home to three breeds, the Jersey, the Guernsey and the Alderney (now sadly extinct). The Jersey diaspora rivals that of the Holstein and the Hereford, also proving adaptable to hot and difficult conditions. Her coat is typically light brown with white patches, but it can also be redder or darker, with less white. She yields less milk than the Holstein – about 4,000 litres a year – but it is higher in butterfat, hence the cream fame.

**The Highland.** Sports a shaggy coat, which is usually reddish-brown, occasionally paler, occasionally jet-black. Long handsome horns. Very rugged in line with Scottish landscape. Forages across a wide range of plants. Increasingly deployed as a conservation grazer. Bred for meat.

# Bovinophobia

Absent hippopotamuses, malarial mosquitoes et al., cattle are our deadliest mammals, killing *twice as many* people per year as dogs. Remember Shere Khan, trampled to death in a buffalo stampede, a 'torrent of black horns, foaming muzzles, and staring eyes'? You (puny human) stand no chance. The protocol:

1. Large cows *and* small cows? **Calves.** DO NOT PROCEED. A large cow with a large penis? **Bull.** DO NOT PROCEED. Jaunty, japesome cows with small penises? **Bullocks.** DO NOT PROCEED. Nice grown-up lady cows quietly munching grass? **Common or garden cows.** PROCEED WITH CAUTION.

2. Assess the field for escape routes. If the cows do attack, is there a hedge or fence you could conceivably vault over or crawl under? Note: this will be a lot harder if you are nine months pregnant.

3. If you have a dog, decide which of you is prepared to make the ultimate sacrifice. Ideally, he will beg you, should it come to it, to drop his lead, whereupon he will charge the herd, barking madly, drawing their ire, so you can escape.

4. Deep breath. Head up. Shoulders back. The ominous clink of the gate shutting behind you will cause one of the cows to look up. Her tail will flick significantly. Don't let her psych you out.

5. Your dog is now likely straining upon the start. The game's afoot! Scurry around the perimeter of the field. Fling yourself through the far gate. Punch the air in triumph.

# FROM *PRIDE AND PREJUDICE*

by Jane Austen

'She has nothing, in short, to recommend her, but being an excellent walker. I shall never forget her appearance this morning. She really looked almost wild.'

'She did indeed, Louisa. I could hardly keep my countenance. Very nonsensical to come at all! Why must she be scampering about the country, because her sister had a cold? Her hair so untidy, so blowsy!'

'Yes, and her petticoat; I hope you saw her petticoat, six inches deep in mud, I am absolutely certain; and the gown which had been let down to hide it, not doing its office.'

'Your picture may be very exact, Louisa,' said Bingley; 'but this was all lost upon me. I thought Miss Elizabeth Bennet looked remarkably well, when she came into the room this morning. Her dirty petticoat quite escaped my notice.'

'You observed it, Mr. Darcy, I am sure,' said Miss Bingley; 'and I am inclined to think that you would not wish to see your sister make such an exhibition.'

'Certainly not.'

'To walk three miles, or four miles, or five miles, or whatever it is, above her ankles in dirt, and alone, quite alone! what could she mean by it? It seems to me to shew an abominable sort of conceited independence, a most country town indifference to decorum.'

'It shews an affection for her sister that is very pleasing,' said Bingley.

'I am afraid, Mr. Darcy,' observed Miss Bingley, in a half

whisper, 'that this adventure has rather affected your admiration of her fine eyes.'

'Not at all,' he replied; 'they were brightened by the exercise.'

# WALKING CHILDREN

..................................................

*But Nature is so uncomfortable. Grass is hard and lumpy and damp, and full of dreadful black insects.*
Oscar Wilde, 'The Decay of Lying' (1891)

When it comes to walking, children are resolutely apolitical and unRomantic, and it's up to you to bring them speedily up to scratch. Enjoying a walk is a culturally learned experience and needs to be inculcated like any other, but the earlier you start the easier it is.

Never debate the fact of the walk, only haggle about the details. So – cake or biscuits? Boots or trainers? Turnips or llamas? Never – walk or no-walk? The answer will always be no-walk.

But don't spring a walk on them too suddenly. Seed it well in advance. Like death and taxes, it must come to feel inevitable. If you foist an impromptu outing on them, the foot-dragging and bellyaching are your just desserts.

Pace yourself, but remember the pain barrier is probably psychological not physical. And be precise with times and distance. Don't fib 'oh, half an hour or so' when you know damn well it's three miles over rough country.

A dog is helpful. Walking a dog is a comprehensible goal and children like those. Admire the frequency and height of its pees, the inquisitiveness of its nose, the jaunty angle of its tail. Agree that your dog is better than all other dogs despite mounting evidence to the contrary.

Food is vital.* You can spend the first half-mile discussing what will be eaten, when and where. But be careful of over-promising and under-delivering. Unless you personally own an ice-cream van, do not guarantee it will be waiting in the car park.

Make sure you know where you're going. Your authority is essential and too much peering at map or surreptitious checking of phone undermines it.

Include features. Moorland walks are hopeless. They encourage grown-ups to ponder their place in *the grand scheme of things*, and that is much too large scale for your average child. Examples: bridges, lime kilns, rope swings, dog pounds, trig points, cows with unusual horns, beacons, the danger signs around quarries. And they won't notice a view unless you point at it and yell VIEW.

But don't be too quick to point things out. The early broadcaster S. P. B. Mais decreed: 'man has to go through a vigorous training before he can see the country at all', but you may find that *vigorous training* is something to which your children respond ill. George Orwell, right yet again, said: 'A boy [or girl] isn't interested in meadows, groves, and so forth.'

Moderation. We advise you to avoid the uncompromising approach of the writer Paul Kingsnorth's father, who led him on immense walks, while his son fell further and further behind, 'alone, scared, cold, crying', squelching in

..........

* Try DIY chocolate Hobnobs. Not that sweet, but weirdly compelling. Rub 75 g butter through a mix of 100 g darkest rye flour, pinch salt, tsp baking powder. Add 75 g blitzed oats, 40 g soft brown sugar, and use a splash or two of milk to bring it together. Add 50 g or so of chopped-up darkest chocolate. Roll out, slice into squares, bake for 15 mins at 180°C.

'black bog juice', feeling that even the cloud was 'punishing' him, rejoicing that the pylons spelt a return to civilisation.

The critic William Hazlitt said solitary walking is best: 'I cannot see the wit of walking and talking at the same time.' But sweet contemplative silence, reading 'the book of nature' is not child-friendly. You need to chat. If they're really flagging, ask them to list their top 10 favourite *Doctor Who / Friends* episodes. Then ask them to recite the plots. How the miles will unfurl.

Children have terrible thermostats. A grown-up can tolerate feeling a bit hot or a bit cold. Children cannot. Carry a large backpack and make no demur each time hats, gloves and fleeces go on and off. You use the same bag to stow important sticks and stones.

Always a loop, never a there-and-back. The moment you turn around and retrace your steps, you expose the futility of the walk. Never let that happen.

Don't gamify. Plant-spotting apps are amazing; it's great to take photos; to track your distance, but that's the walking equivalent of hiding vegetables in food. At some point you have to pull the wool from their eyes. This is a vegetable: eat. This is a path: walk.

Construct a family mythology of walking triumphs and walking disasters. The time we honestly saw an adder. The time that horrible dog scared our lovely dog and he really did nearly pull Mummy off a cliff hahaha. The time we found a creepy fallen tree in a spooky dingly dell, painted up with eyes to look like a monstrous trippy caterpillar. The time Mummy was so desperate to get to the pub before it stopped serving that she led us on a shortcut through a sea of gorse until we were all embayed and even the dog was crying and Daddy had to piggy-back everyone, including the dog, to safety. Evoke these memories if spirits are flagging.

# LIME, LIMESTONE, LIME KILNS

Lime* kilns are an anomaly: industrial relics which people actually like. Once upon a time, hundreds of kilns, large and small, were built all over the countryside, churning out tonne after tonne of lime, which could be turned into a building trade essential and a hugely popular dressing for farmland. Nowadays, they all lie abandoned. Some are scrubbed and signposted, but we rather like those which, burrowing into shadowy hillsides or lurking deep between the trees, are easily mistaken for goblin lairs at dusk.

**The science.** Limestone and chalk, our most common sedimentary rocks, contain a crystalline version of *calcium carbonate* ($CaCO_3$), the same compound found in seashells. After all, our rolling downlands are, in fact, a vast necropolis of tiny creatures which sank to the bottom of the warm sea which lapped above our heads during the Cretaceous (i.e. chalk-making) era.

If you heat these rocks to 600°C, you will drive off the carbon (C) and two of the oxygen atoms ($O_2$) in the form of carbon dioxide ($CO_2$), leaving behind the calcium (Ca) and the remaining oxygen (O) in the form of calcium oxide (CaO). This compound is known as quicklime,** burnt lime or just plain lime.

It will be:

1. the same volume as your original rock
2. half the weight

..........

\* Zero connection to the fruit. In Old English, *lim* means sticky.
\*\* The same *quick* as in quicksand, meaning alive; as in Jesus sitting at the right hand of the Father to judge *the quick and the dead*.

3. very caustic (it'd work well as an anti-goblin spray)
4. unstable (i.e. it wants to grab $CO_2$ from the air and turn back into $CaCO_3$).

To counter this instability, you must *slake* it. If you're a farmer, you add little bit of water, which will give you a powder. If you're a builder, you add a lot of water, which will give you a putty. Either way, you now have calcium hydroxide or $Ca(OH)_2$, which is known as hydrated or slaked lime.

**The farmer.** Lime makes soil less acidic, which perks up soil bacteria, encouraging them to work harder. In other words, lime isn't a fertiliser *per se*, but it helps a plant's root system make the best of what fertility there is. So if you wanted to make acid soil (which might rather be moor, heath or fen) more economically viable, liming was the way forward. It was often hailed as a cure-all: it made grass tastier, it loosened up heavy soil, it suppressed weeds, it prevented foot rot in sheep. And obviously, it also provided the micronutrient calcium.

Spreading lime used to be a grim job, with farmers applying up to five tonnes an acre, before people worked out that little and often worked better. Nowadays, farmers are more likely to use limey rocks ground to a very fine powder, and if they do use slaked lime, they deploy a whole bunch of safety measures, which we doubt were in place when landowners were improving their newly enclosed fields.

**The builder.** The bricks and stones of country houses and parish churches are stuck together with lime mortar and lime plaster, which is slaked lime mixed with sand and more water. In poorer houses, too, a little lime gave strength to the *daub* (some mix of earth, sand, straw, cow dung and horse hair) that you spread over your *wattle* (coppiced stems woven into panels).

**The jailer.** In Oscar Wilde's 'The Ballad of Reading Jail', guards 'with quicklime on their boots' bury a murderer in a makeshift grave in the prison grounds, a chilling curtain-raiser for his torments in hell. In reality, quicklime doesn't 'eat a body with teeth of flame' – scientists experimenting with pigs discovered that it actually *prevents* decay. It does, however, stop bodies smelling.*

# FARMING: PRESENT

........................................

*The Farmer is to blame. The Supermarket too. And let us not forget*
*the Politician, and the Consumer. Let us not omit Me, or You.*
John Lewis-Stempel, *The Running Hare* (2016)

Our attitude towards farmers and farming veers between two extremes. On the one hand, a gooey Old-MacDonald nostalgia for baa-lambs, smocks, horny hands and hayricks. On the other, an angry polemicism: *you* – with your dirty combine harvesters and your sad little piglets – *you* poisoned *our* land.

'If the people of England knew what was happening to their countryside, they would not stand for it,' Marion Shoard wrote in *The Theft of the Countryside* back in 1980. But for a long time many of us either didn't know – or didn't want to know. After all, the changes were patchy and

..........

* Childhood memory. One long-ago spring, three bullocks fell through the hole at the top of a derelict lime kiln on a Devon riverbank, dying a horrible death. A local doctor, aggrieved that the stench of rotting flesh was blighting her favourite picnic spot, organised a working party, wearing surgical masks, to dig the whole lot out.

piecemeal (let's not get in a state about a hedge here, a pond there). The bugs and birds affected were unglamorous (let's save the pandas, let's save the whales). The government said they had everything under control (intensive farming = food security = a better life for the nation) and the farmers agreed (intensive farming = more subsidies = a better life for them and their families).

But since the early years of this century, there has been a broadening and deepening sense of unease, a sense – backed up by hard evidence – that the relationship between farming and the land has gone awry. In the end, it wasn't the increasingly frantic appeals of environmentalists (where are the birds, the bees, *where???*) that broke through, but rather the one-two punch of mad cow disease and foot-and-mouth. The one was immortalised by a Conservative agriculture minister trying to make his daughter eat a burger to prove British beef wouldn't kill you, and the other by bleak footage of mounds of smouldering animal corpses. Both combined to make us realise that something was out of joint. And so now, when we talk of England's green and pleasant land, nine times out of ten, those resonant little words are laced with irony.

REWIND

William Blake wrote the poem 'Jerusalem' in 1804, the same year a man called Richard Cobden was born. He fronted the Anti-Corn Law League, which was on one side of the great political and economic dust-up of the nineteenth century. Should the government protect British farmers by putting up import barriers on wheat? Or should the farmers be forced to compete with producers overseas? It's an argument we're still having.

Grain prices and farming profits remained high during the Napoleonic Wars, but fell sharply come 1815 and the restoration of peace. The landed interest, giddy with relief that they'd not been guillotined like their French cousins, weren't having it. Parliament, still totally unreformed, passed a series of laws, essentially banning imports until domestic prices hit a certain level. People went hungry. People rioted. People, including the growing middle classes of the new industrial towns, got together to demand affordable bread. Their victory came in 1846 when Robert Peel repealed the Corn Laws, torpedoing Tory party unity for a generation.

Imports boomed. And by the end of the century it wasn't only possible to buy in food from Europe, but also from further afield. Think of all those homesteaders in the United States setting off in wagons to 'open up' the prairie. By the end of the century they were big players in a globalising food market, with Australia, Argentina and Brazil also getting in on the act. The effect on British farming was catastrophic.

H. Rider Haggard, in journalist not novelist mode, travelled round the countryside in 1901–2 in dismay. 'Whatever free trade may have done for the country at large,' he wrote, 'it has brought the land and agriculture of England very near the brink of ruin.' The First World War and the German U-boat blockades briefly reversed the trend, putting guaranteed minimum prices for wheat and oats in place, but this ran counter to the broader ideology of the time, and soon after the war the policy was scrapped – farmers called it the 'Great Betrayal' – plunging agriculture back into depression.

Ralph Whitlock, a writer and Wiltshire farmer, wrote a book called *The Lost Village* about those interwar wars, based on interviews with the oldest of his neighbours who were still alive in the 1980s.* Back in the 1920s, he reported, the villagers were aware of mile upon mile of dereliction, just over the horizon. 'It was possible to see the outlines of the deserted fields and even of the plough ridges, for they had been abandoned without even being sown to grass.' And by then it wasn't just arable farmers who were being outcompeted. Huge advances in refrigeration meant the Roast Beef of Old England was now being raised on the pampas of Argentina.

Put bluntly, Britain got its money from making stuff in factories and selling that stuff to the world. The factory workers needed to eat, and the cheaper they could buy their food, the less they needed to be paid. Imported food was cheaper than home grown – and all the shipping benefited our merchant navy. 'Against all that,' writes Whitlock, 'home agriculture was an expendable pawn. It was as simple as that.'

What changed? The Second World War.

The government was terrified that if the country couldn't feed itself, it'd wind up losing the war. Rationing kicked in. The big houses ploughed up their front lawns. Farmers and land girls were the heroes of the hour. And once the war was over, politicians were united in their determination that Britain wasn't going to go hungry *ever again*.

FAST FORWARD

The resolve, enshrined in the 1947 Agriculture Act, was to guarantee prices and boost production: and on that it delivered, 100 per cent. The downside? The countryside, according to a medley of qualitative and quantitative measures, was comprehensively trashed.

..........

* There's a beautiful picture in our copy, showing him cuddling a tame badger called Barney, which makes us inclined to trust every word he says.

Oliver Rackham, in *The History of the Countryside* (1986), is clear where the blame lay. (Hint: not with the farmers.)

> I am not attacking farmers in general; the severest critics of recent practices are themselves farmers. The trouble lies with that powerful lobby which insists that farming is an industry (by which is meant *merely* an industry) and yet requires it to be subsidised, and allowed to do anti-social things, to a degree which no other industries enjoy.

In other words, don't blame individuals; blame the system. Farmers were asked, and heavily incentivised, to make as much food as possible using all the means available. If you know you're going to get paid a fixed sum for what you bring to market (in other words, if you no longer have to worry about the market) – and if, moreover, you're being told that maximising output is the right, the responsible, the moral thing to do – well, of course you're going to do it. It was national policy. Later, when we signed up to Europe, it was part of the Common Agricultural Policy. It was taught in agricultural college and written about approvingly in books. It was what your neighbours were doing, and if you didn't get with the programme, you'd be seen as a crank, an oddball, a relic.

Farming this intensively would, historically, have stressed crops and animals alike. But by then there was an increasing array of technological solutions: fertilisers, pesticides, fungicides, antibiotics, vaccines, drenches, wormers, dips, which could be applied to keep your crops growing and your animals milking. But this system – ramped-up productivity buttressed by science – came with a slew of drawbacks.

## LAND INTENSIFICATION
Farmers ploughed up marginal land and crowded more

animals on to what land they already had. It was as though we were still at war, and had to keep digging frantically for victory no matter what. Guaranteed prices for all those crops, for all that meat, inevitably led to chronic over-supply: the second half of the twentieth century was the age of butter mountains and milk lakes. Policymakers realised this was ridiculous, and in 2003 replaced direct price intervention with something called the single farm payment, which basically gave farmers a lump-sum subsidy per hectare. The effect on land use was the same: cultivate more land, get more money.

Delicious green patches teeming with what we'd now call biodiversity were no use to anyone. Anything that got in the way of big machines and straight lines was tidied up – or, to put it another way, destroyed. These changes, repeated over and over across the country, a steady accretion of small decisions, all of which would have seemed sensible at the time, meant that woods, heaths, ponds, meadows, hedges, were all going ... going ... gone.

## SYNTHETIC FERTILISERS

Imagine, if instead of having to drive your animals on and off your fields, or pitchfork trailer-loads of manure, you could simply sprinkle magic pellets to make everything grow good and green and strong, like Sam Gamgee's box of earth from Lothlórien. You'd be interested, right?

By the 1940s, magic pellets were readily available.

Before we go into the downsides, it's very important to say that without synthetic fertilisers, hundreds of millions of people would not have been able to eat. It was the keystone of the Green Revolution (which, confusingly, wasn't green in the sense people mostly understand the word today), which massively boosted food production in developing countries. Back in Britain, describing his own smallholding in *The Fat of the Land* (1961), the self-sufficiency pioneer John Seymour wrote with disarming truthfulness: 'If we were growing crops to sell to the public [...] we would certainly use artificials and plenty of 'em.'

What, then, is not to like?

1. When it rains, artificial fertilisers run off fields and into rivers, creating *algal blooms*.* You're turbo-charging your crops – and aquatic plant life. The delighted phytoplankton proliferate, hoovering up all the oxygen, blocking out the sunlight, choking off all other life. What starts as merely gross for the swimmer (and confusing for dogs who think there's green sward ahead and take a flying leap), ends up as a fish killer.

2. It's like croissant versus porridge. Sure we'd *rather* eat a croissant for breakfast, but come 11am we'll wish we'd plumped for porridge. In other words, it works to start with. But it doesn't go on working.

3. You're not putting organic matter back into the soil, which is a mistake in the longer term. Organic matter makes soil easier to work (i.e. you can drive a tractor over it without it compacting); it boosts bacteria, fungi and earthworms; it holds on to more carbon; it reduces problems with run-off or waterlogging; and it makes soil more resistant to drought.

4. Atmospheric nitrogen is in some ways a dream raw material: free and unlikely to run out any time soon. Unfortunately, you also need a *lot* of natural gas to turn it into fertiliser, which has a knock-on effect on carbon emissions. Plus, fertiliser prices rove up and down

..........

* Possible plague no. 1 in Exodus: 'With the staff that is in my hands I will strike the water of the Nile, and it will be changed into blood. The fish in the Nile will die, and the river will stink and the Egyptians will not be able to drink its water.'

depending on gas prices, which in turn are linked to the geopolitical hellscape, which is totally and utterly beyond any individual farmer's control. Phosphorous and potassium, on the other hand, are quite simply finite resources. That's right: you can add peak phosphorus and peak potassium to your worry list.

PESTICIDES

The classic farming manual, *The Complete Farmer* by Primrose McConnell,* had the truth of it back in 1910: 'It appears as if the very fact of our crops being highly specialised or developed plants has made them more subject to [pest] attacks, or at least they suffer more than the natural, uncultivated vegetation does.' The solution, everyone knew, was to spray.

In his farming memoir, *The Worm Forgives the Plough* (1975), John Stewart Collis remembers having to douse apples with 'a combination of such a poisonous complexion that even to look at it was mentally disturbing'. But he did it. Of course he did it. It was the thing to do: 'a field of kale, though it glitter with the scarlet, the red, the blue, the yellow and other shades of pretty flowers, is disgustingly dirty to the agricultural eye'. And what was the alternative? Go *backwards*? Back to children rummaging around the fields looking for thistles, looking for nettles, teasels, docks. Good luck with that.

And if you've ever cherished a row of broad beans, sowing them in mid-November, cheering the first shoots on Boxing Day morning, weeding them lovingly once the days lengthen, staking them just in time to save them

..........

* We were initially delighted that a woman had authored such a benchmark book; we were disappointed and delighted in equal measure to discover that Primrose here refers to a man.

from a late-spring gale, if after six months of pouring your love into them, you've watched blackfly turn your hopes and dreams into a sticky, sickly travesty, you will instantly be able to capture the joy farmers felt when scientists told them: *we can fix this.*

So yes, the chemicals killed weeds, bugs and blights, but, as documented so powerfully in Rachel Carson's 1962 game-changer *Silent Spring*, they killed an awful lot of other plant and animal life as well. When H. G. Wells wrote in *The Time Machine* (1895) that the air in the far-future was free from gnats, the earth from weeds or fungi, he thought he was painting a prescient picture of future perfection – only now do we properly understand that if the air and soil is denuded of life, it is, in fact, a disaster.

Sarah Langford, a barrister-turned-farmer, illustrates this perfectly in her memoir. A farmer, looking down from the back of his tractor, sees that the stubble from the last year's harvest is still lying on the ground, months later. 'The truth of what he is seeing hits him with a great force. This earth – his earth – is so empty of life it cannot even decompose plant matter any more.'

SYNTHETIC FERTILISERS AND PESTICIDES

In *The Killing of the Countryside* (1997), Graham Harvey* explains how the two things work in uneasy synergy: 'High levels of nitrogen fertiliser render crop plants more susceptible to disease. So if farmers can be persuaded to push up their nitrogen inputs in pursuit of yields, they are, at the same time, increasing their dependence on fungicides.'

It's like being dog tired, but instead of going to bed, you drink more coffee, eat more biscuits, thinking *I can I can,*
..........

---

* As well as his work as a writer and journalist, Graham Harvey has written hundreds of episodes of *The Archers*, and has also acted as the show's agricultural adviser.

until you can't any more, and you pass out and wake up feeling terrible and swill a load of headache pills, eat two croissants, drink a fat Coke and round and round it goes until eventually you crash.

But if you *didn't* fertilise, *didn't* spray, and your crop was lost – and your neighbour *did* fertilise, *did* spray, and their crop flourished, what were you going to choose the next year?

### SPECIALISATION, CONSOLIDATION, MECHANISATION

'The government,' wrote John Seymour, who was very much swimming against the tide, 'the agricultural supply industries, the agricultural press, all carry on a holy crusade nowadays to persuade farms to specialise.' The classic mixed farm, a bit of this, a bit of that, some arable, some cows or sheep, was increasingly seen as out of date, inefficient. Bolstered by scientific innovation and the subsidy regime, farmers didn't need to hedge against bad years by spreading their risk across a variety of crops and stock. Goodbye mixed farms; hello monoculture.

In addition, sectors which had once been the preserve of the smallholder – poultry, pigs – were increasingly taken over by bigger operations, which ushered in the depressing world of battery chickens and sows suckling their piglets in pens so small they can't turn around.

Farms, fields, machines, all of them got bigger and bigger, but fewer and fewer people were employed, and if you did have a job, it was more and more lonely. And for every agri-business making money, capitalising on economies of scale, the appliance of science, the latest machines, there was a small family farm struggling to make ends meet. Even with subsidies, you have to factor in seeds, fertiliser, sprays, fuel, machines, machine maintenance, rent payments, mortgage payments, loan payments, contractor payments. The constant juggling takes its toll: there's a nook at our local livestock auction site, an *ad hoc* consulting room, covered in posters begging farmers not to be proud, to please see somebody about their physical or mental health.

Melissa Harrison's novel *At Hawthorn Time* (2015) tells how when teenager Jamie was a little boy, he'd liked to make-believe he'd work as a herdsman for his best friend, Alex, the farmer's son, when he grew up. But then the farmer and his wife got divorced, and Alex and his mum moved away, and the farmer killed himself, and so now the farm's standing empty, and Jamie's a picker and packer at a distribution site. 'It seemed impossible, as though so many centuries of productivity, so many hopes, should leave an echo; as though a working farm could not so quickly die. And yet it had.'

Looking back over this period, the Lake District farmer James Rebanks says the economics books were all about how things changed for the better: 'they didn't say much about the losers, the misery, and people hanging on for years, sometimes decades, because they knew nothing else'. His community, he says, was fracturing and breaking. Farming, after all, is often so much more than a job. It might be knackering, all-consuming, poorly paid, but for many farmers no other line of work was even going to begin to compare.

We have, now, finally reached a point where it is clear that for both the good of the land *and* the good of the people who work on it, things need to change, but exactly what that change should be, how it should be brought about, that answer is still being tossed around between politicians and civil servants, between vociferous campaigners – and the bewildered farmers themselves.

# TO A MOUSE

by Robert Burns

*On turning her up in her Nest, with the Plough,*
*November 1785.*

Wee, sleeket, cowran, tim'rous beastie,
O, what a panic's in thy breastie!
Thou need na start awa sae hasty,
　　Wi' bickering brattle!
I wad be laith to rin an' chase thee
　　Wi' murd'ring pattle!

I'm truly sorry Man's dominion
Has broken Nature's social union,
An' justifies that ill opinion,
　　Which makes thee startle,
At me, thy poor, earth-born companion,
　　An' fellow-mortal!

I doubt na, whyles, but thou may thieve;
What then? poor beastie, thou maun live!
A daimen-icker in a thrave
　　'S a sma' request:
I'll get a blessin wi' the lave,
　　An' never miss 't!

Thy wee-bit housie, too, in ruin!
It's silly wa's the win's are strewin!
An' naething, now, to big a new ane,
    O' foggage green!
An' bleak December's winds ensuin,
    Baith snell an' keen!

Thou saw the fields laid bare an' waste,
An' weary Winter comin fast,
An' cozie here, beneath the blast,
    Thou thought to dwell,
Till crash! the cruel coulter past
    Out thro' thy cell.

That wee-bit heap o' leaves an' stibble
Has cost thee monie a weary nibble!
Now thou's turn'd out, for a' thy trouble,
    But house or hald,
To thole the Winter's sleety dribble,
    An' cranreuch cauld!

But Mousie, thou art no thy-lane,
In proving foresight may be vain:
The best laid schemes o' Mice an' Men
    Gang aft agley,
An' lea'e us nought but grief an' pain,
    For promis'd joy!

Still, thou art blest, compar'd wi' me!
The present only toucheth thee:
But Och! I backward cast my e'e,
    On prospects drear!
An' forward tho' I canna see,
    I guess an' fear!

# GOOD FENCES MAKE GOOD NEIGHBOURS: POSTS AND WIRE

Deer vs baby trees?
Fox vs baby chickens?
Puppy vs baby leeks?
You need a fence in a hurry.

Round up:
- a friend
- posts (you need enough to go every 3/4 yards along your fence-line, plus a couple of extras for either end)
- a roll of wire mesh
- a roll of wire, plain or barbed
- a crowbar
- a rammer
- a mallet
- a hammer
- a drill and screws
- a tape measure
- a spirit level
- a chainsaw
- a fencing tool
- rope

1. **Sink the first post.** Make a small indentation with your crowbar. Insert post into indentation. Place rammer on top of post. With your friend, ram four times. Use spirit level to check it's going in straight. Adjust as necessary. Ram a further eight times. Check level again. Check depth: in at least 18 inches? No? Couple of final rams.

2. **Prop the first post.** Use your mallet to drive a second post into the ground at a 45° angle. With your chainsaw, carefully nick a wedge out of the first post. Tuck the diagonal post into the wedge.

3. **Sink the rest of the posts.** Lay the rope down your fence-line to act as a guide. Remove any obstructions (brambles, stones, old bits of rotten post). Ram your intermediate posts. Prop the final post.

4. **Wrap the mesh around the first post.** Hammer staples top, middle and bottom: you really don't want the mesh pinging off when you tension the fence. Continue down the fence-line, unwinding (your friend) and hammering (you) as you go.

5. **Tighten the fence, starting at the midpoint.** This is what your fencing tool is for.*

6. **Unroll your top-wire, very very carefully.** (It will try to go angry snake on you.) Same drill as with the mesh. Attach. Tighten. Admire.

..........

* YouTube this. Pithy explanation of how to use a fencing tool: impossible.

# MEADOWS, ANCIENT AND MODERN

...................................................................................

*Achieving an image of nature as we might dream it to be is not as easy as it looks.*
Christopher Lloyd, *Meadows* (2004)

Natural grassland (called savannah, prairie, pampas, veld or steppe in other parts of the world) isn't a common feature of our countryside. It tends to develop in places that are too dry, too high, too windy or too salty for trees to take hold. Our grassland, on the other hand, tends to be man-made, either because we encourage our animals to graze it (*pasture*) or because we cut it down every year to make hay (*meadow*).*

An ancient meadow, then, which looks like nature in fullest and most glorious spate, is actually one of our most meticulously managed habitats. This can lead to confusion.

The nature writer Helen Macdonald admits she was so horrified – in younger days – by the sight of a farmer about to mow a meadow that she hurled herself in front of his tractor. 'I didn't,' she explains in her essay collection *Vesper Flights* (2020), 'understand how hay meadows work. All I saw was destruction. How could I know that the mower's job was to hold history in suspension, keeping the meadow

..........

* Many languages have two words to show the distinction:

| English | meadow | pasture |
|---------|--------|---------|
| French | pré | pâturage |
| German | wiese | weide |
| Latin | pratum | pascuum |
| Russian | луг | пастбище |

exactly where it was against the encroachment of heather and birch and time?'* This, then, is how, for centuries, we made time stand still:

**Early spring.** Turn your animals out from their winter quarters and let them feast on the sweet new grass.

**Late spring, early summer.** Move the animals to pastures new, leaving the meadow to grow. Over the centuries, long-stemmed flowers (i.e. flowers which can hold their own) will have established themselves amidst the grass, earning themselves any number of pretty names: ox-eye daisy, meadowsweet, confused eyebright, ragged robin, cinquefoil, lady's bedstraw ...

**Late summer.** Cut your grass – which, fortuitously, is ready *after* the flowers have set seed. Use a scythe if you're really hardcore. Don't leave it too late or the grass will form a dense thatch above its root system, making it harder for the flowers to germinate next year. Allow the grass to dry and, depending which century you're living in, rake it into windrows, build a hayrick, or simply bale it up and drive it to your haybarn.

**Autumn.** Return your animals to the meadow to graze any regrowth. Their manure keeps the soil's fertility topped up, without enriching it so much that the grass becomes too dominant. Their hooves will also churn the soil – known as poaching – leaving ruts and bare patches which are the perfect spots for flowers to flourish next year.

..........

* *Rivals* (1988), the most perfect of Jilly Cooper's perfect novels, features a different misunderstanding. Taggie, our grey-eyed heroine, notices that Rupert Campbell-Black's fields are on fire. She races to tell him (past red admirals gorging on white buddleia: great foreshadowing). He pauses his (naked) tennis game to tell her (caddishly! so 80s!) that they're burning the stubble. 'What about the rabbits?' asks Taggie, whose grey eyes are probably a bit like a frightened rabbit's. 'They've got legs,' says Rupert, 'they can run.' Stubble burning was, as it turns out, banned a few years after publication.

**Winter.** Many meadows were once purposely situated near riverbanks, with special sluice systems that meant they could be flooded on demand (by a man called a drowner). Soaking a meadow ahead of the spring warmed the soil, encouraging an earlier new crop of grass: fresh food for your animals at exactly the moment your hay stores were running low.

But these meadows have nearly all gone: since the 1930s, we've lost *97 per cent* of them. What happened?

Firstly, **specialisation**. Meadows made sense if you ran a traditional mixed farm. A purely arable farmer, however, has no animals to feed. No animals, no hay, no meadows. A purely livestock farmer, on the other hand, could choose to focus on what they knew best – their animals – and simply buy in winter feed, rather than going to the trouble of haymaking.

Secondly, **yield**. Farmers who still needed hay often opted to plough up their meadows and re-plant them with specialist grasses, an annual crop to be fertilised and sprayed like any other. The yield is much greater – wonderful thick lush green grass – but the biodiversity, i.e. the pretty flowers, was gone.

Thirdly, **silage**. In the dark days before you could check the Met Office rain radar on your phone, haymaking was a tense business. Farmers spent nail-gnawing hours thinking *is it going to rain, is it, shall I cut, shall I wait, yes, yes, arrrrrgh, bollocks, no* – and all during British summers which, as we all know very well, can go tits-up at the drop of a hat. If rain was the enemy, silage was the cavalry, riding to the rescue. You no longer need a run of bright blue breezy days to dry your grass; instead, you can simply cut it, scoop it up and squish it down in a clamp or wrap it up in plastic.

By winter, it will have fermented,* giving your animals tasty food that's a) nutritious and b) easy to digest. Plus, because you've sown robust ryegrass into fertilised soil, you can get two or even three cuts of silage, versus one cut of hay.

Given the above, it's hardly surprising that meadows are now a romantic memory, a relic, a daydream of buzzing bees, flickering butterflies, ticking grasshoppers, aching work and moonlit play at hazy sweet-smelling summer's end. A hundred years ago, Sylvia Townsend Warner's heroine, Laura/Lolly, walked into just such a meadow, blooming with flowers:

> She knelt down among them and laid her face close to their fragrance. The weight of all her unhappy years seemed for a moment to weigh her bosom down to the earth; she trembled, understanding for the first time how miserable she had been; and in another moment she was released. It was all gone, it could never be again, and never had been. Tears of thankfulness ran down her face. With every breath she drew, the scent of cowslips flowed in and absolved her.

We experimented. There's no absolution in ryegrass.

Here, then, is how to (try to) **make your own wildflower meadow**. Informal, unfussy, natural, *wild* – they are, after all, extremely fashionable: the gardener's darling, you could say, rather than the farmer's duty. Sadly, though, it's not always as simple as #NoMowMay.

1. It might seem easier to try to **revive** a meadow where there was one before, but first a word of warning from Pam Lewis, meadow expert: 'As with antiques, copies

..........

* It smells ... sort of weird, but sort of nice. A bit like a sourdough starter. Silage is, in fact, an unsung trailblazer for foodie interest in kimchi, kefir, sauerkraut et al.

of fakes may be attempted but the original can never be replaced.' Once a meadow has been ploughed and resown, you can't just stop ploughing and guarantee that it will reappear, looking just as it did a hundred years ago. You can't rewind. Nor can you sow wildflower seeds and guarantee that a beautiful meadow will magically emerge. You can't fast forward. The delicate dance between grass and flowers evolved over centuries, and it might take years, a decade or more, for them to re-learn the steps. Until then, your wildflower meadow might largely feature buttercups, dandelions and thistles.

2. You also can't **establish** a new meadow anywhere you think it might look nice. If you're starting from scratch, the gateway to wildflower nirvana is thin, nutrient-poor, free-draining soil on chalk or limestone bedrock. (It's not that wildflowers like poor soil, it's just they can cope with it better than grass, nettles, etc., so they don't get crowded out.) Unfortunately, if you live on half-decent land, your meadow ambitions are going to be stymied by your soil's fertility. You'll be battling brambles, thistles and ragwort into submission for *years*.

3. If you think you're in with a chance – or if you're determined to defy the odds – preparation is vital. You must suppress the existing flora:
   **Poison.** Drench your proto-meadow with glyphosate in the spring. Repeat two or three times more over the summer to kill any regrowth. It works a treat, but unless you lie through your teeth, your green halo will have lost some of its lustre.*

..........

* The World Health Organisation has said glyphosate is a probable carcinogen; many campaigners want its use banned.

**Strip.** Remove a 15–20 cm layer of topsoil from your proto-meadow. Sell it – or mould a mysterious tumulus whose purpose will fox future historians.

**Dump.** Concoct 15–20 cm of the most degraded 'soil' imaginable. Cover your proto-meadow with some old carpet. Cover the carpet with sand, gravel, rubble, lime-stone chippings, mimicking the sort of post-industrial landscape where wildflowers flourish. In fact, the best place for a meadow is not an unloved paddock, but a front drive.

4. Buy **seeds**, British seeds, ideally collected from the ancient hay meadow down the road. You need a mix of grasses, plus both perennial and annual flowers. You can also decide to eschew the grass, because it'll very likely turn up on its own. You definitely want some yellow rattle, which is hemi-parasitic on certain grasses, pen-etrating their roots with its own, nicking their nutrients, and thereby giving wildflowers a headstart. Cornfield annuals (cornflowers, marigolds, poppies) will provide some colour while you're getting going.*

5. **Scatter** your seeds at summer's end, raking them into your hopefully thin and unwelcoming soil. Exposure to the cold over the winter will remind them to germinate. Watch and wait. Once they appear, you need to decide what's flower and what's noxious weed, because this year (and the next and the next) you must uproot the muscular thugs to ensure the survival of their meeker brethren.

6. After your flowers have set seed (here's hoping), you **mow**. Gather up every last scrap of grass. Leaving it

..........

* Some people plant annual meadows, which are different from classic meadows. They rely on the sorts of flowers that traditionally thrived ephemerally on the margins of ploughed fields – before enthusiastic spraying did for them.

would increase fertility and you don't want that. If it's a warm autumn, mow again.

7. Stick at it. Eventually, you'll have something that, honestly, people will come from miles around to **admire**.

# THE WOODS AND THE TREES

...........................................................

*La nature est un temple où de vivants piliers
laissent parfois sortir de confuses paroles.
L'homme y passe à travers des forêts de symboles
Qui l'observent avec des regards familiers.**
Charles Baudelaire, 'Correspondances' (1857)

Once, there was ice.**

Then, 12,000 years ago, it started to melt, and our woodland history began, with pioneer trees chasing the ice as it retreated northwards. You can think of them as waves of invaders – coming by land not sea; we weren't an island then – starting with birch and pine, followed by hazel, followed by oak, alder and lime, then elm, then ash, and finally holly, beech, probably rowan, probably hornbeam, before the rising seas (all that ice melting) cut Britain off from the

..........

* Very rough translation: 'Nature is a temple whose living pillars sometimes let slip crazy words. We walk through forests of symbols: they see straight through us.' (God, we love the French.)
** What follows is indebted to Oliver Rackham's engrossing *Woodlands*. We could say something like 'he towers over the study of the countryside like an ancient oak', except he comes across as a singularly modest, if unbelievably knowledgeable, man. His *Economist* obituary (he died in 2015) describes him as a 'shyly smiling wild man of the woods [...] with a lengthening and whitening beard'.

rest of Europe. Any trees that came thereafter came as seeds in Roman pockets (did they have pockets?); as lovingly wrapped saplings in explorers' sea-chests; as UPS deliveries from nurseries in Holland.

Today, we call this post-ice landscape the *wildwood*, and we can only wonder how much of a shock it was for our very distant ancestors, whose way of life had developed hunting game across the open tundra, to find a tree-wall growing up all around.

As to what this wildwood (or wildwoods) looked like, there are two takes. For a long time, we assumed it was dense trees, thick undergrowth, a dark, tangled and impenetrable place. Not so, say more recent studies. They invite us to envisage it as more like savannah, lots of trees, yes, but lots of clearings too, open spaces where the big beasts could stomp and graze.

There are problems with both theories, but we can leave those to the experts, because everyone agrees that by the closing chapters of pre-history (roughly 3,800–2,000 BCE), the wildwood was on its way out. The Mesolithic hunter-gatherers left only the most tantalising of traces upon our landscape, but the Neolithic farmers who followed them had grander designs.

These men and women, migrants from the central and eastern European steppes, brought new skills and new ideas to our islands. Their societies depended on arable crops, and so they had to do everything they could to make wheat and barley feel at home: they had to get rid of the trees. They also needed space for houses and animal pens, for tombs and temples, for all the things we recognise as civilisation. The Bronze and Iron Age peoples who followed them were culturally very different, but they too managed the land by suppressing its trees.

Fast forward to the arrival of the Romans, and our tree cover was, believe it or not, only a little bigger than it is today. Some say 20 per cent, some as little as 10 per cent. Nor, as we once thought, did the Romans' departure (they pulled out in the fifth century) trigger a literal Dark Ages: a great green roof *didn't* grow up over King Arthur's head. Some fields might have been abandoned. Some trees might have regrown. But the wildwood didn't return.

How do we know for sure?

Well, if you have the skill and patience to fillet the Domesday Book, you can say with reasonable confidence that by the 1080s, tree cover stood at 15 per cent, perhaps a little less. Obviously, some bits were woodier than others, with the west and the southeast of England woodier than the middle. So if the wildwood *had* existed during the Dark Ages (now more politely called the Early Middle Ages), somebody would have needed to fell a *huge* number of trees to hand the Normans the landscape they so meticulously recorded. But, says Rackham: 'The entire corpus of Old English writing makes no direct mention of woodland being destroyed.' That doesn't mean woodland was never grubbed, he adds, but we can infer that the Germanic settlers who followed the Romans took over the landscape as 'a going concern'. Plus, Old English legal documents show woodlands as both defined and owned. In other words, the woods were exploited – *farmed* even. They weren't some great big amorphous creepy wild Other.

Or, to put it another way, an Angle Hansel and a Saxon Gretel would have been hard put to get lost in the woods. 'The trail of white pebbles,' writes Francis Spufford in *The Child That Books Built* (2002), 'would really not have been required.'

Nevertheless, the *idea* of the wildwood has lived on – for centuries. From Gawain questing after the Green Knight, dodging wolves and wodwos,* bulles and beres and bores, to poor old Moley frightened out of his tiny mind by the faces in the trees, we still think of woods as places of fairytale, of magic and freedom, of awe and dread. And that's fair enough. If you walk into a darkling wood before the moon is up, after the chainsaws have done their worst, the pools of sawdust glow like phosphorescent tree-blood, a winding pathway leading you – where? Spufford reckons that, in fact, we *need* to go down to these metaphorical woods, that they are – if you're in a Freudian mood – 'the mind's necessary wilderness'.

The US academic Robert Pogue Harrison, in *Forests: The Shadow of Civilization* (1992), suggests that it was only later, when the *city* started to be seen as more threatening, more dangerous – a site/locus/signifier of jeopardy, of moral, financial and physical corruption – that the woods could be reimagined as somewhere inviting. By Tudor times, therefore, an English wood could also be innocent, diversionary, comic, a place of improbable disguises and big reveals, a place where you could bend identities, blur categories, the world of *As You Like It* and *A Midsummer Night's Dream*.**

Another way for a wood to become more fun (for some people) was for it to become a *forest*, a controversial innovation which we owe to William the Conqueror. A millennium ago, you see, forests weren't forests; forests were game reserves, tracts of countryside demarcated for the king's hunting pleasure. In a forest, the animals (deer, boar, hares, wolves) were not to be touched (apart from by the king and the king's friends) and if anyone *did* touch

..........

* Hairy, scary quasi-satyrs; very popular in medieval Europe.
** The Big Bad City, in other words, became scarier than the Big Bad Wolf. Coincidentally, by Shakespeare's time, wolves were extinct in England.

them: retribution. 'His rich men bemoaned it,' reports *The Anglo-Saxon Chronicle* (after his death), 'and the poor men shuddered at it. But he was so stern, that he recked not the hatred of them all; for they must follow withal the king's will, if they would live, or have land, or possessions, or even his peace.'

Whether or not anyone ever actually had their eyes put out for killing a stag is up for debate, but there's no doubt that in creating forests, William created a prestige activity, as well as a whole system of patronage he could exploit: food to feast his nobles; carcasses and hunting rights to bestow as gifts; cash from fines to fill his coffers. It was, in effect, a bold opening gambit in a war we're still fighting today: who gets to hunt what, where, when and why.

The first Royal Forests included large areas of farmland (New Forest), woodland (Epping Forest), moorland (Dartmoor), marshland (Lincolnshire) and heath (Sherwood Forest)*, anywhere, in fact, that might offer deer or other desirable game. When an area was turned into forest, the people who lived there became subject to strict forest law, which brought in a whole raft of new rules (no messing with the *vert* (vegetation) or *venison* (game), no farming, no grazing, no weapons, no dogs), plus severe penalties if you disobeyed. Local landowners could buy a licence to hunt, and commoners might be granted grazing or farming concessions, but rich and poor alike saw the king's move as a massive abuse of power. (Which, of course, it was.)

A century or so later, soon after the Magna Carta limited King John's power over his nobles, the Charter of the

..........

* 'I fear,' says Oliver Rackham, 'that the popular confusion between Forests and woodland is by now ineradicable. I have no more chance of persuading the public that Sherwood Forest was not a wood than Professor J.C. Holt has of getting people to believe that Robin Hood really lived in Barnsdale (West Yorkshire). But I must try.'

Forest rowed back on some of the forest law. The overall *afforested* area was reduced. No-one was to lose life or limb over venison; just prison or a fine. People could graze their animals, dig ponds and gather birds' eggs. And they could legally continue to practise the woodsmanship that was once such an essential part of the economy.

From today's standpoint, it can be tempting to put trees in one of two boxes: wild broadleaf woods vs cultivated conifer plantations, but the reality is that many of our most 'natural'-looking woods were once farmed. In the past, however, managing woodland wasn't primarily about clear-felling for timber. Instead, a tree's limbs were harvested, without killing off the tree itself. The aim was to provide small-to-medium lengths of wood for cooking, for tool handles, for building and fencing, for charcoal burners and lime kilns, for shipyards – and, later, for coal mines and train tracks. There were two chief methods:

**Coppicing.** You cut a tree back to its stool or stump, on rotation, anywhere between every five and twenty years. The tree then regrows quite happily. The unintended benefit is the creation of sunnier and shadier patches, which encourages a mix of plants to flourish. If a wood isn't coppiced, the floor is soon awash with shade-loving plants: wild garlic and dog's mercury prospering at the expense of wood anemones and bluebells, which need a touch of sun.*

**Pollarding.** You cut a tree down not at the base, but *above the height of a red deer*. Safe from herbivores, the tree then regrows from there. This creates a lovely habitat known as *wood pasture*, where there's enough light for cows

..........

* Being able to distinguish between the English and the Spanish bluebell is a key skill. If you want to display what the nature writer Richard Mabey calls *aesthetic patriotism*, then nod approvingly at the 'soft Celtic curves' of the former and sniff at the 'brasher bells and angular stalks' of the latter.

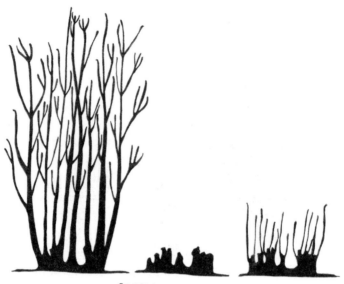

COPPICING

and sheep to graze beneath the trees, enjoying the shelter and the shade.

It's important to stress that where we have lost ancient woodland (woods that existed in 1600), this domestic or light-industrial use wasn't necessarily to blame. 'The woods,' says Rackham, 'did not disappear from the industrial Weald or the Lake District, or the Forests of Dean or Wye. It was non-industrial Norfolk, the land of agricultural innovation and prosperity, that lost three-quarters of its medieval woods between 1600 and 1790.' Of course this wasn't early modern tree-huggery, but sound commercial sense. It was far more profitable to treat trees as a perennial crop to be prudently husbanded (like very large asparagus), rather than as a one-off resource to be extracted (like seams of dead trees, i.e. coal). Instead, it was ambitious farmers, enclosing and improving, who could turn the destruction of woodland to their advantage.

POLLARDING

Equally, the Royal Navy can have many sins laid at its door, but it didn't hoover up all our oaks. The Admiralty did moan about a lack of trees, true, but what they were really moaning about was a lack of money: oak was available, but other industries could outbid them when it came to prime timber. However, riding high after the Napoleonic Wars, the navy eventually strong-armed the government into replanting great swathes of the Forest of Dean with trees reserved for them – but that turned out to be disaster because a) they planted the wrong sort of oak and b) by the time the oaks were mature, wooden ships were practically museum pieces.

Gradually, though, from the middle of the nineteenth century, this relatively creative and sustainable use of woodland came to an end. People were heating their houses with coal not brush-wood. Tools were made in factories not village workshops. And who would go to the trouble of weaving fencing hurdles out of hazel when there was barbed wire for sale? The woodsman's work dwindled, and arboriculture began to be associated more with aesthetics: a hobby for people in big houses, who planted interesting specimen trees designed to be admired.

After the First World War, however, our fear of scarcity and passion for productivity brought about what amounted to the biggest change in forestry since the Neolithic.

Policymakers estimated that each soldier on the Western Front (propping trenches, laying duckboards, lining dug-outs) had got through an average of five trees. What, they asked themselves, if there was another war? What if we lost because we didn't have enough wood? And so, in 1919, to ward off this danger, the Forestry Commission was created. But again, as with the navy's ships, this was meticulous forward planning for the *wrong war*: trenches were soon as dated as Nelson's *Victory*. Nevertheless, the commission is now the country's biggest landowner, bigger even than the king, and its impact on our landscape has been enormous.

It what seems pure madness to us now, the Forestry Commission set about felling acre upon acre of woodland, digging out ancient stumps, poisoning ancient roots, and planting in their place regimented blocks of conifers. According to the imperative of yield, it was a good call: conifers grow much, much faster, and so conifers it was. This means that the UK's tree cover has *more than doubled* in the last century, but much of this increase is made up of these unprepossessing – even ugly – plantations.

Today, more than half of our trees are conifers, with that figure rising to 75 per cent in Scotland, whose 'emptiness' meant it bore the brunt of twentieth-century block-planting. Private landowners also got in on the act, spurred on by fat tax breaks, which they claimed to need because otherwise why would they do something as altruistic and future-minded as plant lots of sitka spruce? (Yes, they got paid twice over: first when they planted the trees, second when they felled and sold them.)

If you've walked into a sitka plantation, you'll know how weird it can feel. The trees are native to the west coast of America but, superficially, they evoke a quasi-Germanic wildwood. Wander inside, however, and something feels *off*. They're so densely planted that there's no understory; nothing has figured out how to grow in the gloom at their feet. So shadowy. So stygian. So quiet. There's a patch on the north side of our hills where *all colour disappears*. It feels like you're walking back in time – or into another time – as if the air around you might shimmer and crack, and suddenly you'll find yourself in mid-winter Narnia before the return of the Lion. If a child runs away from you, deeper into the plantation, within 30 yards they all but vanish from view, and you want to shout and shout to bring them running back into the green and gold.

Happily, in recent decades there has been a massive about-turn. 'A new generation of foresters had arisen,' says Rackham, approvingly, 'with better things to do with their lives than growing millions of identical trees.'

When we visited the Forestry Commission's homepage, we were met with six images, and of those six, every single one was a broadleaf tree. This is part PR (oak-washing?), part truth: the commission is now focused on biodiversity and habitat preservation in ways that would have been unthinkable a generation ago. In her study of the relationship between trees and stories, *Gossip from the Forest*, Sara Maitland suggests that the commission might no longer be a wicked stepmother, but instead a wise animal or a rescuing prince. For as well as producing timber, it's busy opening up its land for walkers and picnickers, for bikers and campers: a bonus harvest of human happiness.

'Every generation,' writes John Lewis-Stempel in his close study of a wood in Herefordshire, 'looks at the trees, and takes what it wants.' Once, he says, we saw heroic individuals. Now, though, we're much more likely to be enchanted by evidence of the *wood-wide-web*, to delight in stories of connection and mutual aid, balm to our fears that the digital world has left us atomised, cut off from each other and the natural world.

Woods can also become places of prayer and pilgrimage in a largely secular society. And no wonder. Gothic cathedrals, posits Robert Pogue Harrison, are reproductions of the forests which were once places of worship, their high windows letting in light like breaks in the foliage. Nature, he says, isn't just like a temple, it *is* a temple. And so now, instead of seeking peace, solitude and a connection with something larger than ourselves in church, we go down to the woods – call it self-care, call it mindfulness, call it forest bathing, call it what you will, time spent beneath the trees can be an almost spiritual act.

One Easter Sunday morning, we followed a trail of people – couples in fleeces, children in sequins, an earnest young man with something by Edward Thomas poking out of his slimline backpack – all of them going to pay homage to a scrap of ancient Dartmoor woodland, to sit on mossy boulders, staring at the sky through the bare branches.

'Truly,' writes the ecologist John Stewart Collis, 'trees are Beings. We feel that to be so. Hence their silence, their indifference to us is almost exasperating. We would speak to them, we would ask their message; for they seem to hold some weighty truth, some special secret – and though sometimes we receive their blessing, they do not answer.'

# OLD-SCHOOL TREES

### ALDER (*ALNUS GLUTINOSA*)

Alders like water, so you'll find them leaning over streams, trailing along riverbanks and lurking in marshy country. They have shiny, you could even say leathery, dark green leaves, which are racquet-shaped with serrated edges. Sensibly, the seeds float, allowing the next generation of trees to germinate along flood-lines. Also sensibly, the timber gets tougher when waterlogged, rather than rotting. Overall, though, alders are a bit unloved and Eeyore-ish.

### ASH (*FRAXINUS EXCELSIOR*)

In summer, ash trees are easy to spot because of their distinctive *pinnate* leaves, three to six pairs of fingers per stem. In winter, their gnarly bark might trick you into mistaking them for an oak, but there won't be acorns underfoot, so you won't be fooled. Their winged fruits or *keys* travel far on the wind, allowing them to germinate with gay abandon.

But, and it's a horrible but, the ash is currently in trouble. Ash dieback (*Chalara fraxinea*) is a fungus originally from Asia where its native hosts (the Manchurian and Chinese ash) don't mind it. Here, however, it's another story. First recorded in 2012, the fungal spores, which blew across the Channel from infected trees in Europe, stick to leaves and slowly penetrate the tree itself, blocking its water transport systems, slowly killing it. It's easy to spot a tree that's suffering: discoloured, wilting leaves; early shedding; lesions where branches meet the trunk; new, *epicormic* growth from dormant buds further down the trunk.

International trade is, sadly, to blame for the spread of pests and pathogens. 'If you are a tree,' writes Helen Macdonald, 'death comes hidden in wood veneer, in packing material, in shipping containers, nursery plants, cut flowers, the roots of imported saplings.'

It's hard to think of anything positive to say: as many as 80 per cent of our ash trees might succumb. 'From now on,' says Macdonald, 'each one I saw would mean death, no matter how healthy it might be,' and she is, sadly, quite right.

### BEECH (*FAGUS SYLVATICA*)

A grand and regal tree – some say a bit *too* grand. Technically it only counts as native in the southeast, but with our help it (or she; the beech is often gendered female) has been delighted to drift north and west.

Few species grow well beneath her canopy, which means you'll always know when you're walking through a beech wood: it'll feel light, airy, like the nave of a great cathedral, which can inspire both awe and a strong sense of your own insignificance. Her seeds or *mast* crunch satisfyingly underfoot, and in late April, her new leaves, which look exactly like leaves are meant to look, of the lightest green, borne on feathery branches, are the magnanimous herald of the warmer days to come.

Unsurprisingly, her lofty demeanour made her a very popular choice for ornamental avenues, so come the apocalypse, if you're a hunting a big house to hole up in, *follow the beeches*. (This will admittedly work less well on the Quantock Hills, where beeches were planted in hedge banks, marking boundaries and shading the drove roads to market.)

Some remain wary. We have a book which gives us advice on how to talk courteously to all manner of trees, but it doesn't include the beech. We wondered why, until we read Sara Maitland's characterisation of the beech as the 'imperious and very beautiful' stepmother of fairytale, and you're not going to confide in her, are you?

### BIRCH (*BETULA PENDULA*)

The silver birch, on the other hand, is a *great* tree to talk to. She (also female; but more of an Anna than an Elsa) was one of the plucky pioneer trees which made good in Britain when the ice retreated. She was driven out of the big woods by more robust species, but clung on, thriving in a scrubby sort of way, on our uplands.

The druids appreciated her, seeing her as sister to the oak, and she still does excellent service as a witch's broom or maypole. You can find her today, haunting the fringes of felled or abandoned woodland, her silver bark glittering under the Hunter's Moon, red-and-white toadstools clustered at her feet.

### WILD CHERRY (*PRUNUS AVIUM*), BIRD CHERRY (*PRUNUS PADUS*)*

These are *not* the ancestors of the blowsy hybrids whose searing-white and shocking-pink flowers erupt in springtime. Cherries do nonetheless provide a very pretty display

..........

* Footnote for eagle-eyed Latinists. We haven't muddled this. *Prunus avium* means *bird cherry* but is the Latin name for the *wild cherry*. Gah.

of white flowers followed by cherries of every colour and flavour for the birds to eat in summer. The bark is a distinctive, shiny dark reddish-brown, with lots of what look like horizontal scars or cuts, known as *lenticels*. If you're a beginner, you could muddle cherry leaves with beech, so if you think *hmmm ... beech?*, but there's no mast on the ground and no awe in your heart, then it's cherry. A genial sort of tree, in short, which gets on nicely at the edge of woods and in hedgerows.

Foxes and badgers love cherries, as evidenced by their poo. Nothing stopping you eating them either, although they can be a bit sour.

ELM (VARIOUS *ULMUS*)
The wych elm was another pioneer species, whereas the field and English elms were introduced, but so very long ago it seems churlish to leave them out. They have an asymmetrical base, tapering to – but, stop, why are we telling you this? They're gone.

Once upon a time, the English elm, in particular, was a towering presence in the English countryside – and in the English imagination. The poet and pin-up Rupert Brooke, sick and grumpy in Germany, dreaming of Grantchester, wanting his tea, asked:

> Say, do the elm-clumps greatly stand
> Still guardians of that holy land?

The answer is: *no*. Millions upon millions of trees were wiped out in the 1970s by Dutch elm disease, caused by the fungus *Ophiostoma novo-ulmi*, spread by the elm bark beetle. A few still cling on in hedgerows, but they always struggle to grow more than a few metres tall. Don't blame the Dutch; they just carried out the crucial research in the 1920s. The disease actually arrived on timber imported from Canada, part and parcel of the same issues that are doing for our ash.

'Normal dynamics', says Oliver Rackham, 'are circumvented by modern humanity's flair for mixing up the world's pathogens – human, animal and plant.'

Tolkien's tree shepherds, the ents, would agree that we are too *hasty*. They'd advise us not to go rushing round the world. But we love travel, trade, adventure, *new things*, and so the sorry tale of elm, of ash – of the North American chestnut – will happen again and again. However vigilant our foresters are, we're unlikely to spot the first sick tree, nor the first hundred, nor the first thousand – and so we can't stop the spread until it's much too late.

Somewhere in Middle Earth, the ents are still wandering, looking for their lost ent-wives. Just as boomers mourn the elms of their childhood, so too their grandchildren will search the woodlands of the 2050s for ash in vain.*

HAZEL (*CORYLUS AVELLANA*)
Hazel is a cheerful, unpretentious sort of multi-stemmed shrub, rather than a tree proper. It's prime coppicing material and a great renewable resource: the stools sprout multiple stems and grow 4 feet a year. Knot them, twist them, the stems you lop off are very versatile. Think fence

..........

* The acronym for the government's post-Brexit agricultural policies is Elms (environmental land management schemes); we hope their choice averts rather than courts disaster.

hurdles, bean poles, thatching spars, water-divining sticks and the ribs of a Traveller's bender tent. The brush-wood used to be saved too, and tied in bundles called *faggots*. When burned, they produced an intense heat, so they were used in bakeries to fire ovens. More useful nowadays to support your pea crop.

The leaves are heart-shaped, with a pointed tip, and soft to the touch. The underside is covered in fine white hairs. Its bright-yellow catkins light up the dark days of late winter.

## THE HOLLY (*ILEX AQUIFOLIUM*) AND THE IVY (*HEDERA HELIX*)

Holly and its BFF ivy, unlike other evergreens, are both good to eat (pine tastes gross) and safe to eat (yew is poisonous), making them the perfect emergency food supply for sheep in snowy winters.

The holly, smothered in bright-red berries until the birds grab them in mid-winter, can be a fine specimen tree – or, alternatively, a highly effective hedging plant, an impenetrable wall of prickly leaves.

Ivy, obviously, is not a tree, but a riotously successful woody vine. It climbs up tree trunks in search of extra sunlight, but it's not a parasite, because it has its own roots. Even though some trees look absolutely choked, they're honestly fine. Some people strip ivy for the aesthetics; your call.

## HORNBEAM (*CARPINUS BETULUS*)

The guy on the rugby team who's actually really sweet: Nick Nelson in *Heartstopper*. A massive spreading tree, which looks splendid in manorial parkland, providing shade to a herd of cattle. Also works as a dense, formal hedging plant, keeping hold of its leaves throughout the winter. It's also *hard* – the hardest tree in Europe – which means it was once used for ox yokes.

## LIME (VARIOUS *TILIA*)

There are two main native limes, the small-leaved and the large-leaved, which hybridise to create the common lime. It's a great summer treat to stand under a lime's spreading branches, soaking up the intoxicating honeyed scent of its yellow flowers, listening to the mob of bees buzzing with nectarious joy. (Unless you're Coleridge, grumpy because his friends have gone on a walk without him, who calls his lime-tree bower a prison.)

For a very formal look, it's possible to train lime trees to create a narrow screen or hedge, twisting and tying young shoots on to a frame, a technique called *pleaching*. It can look excessively contrived, like the lines of crucifixes in *Spartacus*.

Soft and smooth, neither knotty nor grainy, lime wood is also ideal for elaborate carvings, whether Grinling Gibbons's famous work for St Paul's Cathedral – or the face of a *green man* on sale for a tenner on Glastonbury High Street.

## OAK (VARIOUS *QUERCUS*)

Again, there are two types: *Quercus robur*, aka the pendunculate or mighty English oak, and *Quercus petrea*, aka the sessile oak. The sessile is skinnier, with stalkier leaves and stalk-free acorns, and generally has a more Celtic vibe, preferring the north and west, perhaps atop a high and windy heath or leaning a bit mysteriously over a winding river. The robur, by contrast, is a more upright and proper sort of chap; Keats called him a green-robed senator.

However, we're sorry to tell you, there's a thing called *oak change*, which is worrying, if not (yet??) catastrophic. For the last hundred years or so, oaks no longer grow from acorns within existing woodland. Around the edges, yes, on open ground, heathland, farmland, yes, but not under their parent trees. One possible reason is oak mildew (*Erysiphe alphitoides* or *Microsphaera alphitoides*), which doesn't kill off mature trees in the open, but is fatal to a baby oak lacking sunlight.

### ROWAN (*SORBUS AUCUPARIA*)

You might meet a rowan tree on the heights, in the north or west, hardy yet graceful, her bright-red berries a joy. Or maybe she's standing discreetly outside your door, a small and friendly sentry, keeping you safe from all manner of goblin tricks and witchy spells. Her slender branches are an excellent choice for a wand or a druid's staff, for a set of dousing rods or divination runes. For a power boost, use wood from a *flying rowan* growing, as if by magic, out of a remote and rocky cleft. Just make sure you ask the tree's permission first.

(Rowan is sometimes called mountain ash, which is a little bit demeaning, but rowans, on the whole, are very forgiving.)

### SCOTS PINE (*PINUS SYLVESTRIS*)

The beauty of a Scots pine is unrivalled, says Hugh Johnson, moonlighting from his other speciality, wine.

> The richness of its colouring, its wild poise set it apart. No matter how grey the winter's day, the papery bark, flaking in butterfly

wings of salmon and green, glows with the warmth of a fire in the sky. And if the bark is richly red, the leaves are no less richly blue. To handle a heavy resinous spray and see the unripe cones, little jade carvings in the deep sea lights and shadows of the needles, is an intoxication.

The Scots pine was only just behind the silver birch, following the ice north, and for a long time it only grew in its Scottish redoubt. Today, plantations have been established on thin-ish soil in the south and east, but it really does best as a noble sentinel on a grassy knoll or lakeside promontory. If you have one of those to hand, it is your solemn duty to posterity to plant it with Scots pine: a dozen or so on a knoll, perhaps three times that on a promontory. Even a single Scots pine, perfectly placed, is one of nature's most romantic landmarks.

You might only get to see it in its youth, when its dense foliage is carried on branches stroking the ground, but those who follow you can watch the branches recede to reveal its heart-warming trunk.

ENGLISH YEW (*TAXUS BACCATA*)
'Yew trees,' says Justin Hopper, whose *The Old Weird Albion* (2017) is an eerie treat, 'stand guard over churchyards and are entrances to the afterlife, signposts left to remind the clergy who is *really* in charge.' That's one idea anyway.

Or perhaps – their evergreen leaves and berries being seriously poisonous – they were planted to discourage farmers from grazing their cattle on sacred ground.

Or was it something to do with the army? Yew branches were the no. 1 choice for longbows – but why then in *churchyards*? So people wouldn't steal them? It's baffling.

Or perhaps they're simply there to help us reflect on that end to which all paths must tend. After all, nothing says Grim Reaper more clearly than a louring yew.

We're accustomed to seeing them in churchyards (or as ornate hedging back when topiary was a thing), but if you get rid of sheep and/or rabbits, yew woods do grow on chalky grassland. Juniper and hawthorn come first, and yew seedlings flourish in their shade, before eventually overtaking them.

Unlike us, yews live forever. Thousands of years forever.

POSTSCRIPT

If you find that no matter what you do, the different trees refuse to stick in your head, and you can only really manage a) oak and b) not oak, then feel free to commit to memory these words of the contrarian and novelist John Fowles, to murmur whenever you feel shown up by a companion:

> Even the simplest knowledge of the names and habits of flowers or trees starts this distinguishing or individuating process and removes us a step from total reality towards anthropocentrism; that is, it acts mentally as an equivalent of the camera view-finder. Already it destroys or curtails certain possibilities of seeing, apprehending and experiencing.

Tl;dr: names are for losers.

# NEW-SCHOOL TREES

### SWEET CHESTNUT (*CASTANEA SATIVA*)

Thank you, Romans. You can grind chestnuts to make flour, which is great if you're gluten-free or the global food supply chain has melted down and you need something to enjoy with your nettle soup and acorn coffee. You only get really good nuts after a hot summer, but that obviously won't be a problem come the apocalypse. Good times ahead.

There is also, incidentally, no more pitiful sight than a dog with a very low pain threshold holding out a trembling paw with a spiky chestnut cupule buried in the pad.

### HORSE CHESTNUT (CONKER TREE)

Comes from the Balkans. No relation to the sweet chestnut.

Important: to win at conkers you really need to harden them off. Keep them for a year, give them a quick bake – or soak them and boil hard in vinegar. (Don't use nail varnish: too obvious.) If you're playing seriously and you can't BYO conkers, some sort of sleight of hand is necessary. Learning how to trouser an official competition conker and replace it with one of your own is a great life goal.

### HOLM OR HOLLY OAK (*QUERCUS ILEX*)

New Year's Eve walk, *check*, acorns on the ground, *check*, evergreen leaves overhead, *check*: that's a holm oak. They arrived from the Med in the sixteenth century, and were widely planted by the coast because they can put up with salty winds.

CEDAR (*CEDRUS LIBANI*)
A truly divine tree. It was planted by God (Psalm 104:16, Isaiah 41:19). It is the first of trees (1 Kings 4:33), strong and durable (Isaiah 9:10), mighty and splendid (Psalm 80:10, Ezekiel 17:23), high and tall (Amos 2:9, Ezekiel 17:22), fragrant (Song of Songs 4:11), an excellent nest (Jeremiah 22:23, Ezekiel 17:23), perfect for building temples (1 Kings 5:6, 1 Kings 6:9–10), palaces (2 Samuel 5:11, 1 Kings 7:2–3) and ships (Ezekiel 27:5) as well as a symbol of the flourishing of the righteous (Psalm 92:12) and of radiance, beauty and sweetness (Song of Songs 5:15).

Cedars have been planted in the grounds of big houses since the seventeenth century, when they were brought here from the mountains around the eastern Mediterranean – and some of them have been standing ever since.

LONDON PLANE (VARIOUS *PLATANUS*)
The London plane is a hybrid between Turkish and American parents, which first arrived in the seventeenth century. Mass planting in the capital in the Edwardian era means

London planes are now some of the city's most iconic and beneficial trees. They shrug off pollution and don't mind being pruned or pollarded to allow red buses to squeeze past. From the winter skyline to summer shade, London would be lost without them.

### WELLINGTONIA (*SEQUOIADENDRON GIGANTEUM*)

These macho US trees pitched up in Britain in 1853, the year after the Duke of Wellington's death (and epic state funeral), hence why they've been lumbered with his name.

### MAPLE (VARIOUS *ACER*)

The field maple (*Acer campestre*) is an old-timer, but the wily sycamore (*Acer pseudoplatanus*, i.e. a maple trying to pass itself off as a plane) is probably more familiar. On its own, it can be a handsome tree, but it seeds freely, grows fast, and takes over anywhere it gets a foothold. Never allow a sycamore anywhere near your garden, or you will be removing seedlings from dawn to dusk. Other maples, by contrast, are pure autumn glory: seek out the red maple *Acer rubrum* (from North America) or the Japanese maple *Acer palmatum* (from the Far East).

### MAGNOLIA (VARIOUS ... *MAGNOLIA*)

Originally from China and the Himalayas, magnolias put forth white, yellow, pink or purple flowers in early spring, when the daffodils have just woken, when the ground is hardening underfoot, when light and hope are returning, and when you no longer need a fire to coax the children out of bed. Their flowers open mostly on bare branches, which looks almost impossibly lovely (which you'll probably already know, even if you're not into trees, because social media goes mad for magnolias).

# A SHROPSHIRE LAD, 2

by A. E. Housman

Loveliest of trees, the cherry now
Is hung with bloom along the bough,
And stands about the woodland ride
Wearing white for Eastertide.

Now, of my threescore years and ten,
Twenty will not come again,
And take from seventy springs a score,
It only leaves me fifty more.

And since to look at things in bloom
Fifty springs are little room,
About the woodlands I will go
To see the cherry hung with snow.

## GOOD FENCES MAKE GOOD NEIGHBOURS: THE HURDLE

These handsome screens or fences makes excellent temporary barriers. Easy to move around, they can plug a hole in a hedge or create a temporary pen for animals or toddlers. If you then slap a mixture of soil / clay / sand / dung / straw over your pen, you've made the walls of your own wattle-and-daub house. Or if it's rained non-stop for weeks, you can lay them flat to create safe(-ish) paths, as people did on the Somerset Levels in prehistoric times.

Your material of choice is coppiced hazel. Use thicker stems, perhaps split in half, for the uprights and the top and bottom bars, and thinner side branches for the woven lattice screen. Weaving the lateral branches in and out of the uprights is a *lot* harder than it sounds, but the results are very pleasing.

Once you've mastered hurdles, don't let us stop you diversifying into basket-making. For that, though, you want willow.

# HOW TO PLANT A WOOD

So many reasons to plant a wood.

A covert for a fox. A tax wheeze. A cover-up for some really toxic fly-tipping. Salve for your globe-trotting conscience.* For firewood, for the sound of a winter storm berserkering the branches, for your great-great-great-grandchildren. For the chance to deploy lofty (but somehow very moving) classical allusions:

> Men seldom plant *Trees* till they begin to be *Wise*, that is, till they grow *Old*, and find by *Experience* the *Prudence* and *Necessity* of it. When *Ulysses*, after a ten-years Absence, was return'd from *Troy*, and coming home, found his aged *Father* in the Field planting of *Trees*, He asked him, why (being now so far advanc'd in Years) he would put himself to the Fatigue and Labour of Planting, *that* which he was never likely to enjoy the Fruits of? The good old Man (taking him for a Stranger) gently reply'd; I *plant* (says he) *against my Son* Ulysses *comes home.***

Once you've wiped the tear from your eye, here's how to make a start.

### APPLY FOR A GRANT
It'll be a massive ball-ache, but if you've got a large-ish piece of land in mind, there will be money out there, but you have to talk the talk and tick the boxes. The more of these criteria your proposed wood meets, the more money you get:
..........

* Note: you'll have to wait a hundred years before you've got a tree remotely big enough to offset a return flight to New York.
** John Evelyn, *Sylva, or A Discourse of Forest-Trees* (1664)

- supports wildlife and nature recovery
- reduces flood risk and improves water quality
- is close to where people live, and you plan to let them visit.

CHOOSE THE TREES

There is a Forestry Commission app which provides a list of species which are likely to do well where you are, taking account of altitude, water levels and so on. In general:

- plant trees
- mostly old-school trees
- but don't get petty about what's old and what's new.

Sadly, you'd better avoid ash. In fact, foresters are planting other trees beneath existing ash in preparation for dieback taking hold. But do keep on planting oak.

You might include pioneer species such as willow and birch, which can then be overtaken by beech, oak, rowan, cherry, hornbeam, lime, sweet chestnut and alder. Ideally, you'll also plant a lower canopy of, for example, crab apple, wild pear, hazel, spindle, dogwood, guelder rose, buckthorn, holly and field maple.

If you go for 40 cm-high cell-grown *whips*, you're looking at about £1/tree. It's uneconomical to try to steal a march by buying 2m-tall *standards*. They're much more expensive, and it's hard to establish them if you get an unusually dry summer. It's also possible to prowl hedges and woodland margins, dig up any saplings you find, and bring them on yourself in pots in dappled shade.*

CLEAR THE GROUND

If you're planting up lawn or pasture, this'll be a cinch. If you're clearing scrub, it might be very hard work.

..........

* Only if you've got permission, obviously, otherwise it's tree poaching.

Paul Kingsnorth, in *Confessions of a Recovering Environmentalist* (2017), meditates ruefully about this when he's hacking down a wilderness (blackthorn, bramble) to plant crops (birch, willow). Factoring in the machines he needs to clear the ground, the factory-made tools, the plastic tree spirals (without which his saplings will get eaten), the plastic gloves (without which his hands will be ripped to shreds), he starts to wonder whether what he's doing is so environmentally friendly after all. Tricky. Easiest to abandon any delusions of green grandeur and tell yourself you're just an honest tree farmer.

### PLANT THE TREES

Cut a V-shaped hole with a spade or mattock. Tuck the whip into the hole with the base of the stem (i.e. the point just above the roots) at ground level. *Never* bury the stem – you'll kill it. Firm the soil with your heel.

If you've got a lot to get through, listen to the audiobook of Thomas Hardy's *The Woodlanders* while you work:

> Winterborne's fingers were endowed with a gentle conjuror's touch in spreading the roots of each little tree, resulting in a sort of caress, under which the delicate fibres all laid themselves out in their proper directions for growth. He put most of these roots towards the south-west; for, he said, in forty years' time, when some great gale is blowing from that quarter, the trees will require the strongest holdfast on that side to stand against it and not fall.

Plant in January or February, when your baby trees are sleepy, keeping your fingers crossed for a warm wet year. In case of drought, you *must* water, or you risk losing the lot.

### PREDATORS, ROUND ONE

The real headache is protecting the trees from predators,

mainly deer and rabbits. It's possible to fence an entire woodland, but that ends free movement for other animals, plus have you seen how high deer can jump? This means individual shelters, which used to mean a forest of green plastic, but biodegradable shelters, thankfully, are becoming a reality.

Make sure your shelters are flush to the ground and supported with a stake. Check in on them from time to time, especially after a gale. For protection against roe, muntjac or Chinese water deer 1.2m is fine; for fallow, red or sika deer you need 1.8m.

You might find that voles (for whose adorable benefit you're planting the wood in the first place) wriggle under the shelters to nest around (and nibble on) your whips, in which case you'll need *vole guards* as well – until the owls (for whose adorable benefit, etc.) get their act together.

So much for fauna. When it comes to flora, you'll find yourself doing battle with whatever was there before your whips went in.

If that was brambles, good luck.

If it was grass, you have to decide whether to spray with glyphosate in the first year or two. Consult your inner critic and other stakeholders. Opinions will vary from, 'Oh [brand name redacted] is so harmless you can drink the stuff!' to 'How CAN you?? Have you not READ what the *Guardian* wrote about [brand name redacted]? Put a finger on that nozzle and I swear I'll *never* talk to you *ever* again.'

At this point you might decide to ask around for alternatives to herbicide. *Ah-ha!* 'You can suppress grass with mulch, such as bark chips or straw bales. Apply it to a depth of around 10 cm to prevent it being blown away or dispersed and top it up annually. You can also buy mulch mats and peg them into the ground to keep them in place.'

Count number of trees.

Set out one moonlit night wearing a balaclava, armed with a backpack of [brand name redacted]. *Whispers*: the tree shelters will also protect the whips from herbicide.

## PATIENCE

There follows a long wait. Forest trees take a good few years to get into their stride. You can jolly them along with some judicious pruning of lateral branches and bifurcating leaders: i.e. pick winners. But to be honest, they'll probably get on fine without you. After 5–10 years, remove the shelters; earlier if the trees are obviously getting too big.

## PREDATORS, ROUND TWO

The grey squirrel is enemy no. 1. In spring and early summer, they gnaw tree trunks to get at the sweet, sappy layers (the *phloem tissue*) just beneath the bark. This tissue moves sugars up and down the trunk, so if a squirrel *ring-barks* a tree (i.e. gnaws a complete circle), the sugars can no longer circulate and the tree will die.

Small trees are safe because they can't support a squirrel's weight. Older trees (40+ years) are also fine because their bark's too thick. In between: disaster.

The solution? Unless you can train your dog to *get its act together*, no other top predator will do the job for you. You've got to cull them yourself, by trapping and/or shooting. This, frankly, is an unpleasant task, but if you want trees and you've got squirrels, the squirrel has got to give.*

You need a trap about 50 x 20 cm, made of rigid wire mesh. At one end: a hinged door. At the other: a hinged base-plate. The door is held open by a rod extending from the plate. You've got to persuade the squirrel to enter the trap and stand on the plate. When it does, the rod will release its hold on the door, and the trap will be sprung.

It's best to set the trap off the ground, ideally in the fork of a low-branching tree. A trap on the ground will get unwelcome attention from your *useless* dog. Also, by-catch (such as pheasants) tend not to cooperate when you try to extract them unharmed.

Grabbing a squirrel's attention is best achieved with bright-yellow maize scattered both inside and outside the trap. Wheat works too. Peanuts are excellent, but expensive.

Once the trap is set, regular visits are essential to minimise distress, and you must shoot what you trap. Drowning is illegal; as is releasing the captured squirrel in another wood. A shotgun will kill the squirrel, but will also destroy the trap. An air rifle is ideal.**

..........

* Any Gen-X-er worth their salt will instantly recall the squirrel-hating highway woman in *Blackadder the Third*: 'Bastards ... I hate them, with their long tails and their stupid twitchy noses.'
** If your sensibilities recoil, murmur these words (John Seymour, *The Fat of the Land*) to stiffen your resolve: 'To connive at the killing of animals while being too lily-livered to kill them yourself is despicable.' This is trickier if you're vegan. Just close your eyes and think of the trees? (But for God's sake open them before you pull the trigger.)

Consider eating the squirrel. Very modish. Whatever you'd normally do to a rabbit will work just fine. Easier to skin after freezing.

### FAST FORWARD 15–20 YEARS
GO YOU! You've got a wood!

### AND FINALLY, A LITTLE FINE-TUNING
You may now start coppicing your willow and hazel so they don't overwhelm your oaks.

You may wish to introduce a couple of pigs. You may wish to clear the under-storey in places to promote snow-drops, primroses, bluebells. You may wish to *brash up*, i.e. cut away lower branches to let in more light. You may wish to exploit the trees for firewood.

### BUT WHAT ABOUT NATURAL REGENERATION?
Sure thing, go for it. Let nature do it herself. It might work really well in some places.

But you can't be sure how *well* it'll work. You'll get a lot of thorny scrub (blackberry, hawthorn) before you get trees, and maybe you won't get trees at all unless you borrow an aurochs or two to break up the horrendous sea of brambles.

But you won't get subsidy, which is no good if you're a farmer who wants to turn some pasture over to woodland.

But you need an existing seed source, i.e. woods, within a couple of hundred metres, so natural regeneration won't work so well in places that have been tree-less for centuries, or even millennia.

But don't let us put you off.

# TICKS

................

Ticks are parasitic hematophagic arachnids – the blood-sucking cousins of spiders. The one you're most likely to meet is *Ixodes ricinus*, known as the deer or sheep tick after two of its favourite hosts. But it's not fussy: it's perfectly happy to moonlight on *you*.

A tick lies in wait in a cool, moist place – in leaf litter, on bracken, amongst tall grass, on low branches – clinging to its launchpad with its third and fourth set of legs, ready to ambush you. Quivering with anticipation, it stretches out its first pair (this is called *questing*) alert to your footfall, your smell, your breath. A shy and fleeting touch. Bravely, it scampers from stalk to sleeve. Boldly, it explores this newfound land. Relievedly, it settles in some secluded spot, where the skin is thin and the blood smells sweet. With its doughty *hypostome* (a tick harpoon), it cuts a neat hole. It excretes anti-clotting gunk into the wound. It feeds and feeds for days, before dropping off and *moulting* i.e. transforming from larva to nymph, or from nymph to adult. After its third meal, it mates. If it's male, it dies. If it's female, it lays eggs. The cycle begins again.

Ideally, you'll notice it before it really tucks in. Best is when it's still free-range, scampering up your arm, and you can just brush it off. Good is when its head is burrowing, its rear legs flailing with effort, but it hasn't actually started feeding. Only quite medium is when its back-end is engorged an eerie pearlescent grey. If you spot a fully latched-on tick:

DON'T shriek, flail and tear it out. You'll leave a manky tick-head inside you.

DO take up your tick remover, of which you'll have two, one on your key fob and one in your junk drawer. This will neatly extract the tick, head, legs and all. If you don't have a tick remover, borrow one. If you can't borrow one, use tweezers. If you're all alone, tick-remover-less, in the middle of Dartmoor ... frankly, *more fool you*. On your head be it, then, if you decide to get medieval with booze or a match.

We worry about ticks because they *sometimes* carry the bacteria that *sometimes* gives you Lyme disease. Most ticks  aren't carriers, and if a carrier does feed on you, you won't necessarily get sick, but even so, you really don't want Lyme. It's hard to diagnose and harder to treat, resembling fibromyalgia and long Covid in the way symptoms rove inexplicably and unpleasantly around your body.

It's vital, then, that if you've been bitten, you stay alert for signs of infection, most obviously a red rash around the bite. It might radiate out like a bullseye. It might be hot or itchy. Basically, if you get a weird rash where you've been bitten OR you feel cold-y or flu-y after you've been bitten, *go to the doctor*. If in doubt, *go to the doctor*. They can give you antibiotics that can ward off Lyme disease, but only if you take them early enough.

Tick prevention advice is only moderately helpful. Stick to the path? Wear pale clothes? Tuck your trousers into your socks? It's a bit like hangover advice. Drink a pint of water between each pint? All very well in theory.

Better to aim for a halfway house between hazmat and foolhardy. During the peak tick summer season, check anyone who's been thrashing about in long grass. And keep cats and dogs well doused with tick repellent, otherwise their fur will seethe like a four-year-old with its first bout of nits.*

# FIREWOOD

........................

1. Select tree. Is it your tree? Was it either planted for timber or now growing in some way dangerously? Is it definitely and indubitably *not* an ancient, venerable piece of English rural heritage? Yes, yes, yes? Crack on.
2. Assess tree. Be honest: is it too big? Beginners should aim for a maximum diameter of 18 inches, something you can bring down with a 14-inch chainsaw bar. Anything larger, call a professional. Now, which way is it leaning? Which way is the wind blowing? Is there a clear path for it to fall down? Are there any family members, prized shrubs or electricity cables in the vicinity? (The firework display created by dropping a tree on cabling is spectacular, but very dangerous and very expensive.)
3. Have a good long hard think about chainsaws and chainsaw safety. It helps if you came of age contemporaneously with the release of *The Texas Chainsaw Massacre*.
4. Chainsaw dungarees on.** Helmet on. Visor down.

..........

* A single red deer was once found to be carrying 16,000 ticks!!! Source: an actual study by Imperial College, London.
** If chain meets dungaree, the long, tough protective fibres wrap themselves around the limb-severing blade in a matter of milliseconds, stopping the teeth *almost* immediately. It's what might happen in those milliseconds that should give you pause.

Clamp ear defenders. Start chainsaw. On a cold day, this will be a sweaty and drawn-out process – or smooth, smug and painless if somebody gave you an electric one for Christmas.

5.  Lay the tree in. This means cutting a V at the base of the tree in the direction you want it to fall. The bottom of the V should be cut flat and extend about 20 per cent of the way into the trunk. The top of the V should be cut at about 35° to the bottom. You should now have a satisfying wedge shaped like a slice of melon.

6.  Make a felling cut on the opposite side. The tree will now fall in exactly the direction dictated by the V. (In theory, that is. It might well get caught on another tree, so you'll have to cut the trunk again and again, feeling like you're in that Monty Python scene where they keep chopping bits off a knight until he's nothing but torso.)

7.  Cut off all the side branches as close to the trunk as possible. Be careful! Some of them might be bent backwards under vicious spring loading: when you cut them they whip free. Reserve branches that are big enough to burn. Pile up the rest for chipping.

8.  Cut the trunk into 4-foot lengths, unless the tree's so broad that you'd have a log too heavy to be carried by one person. If that's the case (e.g. when you get to the base of the tree), cut the trunk into rings about 16-inch deep.

9.  Stack and wait – for a year or two. While you're waiting, learn how to sharpen your chainsaw.

10. Fetch a sawing horse and a companion. Your companion holds each log steady on the horse; you wield the chainsaw. (Unless the thought of chopping off your companion's hands feels worse than them chopping off yours, in which case swap.) Cut to a sensible size for

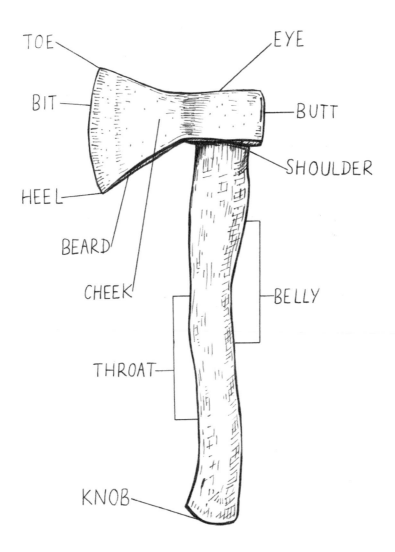

TOE

EYE

BIT

BUTT

SHOULDER

HEEL

BEARD

CHEEK

BELLY

THROAT

KNOB

your stove or fireplace.* Cut them nice and square so they'll stand proud when you come to split them. Be especially wary of light logs being spun by the chain.

11. Dismiss your companion and fetch an axe and a chopping block (a tough old ring of oak). Place first log on block. Raise axe. Feel *awesome*. Swing. Hmmm. That didn't go too well. Get phone out. Watch James Coburn in *The Magnificent Seven*. Wow. Even Steve McQueen looks impressed. Try again. The trick is to hold the bottom (or knob) of the axe handle firmly with one hand, and slide your other hand from the top (or shoulder) as you strike the blow. Beautiful.

12. Stack and wait – for another year.

13. Why all this waiting? Wood needs to have a moisture content of less than 20 per cent to burn efficiently. More than that and you're wasting energy on drying the wood out before it burns properly and puffing pollutants into the atmosphere. You can buy a firewood moisture meter to check your progress.

14. Meanwhile: kindling. Gathering twigs is the perfect job for children too young to wield an axe or a chainsaw. Pay per bag. Pine cones and fallen lime branches are particularly good. Also a quick shout-out to Dr Heat eco-friendly firelighters, made from miscanthus grass and recycled scented candle wax. (No commission. They're amazing!)

..........

* Stoves are more efficient. They convert 70 per cent of the organic matter in wood into heat, whereas an open fire might achieve 25 per cent at best.

# Stacking wood

1. If you're into stacking wood, you should read Lars Mytting's *Norwegian Wood*. But, to be honest, if you're into stacking wood, you probably already have. If, however, you're not yet sure whether stacking wood is your thing, 192 pages of a tall strapping Scandi silver-fox delivering the goods will probably convert you.

2. If you're happy to make do with us, here are some pointers. Wood-piles like sun and wind. They like a nice pallet underneath them. (Airier throughout; no rising damp.) They don't mind being against a wall, but freestanding can be more aesthetic. They like to sunbathe topless in summer, but do cover them up in winter.

3. Start with enough flat-based split logs to create a perimeter on the edges of the pallet. Place the next layer perpendicular to the first, pointing inwards, with the outer edge of each log resting on the perimeter you created. This way you establish an inward slope, mitigating the risk of ignominious collapse. Maintain this slope right to the top. Shove awkward shapes and sizes in the middle. A conical top is always a nice touch.

# FROM *THE RETURN OF THE NATIVE*

by Thomas Hardy

Had a looker-on been posted in the immediate vicinity of the barrow, he would have learned that these persons were boys and men of the neighbouring hamlets. Each, as he ascended the barrow, had been heavily laden with furze faggots, carried upon the shoulder by means of a long stake sharpened at each end for impaling them easily – two in front and two behind. They came from a part of the heath a quarter of a mile to the rear, where furze almost exclusively prevailed as a product.

Every individual was so involved in furze by his method of carrying the faggots that he appeared like a bush on legs till he had thrown them down. The party had marched in trail, like a travelling flock of sheep; that is to say, the strongest first, the weak and young behind.

The loads were all laid together, and a pyramid of furze thirty feet in circumference now occupied the crown of the tumulus, which was known as Rainbarrow for many miles round. Some made themselves busy with matches, and in selecting the driest tufts of furze, others in loosening the bramble bonds which held the faggots together. Others, again, while this was in progress, lifted their eyes and swept the vast expanse of country commanded by their position, now lying nearly obliterated by shade. In the valleys of the heath nothing save its own wild face was visible at any time of day; but this spot commanded a horizon enclosing a tract of far extent, and in many cases lying beyond the heath country. None of its features could be seen now, but the whole made itself felt as a vague stretch of remoteness.

While the men and lads were building the pile, a change took place in the mass of shade which denoted the distant landscape. Red suns and tufts of fire one by one began to arise, flecking the whole country round. They were the bonfires of other parishes and hamlets that were engaged in the same sort of commemoration. Some were distant, and stood in a dense atmosphere, so that bundles of pale straw-like beams radiated around them in the shape of a fan. Some were large and near, glowing scarlet-red from the shade, like wounds in a black hide. Some were Mænades, with winy faces and blown hair. These tinctured the silent bosom of the clouds above them and lit up their ephemeral caves, which seemed thenceforth to become scalding cauldrons. Perhaps as many as thirty bonfires could be counted within the whole bounds of the district; and as the hour may be told on a clock-face when the figures themselves are invisible, so did the men recognise the locality of each fire by its angle and direction, though nothing of the scenery could be viewed.

The first tall flame from Rainbarrow sprang into the sky, attracting all eyes that had been fixed on the distant conflagrations back to their own attempt in the same kind. The cheerful blaze streaked the inner surface of the human circle—now increased by other stragglers, male and female—with its own gold livery, and even overlaid the dark turf around with a lively luminousness, which softened off into obscurity where the barrow rounded downwards out of sight. It showed the barrow to be the segment of a globe, as perfect as on the day when it was thrown up, even the little ditch remaining from which the earth was dug. Not a plough had ever disturbed a grain of that stubborn soil. In the heath's barrenness to the farmer lay its fertility to the historian. There had been no obliteration, because there had been no tending.

It seemed as if the bonfire-makers were standing in some radiant upper storey of the world, detached from and independent of the dark stretches below. The heath down there was now a vast abyss, and no longer a continuation of what they stood on; for their eyes, adapted to the blaze, could see nothing of the deeps beyond its influence. Occasionally, it is true, a more vigorous flare than usual from their faggots sent darting lights like aides-de-camp down the inclines to some distant bush, pool, or patch of white sand, kindling these to replies of the same colour, till all was lost in darkness again. Then the whole black phenomenon beneath represented Limbo as viewed from the brink by the sublime Florentine* in his vision, and the muttered articulations of the wind in the hollows were as complaints and petitions from the 'souls of mighty worth' suspended therein.

It was as if these men and boys had suddenly dived into past ages, and fetched therefrom an hour and deed which had before been familiar with this spot. The ashes of the original British pyre which blazed from that summit lay fresh and undisturbed in the barrow beneath their tread. The flames from funeral piles long ago kindled there had shone down upon the lowlands as these were shining now. Festival fires to Thor and Woden had followed on the same ground and duly had their day. Indeed, it is pretty well known that such blazes as this the heathmen were now enjoying are rather the lineal descendants from jumbled Druidical rites and Saxon ceremonies than the invention of popular feeling about Gunpowder Plot.

Moreover to light a fire is the instinctive and resistant act of man when, at the winter ingress, the curfew is

..........

* Dante btw.

sounded throughout Nature. It indicates a spontaneous, Promethean rebelliousness against that fiat that this recurrent season shall bring foul times, cold darkness, misery and death. Black chaos comes, and the fettered gods of the earth say, Let there be light.

## BONFIRES, SEVEN USES, TWO SIZES

1. **Prosaic.** Burning up big twiggy pieces of garden waste i.e. the bits which won't rot down nicely in your compost heap.
2. **Gastronomic.** An entire mammal rather than a bit of halloumi and marinated aubergine seems more appropriate.
3. **Celebratory.** An invasion has been repelled. A traitor unmasked. A monarch crowned.
4. **Military.** Let London know *they're coming*.
5. **Ecumenical.** Good pagans need bonfires to leap over at Beltane. An H&S nightmare. But what you choose to do in the privacy of your own garden etc.
6. **Judicial.** Disposal of witches. Illegal since 1735.
7. **Valedictory.** Adieu to Grandpa. Illegal since 1930.

A SMALL BONFIRE

**Timing.** If you have the luxury of choice, select a dry day, but *not* in the middle of a drought. You also want a decent breeze to create a draught, but avoid really windy days, or you'll end up with smoke halfway across the parish. Consider your neighbours. If they're blowing up a bouncy castle for their daughter's birthday party: wait.

**Siting.** Very much purpose dependent. Either somewhere as little irritating to your neighbours as possible or equally somewhere accessible to baying crowds. Make sure there's nothing in the vicinity that'll react badly to whirling cinders, whether power lines or freshly washed druidical robes. Once you've got a site, marshal your combustibles in a semi-circle to windward, piling according to size.

**Ignition.** A bonfire needs serious bottom heat. Lay two logs. Pile newspaper, scraps of waste wood or foraged twigs on top. (The little tunnel under the kindling provides a nice draught of oxygen, and a neat nook to tuck a firelighter.) Set it alight.

**Construction.** Take up a pitchfork and add your smallest, driest material first. Aim for a handsome, compact cone, and whatever you do, make sure everything has *contact with the base*. Patience is your watchword: no smothering. Slowly add bigger and bigger pieces, remembering: contact; base.

**Contemplation.** Once you've added everything, lean on your pitchfork and savour the warmth of the flames on your face. When the centre of the fire has burned through, use your pitchfork to turn in all the unburnt ends. Go and get a cup of coffee. Lean, sip, turn, repeat.

**Application.** Prosaic, gastronomic, ecumenical, definitely; judicial and valedictory at a push.

A LARGE BONFIRE

**Lash frame.** Select three or four branches about 6 metres long and 10–15 cm in diameter. Lash them together in a *sheer-leg knot* just below the top.

**Erect frame.** With the help of family and friends, raise the frame into the vertical position by moving the poles outwards until their feet are far enough apart to be stable. Prop up four or five more branches against the top, so your tripod (or quadrupod) becomes an octopod.

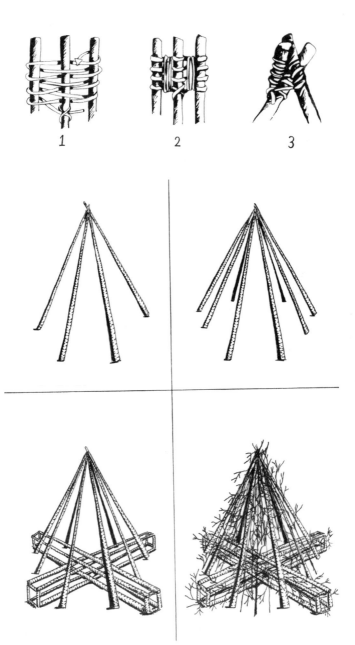

1

2

3

**Build tunnels on the ground inside the octopod.** The tunnels should form an X-shape (aligned southwest/ northeast and northwest/southeast; or whatever suits the prevailing wind) and be about a metre square. They should extend at least a metre beyond the base of your octopod – further, if you've got an awful lot of wood to burn.

**Apply wood.** You can now lean the rest of your fuel as evenly as possible around the octopod, taking care not to destabilise it. Hopefully, your bonfire will now extend to the outer circle created by the four tunnel entrances. This can be done well in advance of the big day; post a guard if your bonfire is in any way politically sensitive.

**Fill tunnels.** Come the day, collect bundles of faggots from dry storage and shove them into the tunnels. Keep access to the heart of the fire open on the side from which the wind is expected to blow that evening. A bale of straw at the centre provides ideal initial combustion.

**Light fire.** The fire is best lit with a giant match, 2 metres long, made using a big stick with a paraffin-soaked beer mat attached firmly to the end.* Even if there's heavy rain, the tunnels feed air into the bonfire and up its internal chimney, drying the fuel out quickly, so you should still have a mighty blaze.

**Application.** Celebratory and military, definitely; judicial if you've got a lot to get through; valedictory if you really loved him.

..........

* Or, as a Somerset headmaster did seventy years ago: attach one end of a zip wire to a tree, the other end to the bonfire; attach a rocket to the zip wire; light; stand well back. We don't often say it, but in this instance, those really were the days.

# BAKING BREAD

......................................

Until the twentieth century, you batch-baked bread in a wood-fired, brick-lined oven, a bit like having a miniature lime kiln in your kitchen. We'll hand over to rural radical William Cobbett, whose *Cottage Economy* (1821) is the original guide to self-sufficiency, aimed not at disenchanted urbanites but at helping agricultural labourers make the best of their bad lot. In it, he condemns the dreadful habit some wives had got into of *buying* bread. This – edited for length and clarity – is his attempt to put a stop to it at once. It's also a pretty workmanlike recipe if you live in a very old cottage or have a mind to build a pizza oven in your garden.

COBBETT'S PRELIMINARIES
As to the act of making bread, it would be shocking indeed if that had to be taught by the means of books. Every woman, high or low, ought to know how to make bread. If she do not, she is unworthy of trust and confidence; and, indeed, a mere burden upon the community. Yet, it is but too true, that many women, even amongst those who have to get their living by their labour, know nothing of the making of bread, and seem to understand little more about it than the part which belongs to its consumption.

How wasteful, then, and, indeed, how shameful, for a labourer's wife to go to the baker's shop, and how negligent, how criminally careless of the welfare of his family, must the labourer be, who permits so scandalous a use of the proceeds of his labour!

## COBBETT'S MATERIALS

Fuel is cheap: the hedgers, the coppicers, the woodsmen have it for little or nothing. It needs to be properly dried faggot-sticks, not brush-wood, with any larger logs split up into sticks not more 2½ inches through. The woody parts of furze (gorse), or ling (heather), will also heat an oven very well.

Fine flour need not and in fact ought not to be used. Besides this, rye, and even barley, especially when mixed with wheat, make very good bread. Half wheat, a quarter rye and a quarter barley, nay, one-third of each, make bread that a man could be very well content to live upon all his lifetime.

Use milk to wet the bread, an exceedingly great improvement in its taste as well as in its quality.

## COBBETT'S RECIPE

1. Light a strong and lively fire in the oven. (Pre-heat the oven to 200°C or 180°C fan.)
2. Hump a bushel of flour into your kitchen. (Cobbett, or rather his wife, isn't messing around here: that's about the same weight as one of today's 25-kg sacks. Feel free to shunt the decimal point one to the left and use a 2.5-kg supermarket bag.) Put the flour into a trough or clean smooth tub of any shape, not too deep and sufficiently large. Make a hole in the middle.
3. Take a pint of good fresh yeast and stir it into another pint of water, milk-warm. (A pint is 570 ml. If you're scaling down, use 4 tbsp. Milk-warm means the temperature of milk straight from a cow, i.e. the warm end of lukewarm.) Pour this into the flour. Take a spoon and work it round the mixture, adding flour, by degrees, to form a thin batter, which you must stir well for a minute or two. Take a handful of flour and scatter it thinly over

this batter, so as to hide it. Cover the whole over with a cloth.

4. When you can see that the batter has risen enough to make cracks in the flour that you covered it with, you can form the whole mass into dough. First scatter half a pound of salt. (Half a pound is 225 g. If you're scaling down use, 3 heaped tsp.) Then, work the salt into the batter. Finally, pour in, as it is wanted to make the flour mix with the batter, warm water or milk. (*As it is wanted* isn't the most helpful measurement. On average, you need 600 ml for 1 kg flour, so that's 1.5 litres for your scaled-down recipe, or 15 litres for the biggie.) Knead it well.

5. This is a grand part of the business for, unless the dough be well worked, there will be little round lumps of flour in the loaves, and the original batter, which is to give fermentation to the whole, will not be duly mixed. The dough must, therefore, be well worked. The fists must go heartily into it. It must be rolled over, pressed out, folded up and pressed out again, until it be completely mixed, and formed into a stiff and tough dough.

6. Scatter a little dry flour thinly over it, cover it again to be kept warm and to ferment, and in this state, if all be done rightly, it will not have to remain more than about 15 or 20 minutes. (This feels like a serious under-estimate unless

your kitchen is roasting hot. We'd say wait until it's nearly doubled in size.)

7. When an oven is properly heated, can be known only by actual observation. Women know when the heat is right the moment they put their faces within a yard of the oven-mouth, and once or twice observing is enough for any person of common capacity. Remove the fire and wipe the oven clean.

8. Cut the dough up into pieces and make it up into quartern loaves (that's a 2 kg-loaf, or twice the size of a standard modern loaf tin), kneading it into these separate parcels, shaking a little flour over your board, to prevent the dough from adhering to it. The loaves should be put into the oven as quickly as possible after they are formed.

9. If all be properly managed, your loaves will be sufficiently baked in about two hours. (His loaves take two hours because old bread-ovens cook with residual heat. In a modern oven, a big loaf takes about 50 minutes.)

COBBETT'S CONCLUSION

And what is there worthy of the name of plague, or trouble, in all this? Here is no dirt, no filth, no rubbish, no litter, no slop. (There speaks a man who's never kneaded a bushel of flour.) And, pray, what can be pleasanter to behold? Talk, indeed, of your pantomimes and gaudy shows, your processions and installations and coronations! Give me, for a beautiful sight, a neat and smart woman, heating her oven and setting in her bread. And, if the bustle does make the sign of labour glisten on her brow, where is the man that would not kiss that off, rather than lick the plaster from the cheek of a duchess.

# A few country measures

People originally standardised area measurements based on the ground a ploughman and his ox-team could cover in one day: an **acre**, which was 220 yards long by 22 yards wide (4,840 square yards). It's longer than it is wide, because 220 yards was the distance the oxen could cover before needing a break: a **furlong** i.e. a furrow long. After a rest, the ploughman turned the team around and headed back the other way, up down, up down, until the ploughed strip was 22 yards wide – a **chain** – and it was time to go home for tea. (Which hopefully wasn't much further than eight furlongs, or one mile, away.)

Yards and acres have become metres and hectares, but the furlong is still alive and well on the racecourse. Marker posts are placed at every furlong so that the jockeys can judge their final dash to the finish line.

And if you fancy buying the winner, you'll size it up and pay for it using two other retro measures: the **hand** (4 inches) and the **guinea** (21 shillings or £1 1s, back when there were 20 shillings to the pound). This means that your race-horse might be 16 hands tall, as measured from its withers (the high part of its back, between its shoulder blades) to the ground, and cost 10,000 guineas (or £10,500, with the extra £500 going to the auctioneer as commission). Hence, also, the 1000 Guineas flat race at Newmarket, named after the size of the purse (inflated to £500,000 today).

# CHEESE, A GOOD NEWS STORY

*'A corpse is meat gone bad. Well and what's cheese? Corpse of milk.'*
James Joyce, *Ulysses* (1922)

Cheese, once upon a time, was how the farmer's wife stored milk for the winter – when the grass stopped growing and her cows' milk slowed. And she it was who invented our classic hard cheeses: our Cheddar and Gloucester, our Cheshire and Wensleydale, our Leicester and Lancashire, i.e. cheeses from good cow country, where it's wet and grassy and there aren't too many big hills. Her skill was recognised in the capital, because luckily her cheeses travelled well (by boat, back then, if they were going up to town) and did not spoil. But for the last 150 years, a clutch of villains conspired to dismantle this cottage industry, nearly wiping out British cheese for good. *Nearly.* This tale – for once! – has a very happy ending.

But first, those villains:

**Industrialisation, especially trains.** Once the railways arrived, farmers could send their fresh milk to the growing cities, doing away with the need to preserve the fine-weather surplus. It soon became profitable to open commercial dairies at railway hubs, where butter and cheese could be manufactured on a large scale, undercutting the original farmhouse cheese-makers. France and Italy, by contrast, industrialised more slowly, had smaller rail networks and many more remote areas, all of which encouraged localism to prevail. (And by the time France's little producers might have been gobbled up, the government had created the *appellation d'origine contrôlée* (AOC) system, which protected place-specific, traditional know-how.)

**Free trade.** When people quit the countryside, they didn't necessarily go to British towns and cities, but instead sought new opportunities overseas – sometimes out of a sense of adventure but more likely because low wages and high rents left them with no other choice. Some of them (from the Puritan farmers onwards) took cheese-making techniques with them and so, by the mid-nineteenth century, American cheese (including knock-off Cheddar) was starting to flow into Britain: it was pretty tasteless, but cheap. New Zealand soon followed suit. (More appetisingly, we started importing from Italy, which from the 1930s cornered the market in relatively classy cheese.)

**Germs.** Researchers realised we could catch tuberculosis from cow's milk, and the only way to kill off the bacteria was to pasteurise it: 72°C heat for 15 seconds. That certainly finished off the bugs, but it also eroded the distinctiveness of different milk.* At the same time, pasteurisation suited the big dairy businesses, because the kit was large and expensive.

**Westminster.** In the 1930s, the government set up the Milk Marketing Board to act as a buyer of last resort for farmers' milk across the country. On the one hand: great. Dairy farmers were protected from the vicissitudes of the market. On the other hand: terrible. The economic incentive for producing cheese vanished overnight – why would farmers go to the effort of making cheese (a complicated

..........

* Milk tastes different depending on what the cow's been eating. (The same holds true for human milk.) If you don't pasteurise, you're giving the milk a better chance to express its unique flavour. You notice this very distinctly with French mountain cheeses, such as Beaufort: the summer version, when the cows are grazing high Alpine meadows, literally tastes more *flowery*. (Think how geology affects the taste of wine; same thing.)

and time-consuming process) when the government would give them a good price for their liquid milk?

**Germans.** During the Second World War, liquid milk took priority, and only long-lasting cheeses made to specific standards were allowed. So you could make Cheddar, but Stilton was discouraged. Cheese was also rationed: just 2–3oz per person per week. By 1954, when Dorothy Hartley published her classic, *Food in England*, she could state quite confidently that 'our really fine cheeses are lost'.

**Supermarkets.** Before the war, there'd still been more than a thousand registered farmhouse producers; by 1960 that number had fallen below two hundred. It's no coincidence that the first supermarket opened its doors in London in 1948 and the first Kraft cheese slices hit the shelves in 1950. Supermarkets wanted homogeneity and long, long life, so a child of the fifties grew up on sandwiches that leered with rubbery, orange-tinted cheese.

So ... what changed?

**A new culture in the country.** Combine the 1960s counterculture with the eye-watering inflation of the 1970s, and you have the makings of the self-sufficiency movement: mostly young, mostly idealistic people trying new ways of

making old things. In 1975, for example, the first year the classic sitcom *The Good Life* aired, the old cinema in the little Somerset city of Wells turned into a self-sufficiency trove that sold everything from cheese moulds to goat tethers, from wine-making paraphernalia to wood-stoves.

**A new culture in town.** The upwardly mobile 1980s was the decade that killed off Britain's reputation as having the most disgusting food on the planet. Chefs became cool. Cooking became cool. Could *cheese* become cool too?

**A new culture in Westminster.** The Milk Marketing Board came to an end in 1994 (it fell foul of EU competition law because it was a monopoly buyer and price fixer) which meant farmers now had to sell directly to the supermarkets. They were only offered a pittance, pennies for pints, and so it made sense, once more, for farmers to try to add some value to their milk. Some chose ice-cream, some yoghurts. Others chose cheese.

**A new kid on the block.** The Great Man theory of history weaves in and out of fashion, but when it comes to cheese, Patrick Rance is Mahatma Gandhi and Winston Churchill rolled into one. In 1954 (when he was in his mid-30s) he bought a house in Berkshire that included the village shop, which, at the time, sold three cheeses: Dutch Edam, New Zealand Cheddar and Danish Blue. Writing Rance's obituary in the *Guardian* in 1999, Egon Ronay says: 'It was here that his life's towering achievement originated: the almost single-handed creation of the British farm cheese industry – far beyond the tiny, prewar cottage industry – through advising, encouraging, pleading, coaxing, writing and broadcasting without any financial reward – a singular act of selflessness.'

Others, most notably Randolph Hodgson at Neal's Yard Dairy in London, took up the banner. Together, these cheesemongers gave small producers, who were making distinct, delicious cheeses, what they so desperately needed: a route to market. And so we have cheeses which taste like classics but are actually less than fifty years old, or classic cheeses which have found a new lease of life.

- Stinking Bishop
- Lincolnshire Poacher
- Ticklemore
- Wigmore
- Berkswell
- Colston Bassett Stilton
- Ragstone
- Appleby's Cheshire
- Cornish Yarg
- Kirkham's Lancashire

Pure cheese-y poetry.

# BACK TO THE LAND

*I paint the Cot,*
*As Truth will paint it, and as Bards will not*
George Crabbe, 'The Village' (1783)

Since the industrial revolution, the overwhelming direction of travel has been

country → → → → → city

but from the early days of European literature, we've dreamt of the reverse

city → → → → → country.

There's an epode by the Roman poet Horace, known as the *Beatus ille*, which starts with an unnamed narrator thinking how blessed (*beatus*) is the man (*ille*) who, far away from the forum, can plough his fields, tend his orchard, pot up his honey, keep a few sheep, do a little hunting, only for a sharp reverse in the final verse where he snaps out of his reverie and gets back to his job as a big city financier. That daydream is as potent today as it was two millennia ago.

Here, for example, is Paul Kingsnorth, writing what might be a twenty-first-century riff on Horace. 'These days my desire, overpowering sometimes, is for some land. An acre or two, some beans rows.* A pasture, broadleaved trees, a view of a river. A small house, my kids running around.'

What drives people to dream of leaving the city behind? To do without all those shops, all those jobs, all those pubs and clubs full of interesting strangers? Wars, recessions, pandemics, yes, yes, yes. But more often, it's a malaise with modern life (whether your modern is 1800, 1900 or 2000).

'As they walked through the everlasting streets they began to pine for the open fields, for the blessed sun, for the realities and simple joys they had left behind,' writes John Stewart Collis. 'They began to declare that civilisation was rotten at the core and perished at the roots, and that nothing could save it except a great Unindustrial Revolution.'

The dream can take different forms: it can mean anything from full-on, prepper-style self-sufficiency, to growing veg and keeping chickens while doing your old job remotely, to

..........

* The US essayist Henry David Thoreau wrote about beans in *Walden* (1854), his account of going to the woods to live 'deliberately'. Those beans are now iconic. You can find them moonlighting in W. B. Yeats's 'The Lake Isle of Innisfree', nine rows of them, plus cabin and beehive.

early retirement with a nest egg and a small-business plan.*
It's a well-worn path, which means there's lots of advice out
there from people who have gone before, advice to help
marry misty dream and muddy reality.

1. **Think soil.** Don't start out on clay. You're an amateur.
   Clay is for pros.
2. **Be self-aware.** John Seymour (who literally wrote the
   book on self-sufficiency) says you must a) be able to
   laugh at yourself, b) not mind if people think you're a
   nutter (he cheerfully calls himself a 'rip-roaring crank')
   and c) never, never preach. There is, after all, as James
   Rebanks puts it so succinctly in *English Pastoral*, 'a very
   thin line between idealism and bullshit'.
3. **But that doesn't mean you can't stick to your guns.**
   A lot of things which once seemed cranky, wacky, far
   out are now mainstream. Organic farming, farming for
   wildlife, animal welfare, regenerative farming: a generation ago it was fringe stuff; now some of it is policy.
4. **Beware too much book-learning.** 'Most intellectuals
   who visit us, alas, although very entertaining, are *practically* speaking quite useless,' says Seymour. 'It is like
   having some more babies in the house to look after.'
   This is problematic, seeing as a certain stripe of intel-
   lectual-ness can be a prime mover behind getting back
   to the land.

   To wit, Coleridge. He wanted (according to his
   letters) to 'raise vegetable & corn enough for myself &
   Wife' and claimed to prefer the 'dear gutter of Stowey'
   to a stream murmuring through an Italian orange grove.
   Unfortunately, he was too busy walking, writing and

----

* What the dream doesn't (often) include is running a serious farm; serious
farming not being seen as long on 'simple joys', nor as an easy gig to take up
later in adult life.

mainlining laudanum to be much of a provider. Mouse traps and weeding were also out: 'I thought it unfair in me to prejudice the soil towards roses and strawberries.'

Jim Crace's narrator in *Harvest* (2013) has some good advice for all Coleridge's heirs. The land, he says, is inflexible, stern and impatient: 'it does not wish us to stand back and comment on its comeliness or devise a song for it'.

5. **You need a certain sort of grit.** Whether or not you're farming livestock, you'll probably need to be able to kill things. Seymour has a milking cow. Turns out she wasn't a *do-er*. Soon, she was no longer a cow, but a nice cowhide rug. And Collis, after his time with the Land Army, is clear that 'an accurate day-to-day account of life on a farm would be almost laughably dull – though I wish someone would do it if only for the benefit of the romanticists'. This is your challenge: to reconcile *pastoral* fancy and *georgic* reality.

6. **Be sensitive to the people who are already there.** The Domesday Book, says Jacquetta Hawkes, is testament to the small-c conservatism of the countryside. 'Any countryman who goes to consult the heavy volumes in the Record Office can expect to find the name of his village written there.'* Visit any parish graveyard, any cricket pavilion, any war memorial, and the same surnames do crop up over and over again.

An old-timer in Max Porter's novel, *Lanny*, set in a village within striking distance of London, loathes middle-class incomers, despising their fantasies of village life: 'you cannot,' she tells herself, 'simply buy a sense of belonging on your mobile phone.' The real

..........

* We checked: it's true! Our village was once: 'Land of William of Mohun. Households: 21 villagers. 2 smallholders. 7 slaves.'

community, she thinks, is dead and gone, thanks to *people like them* buying up houses (and putting in ridiculous open kitchens). The pushback to such prejudice against incomers, says Seymour, is simple. Basically, don't be a dick. Don't *put it on*. Don't patronise people. Don't make fake small talk about turnips.

7. **But you've every right to be there too.** V. S. Naipaul's novel, *The Enigma of Arrival*, dramatises his (or rather a fictional version of his) own complicated feelings about moving to the English countryside, when he himself was born in Trinidad. At first, he assumes everything he sees (his neighbour tending geese, clipping hedges, planting out annuals) is part of something eternal – an eternal which his presence is disrupting. But then he realises that everything, the neighbour, the geese, the hedges, the annuals, everything is individual – transitory – and his conception of an immutable, immemorial way of life was wrong. 'Change was constant,' he says.

In other words, nobody has more of a 'right' to live in the countryside than you do. There's no right face, no right accent, no right family, no right politics. (And if anyone acts like there is, send us an SAE and we'll post you a baggie of *creeping oxalis* seeds, aka the Weed of Doom, and you can scatter them in their veg patch by dark of moon.)

8. **Don't be huffy about the countryside being full of old people and commuters.** Retired people do a lot of the village graft that people working full-time can't do: clerking the parish council, co-ordinating oil deliveries, sorting the village broadband, doing the parochial church council's accounts, volunteering in the community shop, keeping the post office alive, sorting the carol service, the Jubilee picnic, the blocked storm-drain

just down from the lychgate. And, lovely as it would be for everyone to work locally, there aren't the jobs. No blacksmiths, no schoolmistresses – only a pub, a holiday business or two, one or two farming jobs, if you're lucky. So, even with homeworking becoming more realistic for some, most people still need to commute *somewhere*.

9.  **Be prepared to sacrifice some ideals.** If you're growing on a small scale, your product's going to be expensive. Who's going to buy your pricey eggs, your niche mushrooms, your organic flour? Chris Smaje, a grower who's written a book called *A Small Farm Future*, warns that 'our would-be radical agrarian', inspired by the idea of 'sticking it to the man and doing their bit for the new agrarian dawn', often finds the only way to make a living is 'travelling around ingratiating themselves with the head chefs of all the high-end local restaurants while the Wendell Berry books gather dust on the shelf'. *

10. **In a quiet moment, mull your motivations.** Consider how the dream of going back to the land can often (although by no means always) be an impulse stemming from a place of relative ease, of relative security. Rebecca Solnit, in *Orwell's Roses* (2021), which looks at the relationship between power and nature, urges us to reflect on this. Remember, she says, 'the yearning to be more rugged, more rustic, more rough, more scruffy, is often a white and a white-collar yearning'. Adam Nicolson, in his back-to-the-land memoir, also

..........

* Barely a word Wendell Berry (a US farmer, essayist and environmental activist) writes doesn't bear repeating, but this is one of our favourites: 'A protest meeting on the issue of environmental abuse is not a convocation of accusers, it is a convocation of the guilty. The realisation ought to clear the smog of self-righteousness that has always conventionally hovered over these occasions, and let us see the work that is to be done.'

ponders this contradiction: 'Pastoral – the idea that a rural existence can somehow regenerate those who give themselves over to it – carries the seeds of its own failure. It is, by definition, a sophisticated attitude.'*

A sophisticated attitude with a French phrase to match: *Nostalgie de la boue*? Mud nostalgia.

11. **Imagine the boot is on the other foot.** Remember, just as much as you might want to run *to* the country, so an awful lot of people are desperate to run *away*. Here's Thomas Hardy's Jude (the Obscure) standing on a hill, looking down with painful longing on the never-never-land of Christminster:

'It is a city of light,' he said to himself.

'The tree of knowledge grows there,' he added a few steps further on.

'It is a place that teachers of men spring from and go to.'

'It is what you may call a castle, manned by scholarship and religion.'

After this figure he was silent a long while, till he added:

'It would just suit me.'

Or, to quote an addled Civil War soldier at the end of the film *A Field in England*, some people would rather 'die of the fucking plague in the fucking fleet than spend another fucking minute in the countryside'.

..........

* He tells a funny story (cf. being able to laugh at yourself), which we have to share, about the 'long-jawed scepticism' that greeted his attempts to explain to a village-hall meeting why the roughness of a certain local lane was in fact desirable. Wouldn't it be better if the lane remained rough, all the better to encourage children and bicycles, not cars? Oh, please, no, their faces said, not him again. One held his head in his hands, shaking it slowly. We only wish there was a Zoom record of him reading out Rudyard Kipling's description of the lane in question from *Puck of Pook's Hill*. 'None of it,' he admits, 'cut any ice. I was from a different world.'

12. **And finally**, whichever car, truck or tractor you buy, for God's sake make sure you can back it up the twisty lane really, *really* fast – even (in fact, especially) if you've got a trailer attached.

# CHICKENS

*In fact, the world is full of hopeful analogies and handsome dubious eggs called possibilities.*
George Eliot, *Middlemarch* (1871)

Huzzah! Organic eggs every day and not a food mile in sight. What's not to like?

Plenty, that's what.

**The fox.** You can guarantee that the morning you send a friend's innocent little children to collect the eggs all by themselves will be the morning the fox has been. It'll be ugly. Your fox doesn't just eat its fill, it annihilates every hen within reach, ripping their silly heads off and scattering the uneaten carcasses far and wide. One fox can see off a score of chickens in the time it takes for you to neck your third pint at the pub and run down the hill because you've remembered the coop's automatic door's bust. Foxes can dig, foxes can jump, foxes can scramble up wire mesh: sooner or later, the fox will win.

**The mink.** Understudy to the fox. They're escapees from fur farms – back when we had fur farms – so in some ways, fair play to them.

**The rat.** Chicken feed is a rat's delight. They wriggle, they squeeze, they swarm, and they're far too wily to spring your traps. Poison is risky. You need to find a teenager who's good at Fortnite and is keen to go analogue with an air rifle.

**The red mite.** Beastly little sucker. Starts grey and turns red as it gorges on chicken blood. To tackle an infestation, you have to park your chickens somewhere else, torch all their bedding and clean their house like one possessed.

**Feather pecking.** Alpha hens peck beta hens in a grisly homage to the social dynamics of Year 8. (Yes, this is where *pecking order* and *hen-pecked* originate). If it escalates, lowly hens can wind up scraggy and semi-bald or bleeding or dead. And it's no good simply feeding Alpha to the foxes: Beta will step up to the plate. It's worse if they're too confined – *cooped up*, in fact.

**Avian flu.** Borne on the wings of migrating birds, this nasty killer tends to arrive in winter. By law, all domestic bird flocks must be kept indoors when it appears, which can mean no free-range chickens and no free-range eggs for months on end.

**Errant partners.** See above, re: fox and pub.

**Winter.** They stop laying but keep eating. Galling.

Do you still want to go ahead?

**RULE 1.** Do not think of chicken keeping as either a money-saving or a money-making enterprise.

**RULE 2.** Do not cut corners to circumvent Rule 1.

**RULE 3.** You want happy, free-range chickens eating God's free green grass? Remember: happy, free-range chickens are fox food. You need fencing, maybe electric, plus a decent-sized hen-house where they sleep and lay. Chickens put themselves to bed when it's dark, so you can usually get away with an automated light-sensitive door, which saves you the hassle of opening and closing every day. Be wary around midsummer. It's light for longer, plus the vixens are bolder because they're weaning their cubs.

**RULE 4.** Buy *point-of-lay pullets*: young hens who are about to start producing eggs. Buying and raising day-olds involves too much paraphernalia and palaver.

**RULE 5.** No designer birds.

**RULE 6.** No rescue chickens. They'll eat a lot of food without producing a lot of eggs: bad for your pocket and the planet.

**RULE 7.** No cockerel, however handsome. They are vicious and noisy and have horrible sharp ankle spurs. Hens don't need a cock around to be prolific egg producers.

**RULE 8.** Chickens are bred for eggs* or meat, so your ageing layer will make a rubbish roast. Stock or dog-food.

**RULE 9.** Enjoy the eggs. They do taste (a bit) better. (Even if you have to wipe the poo off yourself.)

**RULE 10.** Don't get cocky and diversify into geese. They're bastards.

..........

* What, you might ask, happens to the boy-child of an egg-chicken? In the first few days of a chick's life, it will meet a highly skilled *chicken sexer*, who decides boy or girl by scrutinising its *vent*. Sexers are paid around £3 per 100 chicks examined, which adds up to £40,000 a year. For the boys, it's an immediate death sentence.

# THE FOX

....................

Traditional

The fox went out on a chilly night,
he prayed to the Moon to give him light,
for he'd many a mile to go that night
before he reached the town-o, town-o, town-o,
he had many a mile to go that night
before he reached the town-o.

He ran till he came to a great big bin
where the ducks and the geese were put therein.
'A couple of you will grease my chin
before I leave this town-o, town-o, town-o,
a couple of you will grease my chin
before I leave this town-o.'

He grabbed the grey goose by the neck,
threw the grey goose behind his back;
he didn't mind their quack, quack, quack,
and their legs all a-dangling down-o, down-o, down-o,
he didn't mind their quack, quack, quack,
and their legs all a-dangling down-o.

Old Mother Flipper Flopper jumped out of bed;
out of the window she cocked her head,
Crying, 'John, John! The grey goose is gone
and the fox is on the town-o, town-o, town-o!'
Crying, 'John, John, the grey goose is gone
and the fox is on the town-o!'

Then John he went to the top of the hill,
blew his horn both loud and shrill,
the fox he said, 'I'd better flee with my kill
He'll soon be on my trail-o, trail-o, trail-o.'
The fox he said, 'I'd better flee with my kill
He'll soon be on my trail-o.'

He ran till he came to his cozy den;
there were the little ones eight, nine, ten.
They said, 'Daddy, better go back again,
'cause it must be a mighty fine town-o, town-o, town-o!'
They said, 'Daddy, better go back again,
'cause it must be a mighty fine town-o.'

Then the fox and his wife without any strife
cut up the goose with a fork and knife.
They never had such a supper in their life
and the little ones chewed on the bones-o,
    bones-o, bones-o,
they never had such a supper in their life
and the little ones chewed on the bones-o.

# HUNTING

.......................

*And yet it irks me the poor dappled fools,*
*Being native burghers of this desert city,*
*Should in their own confines with forkèd heads*
*Have their round haunches gored.*
William Shakespeare, *As You Like It* (c. 1599)

The hunting community has felt under attack for generations.*

When the 8th Duke of Beaufort, back in the 1880s, was writing the first of his hugely popular series of sporting books he lamented that it was a 'melancholy pleasure' since the 'brutality of field-sports' was being denounced with 'so much eloquence and energy' that he couldn't believe the world would suffer him to enjoy a pastime 'which so many wise men have agreed to brand as wanton and debasing' for very much longer. As things turned out, it was three whole dukes later, towards the end of the long life of the 11th Duke, that the axe – in the form of the Hunting Act (2004) which followed the 1997 Labour landslide – finally fell.

That duke's obituaries (he moved on to happier hunting grounds in 2017) make compelling reading. The *Telegraph* notes that he was a dashing sportsman, a connoisseur** and a glamorous figure on the London art scene, as well as sympathising with the 'macabre ordeal' he underwent when the Hunt Retribution Squad attempted to dig up the grave of his cousin and ducal predecessor (known simply as

..........

\* We know your violin is probably *tiny*, but bear with us ...
\*\* In obit code, the *of women* is silent.

Master, thanks to his frankly massive hunting chops) with the apparent intention of delivering the head to Princess Anne.*

The *Times* relates that as joint master of his eponymous hunt, the duke clashed frequently with saboteurs, who once tried to pull him from a vehicle with the intention – he believed – of kicking him to death. 'There were,' the obituarist discloses, 'other hunt-related skirmishes, including in 1991 when the duke and [co-master Captain Iain] Farquhar were in court after their hounds ran riot on a wildlife sanctuary. A decade later there were allegations that he allowed deer carcasses to be dumped on his estate to encourage foxes to feed and breed for the hunt.'

There, in a nutshell, is hunting's ticklish PR problem. You can get away with killing animals. You can get away with being posh. But killing animals while being posh? Beyond the pale.

We are, by contrast, predisposed to admire the world's indigenous hunters, noting their physical prowess, their knowledge of the land, their kinship with their prey – the thickness of their social ties, the great age and intricacy of their traditions. And in the United States, it's not seen as remotely posh to go and kill things – it's a normal part of rural, blue-collar life – and a similar attitude holds across much of Europe. In France, the government says different hunters in different regions each have *leur rite, leur implantation locale, leurs particularités techniques*, i.e. their own special way of doing things. Basically, for the French, hunting's a bit like cheese.

But here, we don't have hunting, we have *huntin', shootin' & fishin'*. It doesn't matter that loads of middle- and working-class people hunt: when people think of hunting, they

..........

* No word of a lie! (Her crime was to have hunted with the Beaufort.)

picture a red-faced man in a scarlet coat, and they think ... well, we don't need to tell you. You know it all already.

It's William the Conqueror's fault, originally. When he got *all the power*, he also (remember the forests) got *all the game*, and so hunting had no chance of developing into an everyday, demotic sort of activity, and instead became elite. Taking a step sideways, into the bracing arms of theory, Erich Fromm (a social psychologist of the Frankfurt School) explains in *The Anatomy of Human Destructiveness* that hunting satisfied the elite man's desire to exert power and control, rather than his desire to kill animals. Disliking hunting, therefore, is as much about disliking (the vestiges of) feudalism as it is about disliking grisly animal death in the name of sport.

And indeed, in our experience, people who don't necessarily have a problem with their local hunt on the grounds of cruelty dislike it immensely if they ever feel they are being patronised, talked down to or in any way taken for granted – if, in other words, they're being *feudalised*. The writer Adam Nicolson, who is no fan of hunting *per se*, summed it up very well: 'Has anyone in the saddle ever managed to address anyone on the ground without exuding the whole "my good man" aura that irritates and alienates so much?'*

He's right. The huntsman does exist who will look down at you from a great height and inform you unapologetically that his hounds have gone in your gate – more fool you for leaving it open on a hunting day – and so the fact that they're currently wreaking merry hell amongst your raspberry canes is rather your own fault.

Hunting, you see, didn't (and doesn't) happen in the wild: it weaves in and out of woods, fields and villages,

..........

* Boris Johnson wrote of huntsmen with *glutinous grins*. Would that he had stuck to phrasemaking.

which is why people who run hunts normally put in a lot of spadework to keep their neighbours on side.*

George, the narrator of Siegfried Sassoon's *Memoirs of a Fox-Hunting Man*, a far more subtle work than its title might suggest, says at first he'd been incapable of seeing things from a local farmer's point of view. 'A large crowd of people riding over someone else's land and making holes in the hedges is likely to create all sorts of trouble [...], but I

..........

* The most helpful thing the hunt does is take *fallen stock* (i.e. dead lambs or chickens) off your hands: both make excellent hound food.

had not thought about it that way. The country was there to be ridden over. That was all.' It's only when George moves in with Denis Milden, a young master of foxhounds, that he realises how much time his friend (/object of desire?) spends appeasing the locals. After that, he 'ceased to look upon an angry farmer with a pitchfork as something to be laughed at'.

The 8th Duke of Beaufort could confidently write: 'The bulk of farmers are so sporting and so good-natured that they do not mind.' But when a duke said, 'You don't mind, do you, old chap?' in the 1880s, and probably well into the 1980s, you tended to say, 'No, Your Grace, not a bit, right you are, thanks ever so, perhaps the hounds would like cream with their raspberries?'

Throughout the last century, therefore, the cult and cachet of hunting was so overwhelming that people who fundamentally weren't all that keen kept their heads down for the sake of a quiet life. E. M. Delafield, whose *The Diary of a Provincial Lady* (1930) is both disarmingly funny and still disconcertingly relevant, mastered this once essential country art: 'I sit next elderly gentleman who talks about stag-hunting and tells me there is Nothing Cruel about it. The stag likes it, and it is an honest, healthy, thoroughly English form of sport. I say Yes, as anything else would be waste of breath, and turn to Damage done by recent storms [...]'

You could, however, get away with being rude about hunting if you were very grand. Lord Merlin, the dissolute neighbour in Nancy Mitford's *The Pursuit of Love*, tells (hunting-mad) Linda: 'Hunt as much as you like, but never talk about it, it's the most boring subject in the world.' And Lady Marchmain (same period, same social circle, different novel: *Brideshead Revisited*) says she's always detested hunting because it turns people into cads and Prussians:

'"The evenings I've sat at dinner appalled at seeing the men and women I know, transformed into half-awake, self-opinionated, monomaniac louts!"'

But after the Second World War, when a lot of old money was forced to sell up, the hunt could no longer take local farmers' and landowners' tacit support for granted. Explains the magazine, *The Field*: 'Rural Britain had changed forever and hunts no longer had carte blanche to gallop wherever they wished. Big estates had been broken up and sold to owners who were at liberty to choose whether they welcomed the hunt or not[.]'

Meanwhile, throughout the 1970s and 1980s, anti-hunting sentiment in the towns and cities was building. New technology made it possible for activists to share gruesome VHS tapes of foxes being ripped to shreds, appealing equally to Tory-hating leftists and environmentalists who had been fighting hard to save the whales, but were now happy to zero in on a cause closer to home.

*Riders*, Jilly Cooper's first great Thackerayan drama, published in 1985, was something of a valiant rearguard action for the hunting lobby. Millions of readers were disconcerted to find themselves gripped by Rupert Campbell-Black* ('shrugging himself into a red coat') as he tried to detach the beautiful 'fox-y' Helen from her wet townie *anti* friends, Nigel and Paul. She falls into his arms ('she kept her lips rigid, then, powerless, she found herself kissing him back'), only to ditch him when it dawns on her that he's simply too much of a massive (in eighties speak) *male chauvinist pig*.

As it turned out, the wet townie antis won a landslide in the 1997 general election, and although they were (in the

..........

* We're delighted to report that his character was apparently partly based on the 11th Duke of Beaufort. Small world.

words of New Labour spinner Peter Mandelson) 'intensely relaxed about people getting filthy rich', they were *not* relaxed about hunting. Unfortunately, though, the Hunting Act was not a clean kill. It left hunting bloody and mangled, but still very much alive. In fact, if the Labour government had intended to draft a piece of legislation that absolutely nobody would be happy with, they totally nailed it.

People who **didn't hunt and didn't want other people hunting** said the ban was a bodge, a fudge, a hedge, sludge, riddled and addled and saddled with loopholes. Their criticisms have turned out to be absolutely spot on, as we'll see in a moment.

People who **didn't hunt but didn't mind other people hunting** said the ban was illogical and illiberal. They pointed out that the Burns Inquiry report, commissioned by the government, said that a hunting ban wouldn't necessarily improve fox welfare. Farmers would still be legally allowed to cull foxes, either by shooting them or by using snares, neither of which was demonstrably a better deal for the fox.

What's more, they said, if you're so worried about animal welfare, what about *all the cats*? Cats eviscerate mice, decapitate rabbits, de-wing bats, de-feather birds, all, so it seems, for fun, for sport. And we allow it. Why? Because cats do nice furry tummy rolls and hide amusingly under rugs? Is that seriously a good enough reason?

This was David Cameron's take, back in 2003 when he used to write a regular column for the *Guardian*: 'Set against the cruelty of factory farming or coarse fishing, hunting hardly registers. So while I might listen to a lecture about the cruelty of the chase from a vegan wearing plastic shoes, the calls to ban hunting from meat-eating, leather-wearing, angling-enthusiast class warriors on the Labour benches make my blood boil.'

And even Tony Blair, the man whose political capital got the law through parliament in the first place, wound up thinking it was a big mistake: 'The more I learned, the more uneasy I became,' he wrote in his memoirs after leaving office. 'This wasn't a clique of weirdo inbreds delighting in cruelty, but a tradition [...] integral to a way of life.'

Finally, **people who did hunt**, or who were more broadly part of the field-sports world, were absolutely incensed. They saw the ban as evidence that an urban Labour Party was wreaking a kind of mean-spirited revenge on conservative and/or Conservative rural voters.

Jamie Blackett, whose *Red Rag to a Bull* (2018) is a rural memoir written indefatigably from the right (a rare bird these days), thought the ban was particularly galling because it came hard on the heels of foot-and-mouth. It was, he said, 'a slap in the face for the hunting and farming community, who had saved the Blair government's skin by making the awful sacrifice of slaughtering their sheep and cattle'. Hunt staff, he said, had worked round the clock culling condemned livestock, even travelling to different parts of the country so they wouldn't have to kill animals belonging to their neighbours and friends.

He, and a lot of other people, didn't see the ban as the many versus the few (a category he does admittedly fall into: Eton, Coldstream Guards) but as the centre versus the periphery, the conquerors versus the conquered. He compares the (very large, very pro-hunting, socially and economically very broad-based) Countryside Alliance marches in the early noughties (which did rather startle London in its Cool-Britannia heyday) to 'salt coming out of the earth to shake an angry Saxon fist at the Neo-Normans'.

But, as it's turned out, all across England, men and women are *still* riding to hounds. The ban, you see, isn't really a ban.

Imagine the government banned alcohol. Imagine the Sturm and Drang. Now imagine everyone taking a deep breath and examining the small print. Oooh. You *can* drink if a) you stick to two units on specific special occasions or b) you're not intending to get drunk.

Sounds nuts? Yes. But that, in a nutshell, is how the hunting ban operates.

### SCENARIO A: TWO HOUNDS, WITH KILLING

You can hunt, so long as you meet certain *exemptions* laid out in the Act. If you can show that you reasonably thought your hunting was exempt, you have *not* broken the law.

You can use two dogs (under close control)

- to stalk a fox or a deer
- to flush it out of cover
- if you are preventing or reducing serious damage which the fox or deer might cause to livestock, game birds or wild birds, food for livestock, crops or growing timber, biological diversity
- or if you're getting meat for you or another animal to eat.

So long as you shoot the fox or deer yourself – instead of letting the hounds kill it – you are totally legit.

### SCENARIO B: ALL THE HOUNDS, NO KILLING

You can hunt with all your hounds, provided you're *definitely* not hunting foxes. Instead, you're playing a fun game of hound hide-and-seek, whereby someone has dragged a foxy-smelling something up hill and down dale, and you're *definitely* chasing that and *definitely* not chasing foxes.

Crucially, to make it more natural for the hounds (whose welfare must be considered), the smelly-something-dragging-person will have visited a lot of fox-y copse-y places, raising and lowering the smelly-something so it's not *too* easy for the hounds (whose welfare, we say again, must be considered). And if, very occasionally, by some awful stroke of bad luck, you happen upon the scent of a real fox, then of course the huntsman will sound their horn, and the hounds will stop on a sixpence, no problem, nothing to see here. That, then, is *trail-hunting*.*

The catch, as anyone who's ever watched a dog pick up an exciting scent can all too easily imagine, is that just occasionally a hound might *speak to* a genuine fox trail, and her pack-mates might join in, and they might get really quite a long way before the huntsman, try so hard as ever they might, succeeds in calling them back in. But even if your hounds were indubitably chasing a fox, for you to be convicted of a crime, the prosecutor has to prove *intent* – that you meant your hounds to give chase. And, as anyone who's ever watched a dog take off after a pair of beautifully coiffed ladies in brightly coloured ath leisure wear will testify, sometimes dogs take off after things, after which you honestly did not intend them to take. Finally, even if you are found guilty, the fines are low and one thing hunts are good at is raising money.

In conclusion, it's a ridiculous situation.

WHY DO PEOPLE HUNT?

Because it's pure heart-in-mouth fun: 'the greatest physical pleasure I know', so Friedrich Engels confessed to Karl Marx. Or rather, because it's boring, confusing, stressful, cold, wet and uncomfortable for hour after hour, and then – excitement – adrenaline – FENCE – wind-in-face

..........

* Trail-hunting evolved from *drag-hunting*, which is a long-established, blood-free way to hunt with hounds. Drag-hunting was developed by Sandhurst cadets who wanted to spend more time galloping across country leaping fences, and less time milling around trying to find actual foxes.

– thundering – ha, ha, ha, he fell – FENCE – etc. In short, it's the sort of thing you hate at the time, but looking back on it with a fat G&T, it was actually brilliant.*

### HOW DOES HUNTING WORK?

You need to be able to ride. Really quite well. Then you can **join a hunt**. Some are posher than others. To join a really posh hunt, a ducal sort of hunt, you're looking at £4,000+ a year, and that's on top of everything you're already spending on a horse, bought or borrowed. Most aren't anything like that expensive, though. More like a gym membership.

You also have to **dress properly**, but don't turn up on day one in a red coat: they're often only for hunt officials (aka *hunt servants*), or longer-standing subscribers. But you still need special kit: a tweed *ratcatcher* coat and brown breeches for autumn hunting; black coat and white breeches come the main season.**

**The master of foxhounds (M.F.H.)** is in charge: think of them as the regimental colonel. They oversee the kennels, disburse the money raised by the hunt, possibly contribute some of their own money. Ideally they're very charming, very good at keeping all the local landowners on side. They'll plan fundraising and charity stuff with the secretary and treasurer, tee up the point-to-point, where they'll make sure that the most apple-cheeked little brothers and sisters of the children at the pony club are photographed cuddling hounds. They'll also make sure there's an enthusiastic roster of hound walkers, a popular job because you get to look after a hound puppy at home until it's big enough to join the pack.

That covers a lot of the stuff going on behind the scenes.

..........

* Cf. every SAS memoir ever written.
** Autumn-hunting used to be called *cubbing*, because you're hunting ... fox cubs. You can see why they went for the rebrand.

On the day itself, the **huntsman** is in charge: think of them as the regimental sergeant-major. The huntsman can be the same person as the M.F.H, or they can be two separate people. Whoever it is, when you turn up, definitely don't bother them, beyond saying a polite good morning. Hunts used to get together outside village pubs or on the lawns of big houses, but these days smaller hunts are often more discreet. It's the huntsman's job to decide which coverts to draw, i.e. where to go and look for a fox to chase (or where to go and look for the trail that's been laid). This is the part where you trot along lanes and across fields, smiling courteously at everyone you pass.

At the meet, you might also have noticed the **foot followers**, who don't ride themselves, but get a lot of pleasure out of watching the hounds work. They'll probably pay a small fee or *cap* to be in on the action. Some hunts even have a **car master**, because people who don't get het up about hunting in general do get het up about badly parked cars blocking the lanes. Odds are that your average foot follower is a) passionate about hunting and b) not massively posh.

Working with the huntsman, you'll see the **whippers-in.**\* They focus on the hounds, making sure they don't wander off or chase something they're not meant to chase. When you get to the first covert, there'll be lots of waiting. At this point the **field master**, who's in charge of the mounted followers (or *field*), will be making sure everyone's quiet, not standing somewhere stupid, that nobody's got lost, that whoever's in charge of shutting the gate has done their job properly.

Next, you're hoping, a fox will appear, the hounds will chase the fox, the huntsman will chase the hounds, and

..........

\* Yup, that's why parliamentary whips are called whips.

you'll chase the huntsman, until the hounds get the fox, and you either all go home, or go and look for another fox. But what often happens is that either the hounds lose the fox (cue more milling) or the fox (wisely, but unsportingly) goes to ground. At this point the huntsman deploys their **terriermen**.

The terriermen have been following the hunt on quad bikes, with their dogs in boxes on the back, wearing more casual 'countryman' clothes, not jackets and breeches. Of course, if you've been trail-hunting, there shouldn't be a fox to flush, which makes antis ask what the terriermen are doing. Answers there are many: they're all-round good sorts, checking gates, mending fences, directing lost riders, making the drag extra foxy, picking up injured hounds, filming to prove the hunt's acting legally, politely but firmly informing antis that they're trespassing. The anti would tell you a very different story.

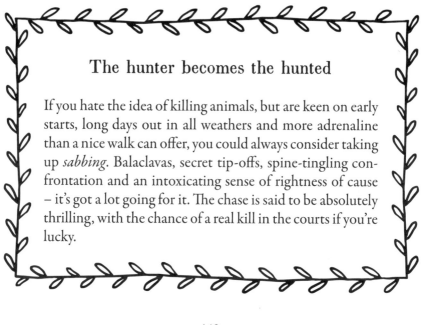

## The hunter becomes the hunted

If you hate the idea of killing animals, but are keen on early starts, long days out in all weathers and more adrenaline than a nice walk can offer, you could always consider taking up *sabbing*. Balaclavas, secret tip-offs, spine-tingling confrontation and an intoxicating sense of rightness of cause – it's got a lot going for it. The chase is said to be absolutely thrilling, with the chance of a real kill in the courts if you're lucky.

# A FATHER'S ADVICE

by Mark Hanbury Beaufoy

If a sportsman true you'd be,
Listen carefully to me ...

Never, never let your gun
Pointed be at anyone.
That it may unloaded be
Matters not the least to me.

When a hedge or fence you cross
Though of time it cause a loss,
From your gun the cartridge take
For the greater safety's sake.

If twixt you and neighbouring gun,
Bird shall fly or beast may run,
Let this maxim ere be thine:
'Follow not across the line.'

Stops and beaters oft unseen
Lurk behind some leafy screen.
Calm and steady always be.
'Never shoot where you can't see.'

Keep your place and silent be;
Game can hear, and game can see;
Don't be greedy, better spared
Is a pheasant, than one shared.

You may kill or you may miss
But at all times think this:
'All the pheasants ever bred
Won't repay for one man dead.'

## SHOOTING

....................

*Oh! if only pheasants had but understanding, how they*
*would split their sides with chuckling and crowing at the*
*follies which civilised Christian men perpetrate for their*
*precious sake.*
Charles Kingsley, *Yeast* (1848)

FIVE METHODS

Very roughly, **rough shooting** means going out, maybe on
your own, maybe with a friend or two, definitely with a
dog, and looking for birds to shoot. You probably won't
get all that many and you're probably not wearing tweed
(not unless tweed is already your go-to look). You might be
doing it on your land, or on a friend's, or you might have an
informal arrangement with a neighbouring farmer: a bottle
or two of spirits at Christmas or some other *quid pro quo*.
If you live near a low-lying and marshy bit of coast, you
might also be wildfowling, which is the roughest of rough
shooting.

Driven **shooting**, on the other hand, means that you
don't have to walk to find the birds – instead, the birds are
brought to you. You're definitely paying. A lot.

Somewhere in between lies **walk-up shooting**, which
combines the romance of the rough with the organisation
of the driven. You or your host will have a well-trained dog

with you to find, flush and retrieve what you shoot. Again you're paying, but not quite as much.

Of course, Britain also has a distinguished tradition of **poaching**, which is both rough and cheap.

Or you can shoot **clays**: driven, affordable, vegan.

## BIRD ONE: PHEASANTS

'Britain,' remarks the *Economist* with customary crispness, 'has an enormous number of pheasants. Whether this is a good thing is a matter of taste.'

Pheasants, you see, make excellent game-birds: they don't mind being reared in captivity and they survive quite competently once they're released into the (semi-)wild.* People have been importing them in dribs and drabs, possibly since Roman times, but their popularity really took off early in the nineteenth century. Pheasants (as will be blindingly obvious if you've ever driven down a quiet lane in shooting country in late July or early August) are now released in *vast* numbers. By vast, we mean 30 million birds a year, accounting for perhaps half of our non-farmed bird biomass, although some estimates put this far higher.

Once upon a time, pheasant shooting was how people in large houses (the sorts of people who had gamekeepers and weekend parties) kept themselves and their guests amused. In fact, an Edwardian pheasant *battue*, explains Jonathan Garnier Ruffer in *The Big Shots* (1977), 'combined the opportunities of a Vimy Ridge machine-gunner with an infinitely better lunch'. Simultaneously, a well-off farmer might have reared a few pheasants for sport, perhaps setting up a syndicate to spread the costs, thereby creating a

..........

* The Balkans and the Caucasus are the nearest places where you might run into a legit wild pheasant. The word *pheasant*, f.y.i, comes from the Latin *phasianus*, which means *Phasian*, which is a reference to the River Phasis, which flows into the Black Sea, which was once in Colchis (which is where Jason found the golden fleece), but which is now Georgia.

few days' fun for his friends. And so, throughout the twentieth century, pheasant shooting was a niche activity for posh and/or country people – until along came Margaret Thatcher and the 1980s Big Bang. Suddenly, there were a lot of people, with a lot of money, looking for high-status ways to spend it.

Nowadays, the sorts of people who live in very large houses still invite each other to shooting weekends but, depending on inclination and cash flow, they're also likely to let shooting days to the sorts of people who work in very large hedge funds and travel by helicopter. Meanwhile, the well-off farmer, or rather his entrepreneurial grandson or granddaughter, has worked out that professionalising the low-key family shoot and selling spots to the sorts of people who can't afford a helicopter, but can still pay hundreds of pounds for a day out, is a superb income stream, especially on more marginal bits of land.*

Running a shoot is a serious – and stressful – business. Throughout the season (1 October – 1 February), you're entertaining a succession of alpha types, people who've paid a lot of money *to be shown some good birds*. If you're the gamekeeper running the shoot, producing those birds, at the right time, at the right height, in the right quantity, demands great skill and artistry.

The gamekeeper either rears or buys in poults over the summer months, making sure they stay put by feeding them, and protecting them from both ground predators and aerial attack. There is, of course, nothing stopping an adventurous pheasant high-tailing it, but they're not very escape-minded. As the winsome Una says in Rudyard Kipling's *Puck of Pook's Hill* (1906): 'Oh, look! The silly

..........

* Bought days are charged per bird shot, so a 200-bird day at £35 a bird (resale value: £1) would cost £7,000. Split that between eight people, add tips, and each person is already looking at pushing £1,000.

birds are going back to their own woods instead of ours, where they would be safe.'

A day's shooting is split into four to six *drives*, which are different places (field, hillside) where the *guns* line up. The drives will be close, but not too close, to the coverts from which the birds will be driven. These coverts might be bits of woodland, old or new, or strategically sited strips of game-mixture crops (i.e. maize, millet, buckwheat, sorghum, kale, mustard, stuff nobody's planning on eating). A drive is divided into *pegs*, which are sticks stuck in the ground, showing each gun where to stand.

Traditionally, a *loader* stood discreetly behind the gun, readying the second of his pair of £100,000-Purdeys while he discharged the first. Nowadays, guns who are a bit clueless have a loader assigned to them, a sort of dedicated wing-man, to make sure they don't do anything dangerous, as well as murmuring important advice like, 'That wasn't your bird, Sir.' (We're told that the number of loaders and the number of helicopters operate in direct proportion.)

All guns, men and women, do honestly wear tweed: jacket or coat, waistcoat or shooting vest, trousers or *breeks*,* plus a tie.

While the guns are getting ready, the gamekeeper will have been deploying their *beaters* to get the pheasants out of cover and into the path of the guns. At all times, the keeper must adhere to Pygmalion's dictum *ars latet arte sua*, which basically means you've got to hide the fact that what you're doing is fake by doing it really well. The guns don't want to be able to see the release pens, the feeders

..........

* Breeks are Bermuda shorts or knickerbockers, which you tuck into stockings. They're much handsomer than trousers stuffed into wellies and easier to move about in. *Plus twos* fall 4 inches below the knee, which'll turn into 2 inches when folded and fastened. *Plus fours* are 8 inches below, four when folded and fastened. You tie off your breeks with rather jaunty tassels.

and drinkers. They certainly don't want pheasants cluck-
ing around their feet. They're after an invigorating flurry
of birds overhead (not an unseemly blizzard). In fact, they
want the ambience of a private family shoot, discreet and
traditional – nothing too commercial, too contrived.*

The beaters, who will know the terrain intimately, form
a line a good distance from the drive and advance slowly,
making their way through cover that is still thick enough for
the pheasants to feel safe, tapping a stick against their boot
(gently, no thwacking) to urge them forwards. Basically, it's
pheasant herding, slow and steady, don't scare the horses.
They have to stay in a neat line (hard if you're negotiating
maize), and move steadily, otherwise the birds try to sneak
back behind them. The gamekeeper will also position some
of their team as *flankers* or *stops* to prevent the birds spill-
ing out left or right, or sneaking off down some gully. The

..........

* A classic cartoon by Norman Thelwell shows a disgruntled gent with one
pheasant perched on his shotgun and another rifling his bag.

pheasants run ahead of the beaters, who are guiding them towards the *flushing point*, which will be very close to the edge of the covert. From there, the beaters drive the pheasants forwards more urgently, encouraging them to take flight into the path of the guns – who've had time to get settled, but haven't been waiting too long.

The birds take flight, the guns bring down as many as they can – and now the dogs take over. A serious gun might have their own dog; others will rely on the shoot's pickers-up. These men and women will have been stationed behind the guns (hoping that none of them is such a moron as to *shoot low behind*) with their beautifully trained gundogs. These dogs, spaniels and Labradors mostly, sit improbably patiently while pheasants whirr and guns blaze overhead, *marking* the fallen birds, until a horn or whistle announces the end of the drive, at which point they dash off to retrieve the dead game – as well as seeing to any *runners*, i.e. birds that weren't killed outright.

Obviously, the whole thing wouldn't work without the beaters and pickers-up. They might get around £50 a day, plus some food, hot drinks and takeaway birds, working from 9am to 2.30–4pm, depending on whether the guns stop for lunch. This might sound like peanuts, but if you're a) retired and living on a state pension, b) a farmworker's wife with kids at primary school, c) in your late teens and keen to get a foot in the gamekeeping door, it's casual, sociable, not-too-strenuous outdoor work, all of which can be very appealing. Or, you might be in it for the love not the money: you want to work your dogs. Plus, at the end of the season there's normally a beaters' day, where everyone who helped out gets a free day's shooting, which for some people counts as a treat.

## BIRD TWO: GROUSE

Pheasants, but posher: if shooting pheasants is winters in Courcheval and summers in Tuscany, then shooting grouse is winters in Klosters and summers, well, on your schoolfriends' grouse moors. It takes place further north (Scotland, the Pennines, the Yorkshire Dales, the North Yorkshire Moors, the Peak District) and higher up (on moorland). And it's much more expensive: at least £3,000 per person per day, plus a fat tip to the headkeeper.

The birds are also (technically) wild, rather than reared and released.* Shooting people love this, talking about how grouse are *really sporting birds*, how they fly *hard and low*. However, because there's so much money to be made out of killing them, grouse don't experience life like most wild animals. Instead, they are coddled by a devoted team of gamekeepers: fed, treated for disease, protected from predators, all so there's a shootable surplus ready for the landowner's friends and clients come *the Glorious Twelfth* (of August, when the season opens).

'There is something beautiful about the purple heather-clad hills in August, with the sport of kings, uniting everyone from the old-school aristocracy to modern-day billionaires,' wrote the *Tatler* magazine recently, summing up the vibe for us nicely.**

Back in the 1960s, the Labour leader Harold Wilson, promising to haul Britain out of the Edwardian era into the jet age, said he represented: 'A chance to sweep away the grouse-moor conception of Tory leadership and refit Britain with a new image, a new confidence.' But both grouse moors (and, *mirabile dictu*, the Tory leadership) are still here.

..........

* People have tried; it doesn't work.
** The word *everyone* is doing a lot of work here.

There are three main charges levelled at grouse shooting:

1. Why are vast tracts of our countryside managed for the benefit of one elite sport?* Why can rich people collect subsidies on land dedicated to fun? Isn't grouse shooting a shocking feudal leftover, 'a line', as Mark Avery writes in his polemic, *Inglorious* (2015), 'of relatively poor people' driving birds to 'a line of relatively rich people'?

2. Wild birds in a wild landscape? That's a con. The landscape only looks the way it does because moorland managers drain bogs and burn heather. 'The average grouse moor' (Avery again) 'is as natural as the average wheat field.'

3. Quite apart from all the dead grouse, gamekeepers deliberately kill endangered raptors, especially hen harriers, who might otherwise threaten 'their' game.**

To which The Moorland Association, aka the grouse lobby, would likely reply:

1. Our industry employs (a few) thousand local people (keepers, loaders, beaters, drivers) who would otherwise struggle to find jobs in these remote parts, as well as providing trade for pubs, hotels and shops. You might get walkers in the summer, but what about the winter? How is the hospitality industry going to survive then? Thank heavens for us! Besides, grouse shooting is a traditional part of countryside culture, which you wouldn't understand because you live in Islington.

..........

\* The acreage of England managed for grouse is larger than Greater London.
\*\* Jamie Blackett observes in *Red Rag to a Bull*: 'In medieval times, if you wanted to ruin a man you accused him of witchcraft; under the Tudors and Stuarts, you accused him of heresy. In Victorian times, you accused him of homosexuality; in twenty-first-century rural Scotland, it seems you plant a dead buzzard on him.'

2. What else do you want us to do with our land? Sitka spruce? Sheep? Wind farms? Besides, the Great British public loves a majestic purple moor, and it only looks like that because we take care of it so nicely.

3. #NotAllKeepers. A few bad apples. We're sorry. Mistakes made; lessons learned. Hen harriers? We *love* them. Please look at this lovely footage of lovely hen harriers nesting happily on our moors. And while you're here, we should point out that our well-paid and nature-loving keepers manage foxes and crows, stoats and weasels so efficiently that ground-nesting birds besides grouse – your curlews, your lapwings, your plovers – are thriving.

To which, campaigners would likely respond:

1. People who are rich enough to shoot grouse don't buy Gingernuts at the village shop or stay in B&Bs. They stay in grand private houses and contribute nothing to the local economy. And I don't live in Islington.

2. Simple! Rewild it.

3. Please stop posting pictures of hen harriers. It's really disingenuous.

We'll leave it there. Suffice to say this is a live debate.

BIRDS THREE AND FOUR: DUCKS AND GEESE

Once upon a time, wildfowling gave people who couldn't get at grouse or pheasants something to shoot. It takes advantage of the fact that around our coastline, the foreshore between the high- and low-water marks is open access. It belongs to the monarch (sort of) but, unlike most landowners, they don't mind you being there.

The original wildfowlers created specialised punts, mounted with crude guns, which they paddled about, staying low in the water. They'd sneak up on *sitting ducks*, blast a good number out of the water, and take them home to eat. The gentry did briefly take up the sport, but wildfowling today is a largely solitary and low-key affair, requiring great skill and tenacity. You need:

- A permit from a local wildfowling club.
- A stalwart, soft-mouthed and water-loving Labrador. Without them, you won't have a hope in hell of recovering what you shoot.
- A gun: a 12-bore, loaded with size 3 shot for geese and size 5 for duck. (Don't try to shoot wading birds. It's easy to make a mistake and kill something horribly endangered.)

You're going to be shooting *flighting* birds, on their way to or from their feeding grounds. In the summer, therefore (when your quarry is holidaying in the Arctic or Scandinavia), you need to reconnoitre spots which might serve as good *hides* at different stages of the tide. You need to be very confident you know where you're going, because you'll be finding your way back there in the dark before a cold grey winter's dawn.

Come the season, keep an eye on wind and tide, on weather and moon. On beautiful still moonlit nights, the birds will fly high, so you won't stand a chance. Geese, in particular, gain altitude fast, so you need to pick your moment. What you're after is a wild and windy dawn, with a new-moon spring tide running hard. In other words, the darker the night and the worse the weather, the better your chance of success. But beware the storm surge. A deep depression, storm-force winds and a big tide can raise sea levels a metre or more: on such a night, it's death to wade into the marshes.

Set your alarm for 0400. Sneak out of your bedroom. Tea, toast, marmalade. Put on many clothes. Load gun and dog into your car and whisk along the silent lanes to the shoreline. Put on many more clothes, plus waders. Extract dog, and make your way through the thinning night to your spot. No torch: your eyes need to be able to pick out birds against the faint lightening in the eastern sky.

Hark! The geese are on the move. The howling south-westerly at your back keeps your quarry low and slow. Lift your gun ... wait ... wait ... NOW! You shoot ... and for once your loyal friend has no cause to doubt your aim. A thud, a splash. A signal, a brief search and your dog is back by your side. One goose or two is plenty.

Back home you go. Your breakfast will taste *delicious*. Now to find a recipe that makes tough old goose palatable. Try currying it?

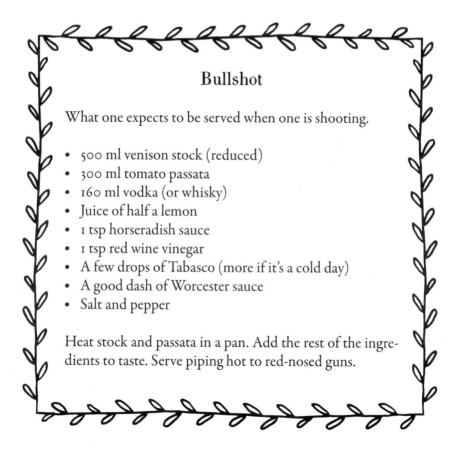

## Bullshot

What one expects to be served when one is shooting.

- 500 ml venison stock (reduced)
- 300 ml tomato passata
- 160 ml vodka (or whisky)
- Juice of half a lemon
- 1 tsp horseradish sauce
- 1 tsp red wine vinegar
- A few drops of Tabasco (more if it's a cold day)
- A good dash of Worcester sauce
- Salt and pepper

Heat stock and passata in a pan. Add the rest of the ingredients to taste. Serve piping hot to red-nosed guns.

# FROM *TESS OF THE D'URBERVILLES*

...................................

by Thomas Hardy

In the midst of these whimsical fancies she heard a new strange sound among the leaves. It might be the wind; yet there was scarcely any wind. Sometimes it was a palpitation, sometimes a flutter; sometimes it was a sort of gasp or gurgle. Soon she was certain that the noises came from wild creatures of some kind, the more so when, originating in the boughs overhead, they were followed by the fall of a heavy body upon the ground. Had she been ensconced here under other and more pleasant conditions she would have become alarmed; but, outside humanity, she had at present no fear.

Day at length broke in the sky. When it had been day aloft for some little while it became day in the wood.

Directly the assuring and prosaic light of the world's active hours had grown strong, she crept from under her hillock of leaves, and looked around boldly. Then she perceived what had been going on to disturb her. The plantation wherein she had taken shelter ran down at this spot into a peak, which ended it hitherward, outside the hedge being arable ground. Under the trees several pheasants lay about, their rich plumage dabbled with blood; some were dead, some feebly twitching a wing, some staring up at the sky, some pulsating quickly, some contorted, some stretched out – all of them writhing in agony, except the fortunate ones whose tortures had ended during the night by the inability of nature to bear more.

Tess guessed at once the meaning of this. The birds had been driven down into this corner the day before by some shooting-party; and while those that had dropped dead under the shot, or had died before nightfall, had been searched for and carried off, many badly wounded birds had escaped and hidden themselves away, or risen among the thick boughs, where they had maintained their position till they grew weaker with loss of blood in the night-time, when they had fallen one by one as she had heard them.

She had occasionally caught glimpses of these men in girlhood, looking over hedges, or peeping through bushes, and pointing their guns, strangely accoutred, a blood-thirsty light in their eyes. She had been told that, rough and brutal as they seemed just then, they were not like this all the year round, but were, in fact, quite civil persons save during certain weeks of autumn and winter, when, like the inhabitants of the Malay Peninsula, they ran amuck, and made it their purpose to destroy life – in this case harmless feathered creatures, brought into being by artificial means solely to gratify these propensities – at once so unmannerly and so unchivalrous towards their weaker fellows in Nature's teeming family.

With the impulse of a soul who could feel for kindred sufferers as much as for herself, Tess's first thought was to put the still living birds out of their torture, and to this end with her own hands she broke the necks of as many as she could find, leaving them to lie where she had found them till the gamekeepers should come – as they probably would come – to look for them a second time.

'Poor darlings – to suppose myself the most miserable being on earth in the sight o' such misery as yours!' she exclaimed, her tears running down as she killed the birds tenderly. 'And not a twinge of bodily pain about me! I be not mangled, and I be not bleeding, and I have two hands to feed and clothe me.' She was ashamed of herself for her gloom of the night, based on nothing more tangible than a sense of condemnation under an arbitrary law of society which had no foundation in Nature.

# POACHING

........................

*But if any dim sense of the uproar did reach the keeper's ear he put it down to the moon, at which dogs will bay.*
Richard Jefferies, *The Amateur Poacher* (1879)

In Germany or Russia, when you talk about animals you're planning to hunt and eat, you say *das Wild* or *дичь*, which are related etymologically to *wildness*. What word do we use here? *Game* ... a word related to *sport*.

That's because, from the Normans onwards, the hunting, killing and eating of game was, legally, an elite pastime. And for it to remain elite, non-elite people had to be excluded, via tough laws and tougher punishments – otherwise it wouldn't have been elite any more. Nevertheless, because killing game is/was a) a free source of protein and b) fun, lots and lots of non-elite people defied every restriction, every deterrent, and carried on hunting regardless. In other words, they poached.

The journalist Harry Hopkins, in his gripping book *The Long Affray* (1985), calls poaching 'a dark red thread' woven into the fabric of rural life in much of England. We tend, he suggests, to see class warfare as an urban phenomenon, but poaching, he reckons, constituted a struggle every bit as bitter as anything you might witness on a Manchester shopfloor. It had its heroes; its spies and traitors; its songs and codes of honour; its weapons – and its martyrs. 'Although fluctuating in numbers and varied in uniform, two hostile forces faced each other down over the years, each believing passionately that it had God and Right on its side, each nourishing a steady hatred of the Enemy.'

Public opinion, moreover, wasn't as anti-poaching as you might think. Indeed, the poacher (in common with the smuggler) enjoyed the support of many outwardly respectable citizens: the shopkeepers and artisans of England's small towns and villages. People never put poaching in the same moral bracket as stealing, which meant they were never inclined to *peach* – to tell. And even when poachers were caught and put on trial, local worthies actually came forward to testify that the defendant was, in all respects, a decent, hardworking, family man.

Certainly, Mary Russell Mitford, writing her portrait of village life in the early nineteenth century, is a big fan of their local (ex-)poacher, Tom Cordery: 'He had a bold, undaunted presence, and an evident strength and power of bone and muscle. You might see by looking at him, that he did not know what fear meant.' And yet, continues Mitford, he was 'of a most mild and gentle demeanour, had a fine placidity of countenance, and a quick blue eye beaming with good-humour'. (He could almost be the prototype for the charismatic father in Roald Dahl's great poaching manifesto, *Danny, the Champion of the World*. A great poacher, he tells his son Danny, is a great artist.)

Why then, this sympathy? Simple: the law was unfair, and everyone knew it.

Poaching, to be clear, wasn't a matter of sneaking into a landowner's pheasant pens. No, poaching was shooting *any wild game at all – even on your own land*. According to the Game Act of 1671, to be legally allowed to shoot a hare sitting on your doorstep (not typical hare behaviour, but you get our point), you had to:

- own land worth £100/year or lease land worth £150/year i.e. be very rich, or
- be heir to an esquire or a person 'of higher degree' i.e. be very posh, or
- hold a royal franchise i.e. be very, very posh.

If you ticked one of those boxes, you were a *qualified person* and could shoot game. If you didn't, which was all but 0.5 per cent of the population, you weren't and you couldn't. This put a lot of people on the wrong side of the law, including tenant farmers who wanted to be able to kill animals that messed with their crops.

The French Revolution stirred the pot, as the contemporary political theorist and activist Thomas Paine explained: 'The French Constitution says there shall be no game laws, that the farmer on whose lands wild game shall be found (for it is by the produce of his lands they are fed) shall have a right to what he can take.' Radical stuff – and parliament responded accordingly: with even tougher game laws, along with a suite of other repressive measures designed to stop *liberté, égalité* and *fraternité* gaining a foothold here.

The 0.5 per cent, of course, continued to shoot and eat game, which made it a fashionable, aspirational food. The expanding upper-middle classes, who had enough money to care about impressing their friends, wanted to serve snipe, partridge, woodcock, etc. at home. But there was a catch: the law forbade game-dealing. You weren't allowed to sell it. Game was always a gift, graciously bestowed, humbly received, *noblesse oblige*. The loyal retainer in the village might get a brace of pheasant at Christmas, but there was nothing for the factory owner in town.

But where there's a will, there's a way.

Game was scarce. Scarce meant expensive. Expensive meant it was worth taking a few risks. Poaching turned from an amateur sideline (literal *pot-shots*) into an extensive and sophisticated supply chain, with innkeepers and coachmen acting as middlemen between the poachers in the countryside and the dealers in the cities.

In 1831, it did become easier to get a game licence (in the same way that the franchise became a bit broader; 'reform that you may preserve'), but tenant farmers were still saddled with game clauses in their leases. These obliged them to manage their land to suit the landowner's shooting agenda: leaving hedges uncut, leaving stubble high after harvest, growing things the game-birds liked. In other words, farmers had to encourage the very animals which were most likely to damage their livelihoods.

Meanwhile, guns were getting more effective, moving from fiddly front-loaders to effective breech-loaders. You no longer had to go through the whole rigmarole of locate bird, load powder, load shot, wad, flush, shoot. You could break your gun, shove a cartridge in, and *boom*. This made it increasingly tempting to rear pheasants – and to design your land to accommodate them by planting game-friendly spinneys, and (to our eyes charming) strips of woodland between fields. As William Cobbett observed in *Rural Rides*: 'I dare say the Duke thinks much more of the pheasants than of the corn.'

Once a landowner spent more money on more pheasants, he was inevitably even more keen to keep poachers out. Threatening noticeboards sprouted in woodlands.

Spring-guns and man-traps lay in wait.* There are dreadful accounts of people – a housewife out mushrooming, a boy cutting sticks from a hedge, a gardener sent to prune a tree – found bleeding, mangled, dead. But the landowners always had the evolving police force on their side. The 1844 Night Poaching Act gave gamekeepers stop-and-search powers on public highways, meaning they could challenge anyone who merely looked like they might have a pheasant down their trousers. And the punishments were severe: 'For every pheasant that flutters in a wood,' said the Reverend Sidney Smith, a nineteenth-century preacher, 'one English peasant is rotting in gaol.'

Reformers tried to compel parliament to acknowledge the insanity of this situation, with the MP John Bright managing to instigate a select committee in 1845 to investigate the issue, but in vain. 'Farmer after farmer,' writes Hopkins, 'told of the hare's diabolical habit of selecting the first – because sweetest – joint of the wheat, so that large areas of ground might be found covered with unripened, snipped-off ears – a heart-breaking sight.'

But the landowners, who still had the loudest voice in parliament, said that was all *poppycock*. Crop damage? Exaggeration. And anyway, game preservation was good for *social discipline*. What did that fellow Bright know? Who was he anyway? A cotton spinner from Rochdale? Pheasants actually ate pests, the black slugs, the wireworms, which Bright would know if he wasn't such a *townie*.

You only need look at a few portraits of Prince Albert to see what the reformers were up against. There's a particularly famous one by Edwin Landseer, titled 'Windsor

..........

* Spring-guns were shotguns rigged to fire when a wire was tripped. Man-traps were like mousetraps, but on a larger scale. In the Ealing comedy *Kind Hearts and Coronets*, Louis Mazzini, our underdog hero, assassinates the vile 8th Duke of Chalfont while he's caught in one of his own traps.

Castle in Modern Times', showing Queen Victoria accepting some flowers, while strewn about the happy family's sitting room are a collection of game-bird corpses. The little Princess Royal is even fiddling with a dead kingfisher.

After a long struggle, though, the Ground Game Act of 1881 represented victory for the reforming faction: henceforth tenants were to have the 'unalienable, concurrent right' to shoot rabbits and hares on the land they farmed. And yet despite this being touted as a great victory, *concurrent* meant the landowner could still pitch up to claim his shooting rights, which was a menace to working farmers; plus the act didn't cover pheasants. John Seymour was still dealing with this in the 1950s: he rented land on what was once a classic pheasant-shooting estate, and the birds were still an unmitigated nuisance – like invading Goths.

Nevertheless, throughout the twentieth century, an increasingly vocal local and national press, as well as fast-changing social and political norms, meant that landowners and their gamekeepers couldn't get away with the same degree of intimidation and violence. And if we hear less about poaching today, that's simply because there are fewer people in the countryside with the skill (or the appetite) to snaffle pheasants – but don't doubt that it still goes on. Often, though, poachers are after more exciting quarry than dopey birds.

Prince Albert would find himself entirely at home on a modern pheasant drive – very little has changed – but a Victorian poacher teleported to the 2020s would be thoroughly discombobulated. 'A hunt in a postmodern forest might begin with the weapons being inspected and made ready, the dogs quietened in their car cages,' write the poets Paul Farley and Michael Roberts in *Edgelands* (2011). 'Next, a few lines of grey cocaine are chopped out with a supermarket loyalty card on the back of a CD case, and, suitably emboldened and excited, the caravan of 4 x 4s switches to full beam and enters the scratchy woodland.'

Farmers and landowners complain about gunning engines, broken gates, churned-up ploughing, damaged crops, distressed livestock, discarded carcasses, not to mention the very real sense of threat. And, it being the digital age, it doesn't take long to find camera-phone footage posted online of 4 x 4s ramming deer, of lamp-lit longdogs* mauling fawns, or to hear reports of men digging out badger setts, the night's work relayed back to a laptop in a pub, with people taking bets on which dog will make the kill.

Hard – even for Roald Dahl – to spin that as art.

# HOW TO PLUCK A PHEASANT

If somebody you know suggests popping in to see you after a day picking up, tell them you're out. *They're trying to palm pheasants off on you.* If it's already too late and they've slung a brace over your gate, then f.y.i the soft brown one is the hen and the fancy one is the cock.

What next?

First check the condition of your birds. Part the breast-feathers. All clean and tidy? A good start. But if they're riddled with shot or badly torn by a rookie Labrador, you might as well bury them 2 feet under your pumpkin patch.

..........

* A longdog is a greyhound crossed with another sighthound, e.g. with a whippet or deerhound.

Next your birds need to be hung. An under-hung pheasant is dry and tasteless. An over-hung pheasant is maggoty. A well-hung pheasant is *just right*. Put them somewhere cool. Maybe the same place you store apples? Warm autumns have shortened the ideal hanging time to three or four days. In December and January seven to ten days would be about right.

When they're ready, don your butcher's apron and settle yourself on a comfortable, upright chair with an old wine box between your feet. Lay the pheasant across your lap and start plucking. Always pull *towards* the head, starting very gently with the breast, working down the wings and legs to the first joint, and finally round the back to about halfway up the neck. With a tough pair of scissors or tin snippers, sever the outer part of the wings at the joint and chop off the legs just below the knee, then remove the head. Move to a suitable work surface, light a candle and lightly singe the body all over to remove any bits of down and bristle still attached.

Now for the less pleasant task: how unpleasant will depend on the length of the hang. Place the bird, breast up, on a chopping board. Locate the anus, insert the point of a sharp knife and slit the skin open to the breast bone. Put your hand in, right up to the neck, and draw out the entrails.* Wipe out the cavity with kitchen paper.

Next you must truss your bird. First push the remaining bit of neck back into the gut cavity so that it's covered neatly by a fold of skin. Then fold the wings and tie some natural twine round the body to hold them in place. Finally push the thighs up towards the body and tie them just above the knee. Dust lightly with plain flour.

..........

* A large hand is a distinct disadvantage here, so why not get the children involved?

Repeat for the second bird.

*Shhhhush*. You can also cheat. Go back to the beginning. Lay your pheasants on their backs. Slice through the skin along the breast line, peel back the skin, cut off the breast meat and dispose of everything else, heads, wings, legs and guts. Admittedly, the flavour won't be as good.

Now to the kitchen. The only way to eat pheasant is with cream and Calvados, channelling one's Norman heritage.

1. Pre-heat a heavy pan with a good slug of butter. Season the meat with salt and pepper and fry for about 45 minutes over a medium heat, turning and basting regularly.

2. Remove the pheasants, pull off the legs and wings and chop up the breast meat. Put them in a pre-heated serving dish in a warm oven.

3. Turn the heat up a bit, return the pan, and add a glass of warmed Calvados to the juices. When the mixture is bubbling merrily, set fire to it.*

4. Turn down the heat and gradually stir in a big pot of crème fraîche, allowing it to bubble gently until it thickens. Pour the sauce over the pheasant pieces.

5. Separately, whizz up some stale brown bread in a food processor, add soft butter and fry the crumbs carefully, keeping a weather eye on them lest they burn.

6. Slice two or three apples – are the breadcrumbs burning?? – and fry until golden.

7. Devour.

..........

* A reward for whichever child put its hand up the pheasant?

# HOW TO HAVE A REALLY
## WELL-BEHAVED DOG

......................................................

*A man who talks to his dog is acknowledging the porosity*
*of the boundary between species. He's taken the first and most*
*important step towards becoming a shaman.*
Charles Foster, *Being a Beast* (2016)

We'll start by sharing an old piece of poker lore: if you don't know who the mug is at the table, it's you. We'll continue by sharing the even older piece of country lore: if you can't instantly name the worst-behaved dog in the village, it's yours. And remember, even if people don't know you, *they know your dog.*

Perhaps he's particularly distinguishable in some way.

Perhaps he's a very large, very over-bred, very preposterous Red Setter.

Perhaps you set off through the village, bright-eyed and bushy-tailed, only to discover that a psychotic hatred of all farm dogs causes him to leap like a slavering hell-hound at every passing tractor, Land Rover and quad bike, in the misguided application of Master Sun Tzu's principle that *in war, victory should be swift.*

Perhaps you hurry off the road to enjoy the pretty walk with the view, only to meet on that narrow and bramble-bound way a benign and peaceable spaniel, and in a flash a red and martial mist descends on your dog, and you're pinning him to the Jubilee memorial bench, while the benign and peaceable spaniel, plus its benign and peaceable owner, flee in horror.

Perhaps you decide it's time to deploy the absurdly

expensive running equipment you bought so that you and he, tethered tight, can run across the hilltops, human and dog in perfect synchrony, far, far from spaniels and farm vehicles, but perhaps you realise that running behind a Red Setter means you are running too fast, and perhaps you trip and fall and bleed everywhere, and perhaps you don't realise for months that your fingers aren't just a bit wonky, but really quite badly broken, and you now have some sort of proto-arthritis and you will certainly never ever be able to open a tight jam-jar lid ever again.

Perhaps you decide a nice game of fetch in the garden is probably for the best, but perhaps somebody-who-shall-remain-nameless has left a gate open, and perhaps he bolts through that open gate, and perhaps he chases down one of your neighbour's ewes, and now you must chase him down, running faster than you have ever run before, tackling him to the ground, rolling in the sodden grass and sheep shit, gasping, shouting, sobbing, trying to get it into his thick skull that he is a bad, *bad*, BAD dog.*

Perhaps, later, while he looks at you dolefully from his bed, wondering why everyone suddenly hates him, you find yourself reading Jilly Cooper's *The Common Years* as therapy, and perhaps you find yourself thinking, well at least *my* dog never rampaged round a hospital like *her* dog – until, that is, you get to the bit where her dog does something so very bad that he has to be put down, and you fall into a despond, a black dog about your red dog.

And then, perhaps, your family summons you to the sitting room, where they've

..........

* Calling up a farmer to say your dog's chased one of their sheep is not something you'd wish on your worst enemy.

teed up a film called *Big Red* about a Red Setter who everyone thinks is really bad – until he saves a man from a lion,
and you think one day, one day, that could be *your dog*, and
you have a little cry, and you call another dog trainer and
you say, you see, I have this very large, very over-bred, very
preposterous Red Setter … and you start *all over again*.

Want a well-behaved dog?

GET A LAB.

## Why does everyone have Labradors?

Labradors were bred for generations to fetch. Bringing
stuff back to you makes them seriously high, which incen-
tivises them to stick close, hoping against hope you'll throw
something. Setters, on the other hand, were bred for generations to hunt and point, i.e. to run off really fast, sniff out
something a long way away, and freeze stock-still, letting
you know they've found it. Setters, in other words, get seriously high standing minimum one furlong away, looking
devilishly alert and handsome. This is super-handy if you
own a grouse moor. Less good in almost all other circum-
stances. (They're also allegedly bred to retrieve. This is false
advertising.)

# RURAL REBELS

............................................

*Get down to Stonedhenge Maggie see your utopia*
George McKay, *Senseless Acts of Beauty* (1996)

The countryside can present a fine, upstanding, prim and proper face to the world. Bluebells, blue-remembered hills, the squiggly blue oak tree of the Conservative logo, bluebirds over the white cliffs of Dover, blue skies marred by nary a cloud. But although you don't see many red flags flying over the green fields, there's always been what Raymond Williams in *The Country and the City* calls 'a precarious but persistent rural-intellectual radicalism: genuinely and actively hostile to industrialism and capitalism; opposed to commercialism and the exploitation of the environment; attached to country ways and feeling, the literature and the lore'.

This rural radicalism does tend to be culturally distinct from the professional, traditional party-political left, from the trade unionist, the university Marxist, the Momentum activist. Indeed, historically, committed and class-conscious members of the urban proletariat might once have looked down on their country cousins, thinking them backward, un-comradely, still dancing the feudal dance, far too likely to doff a cap or tug a forelock.

This friction played out on a tragic scale in the Soviet Union, when the kind of land reform the rural working class (the 'peasants') wanted, namely a dozen acres to call their own, was deemed incompatible with the overthrow of capitalism. The politburo's idea of land reform was *collectivisation*, and those who contested it, who clung on to their smallholdings, were denounced as *kulaks*, and either sent to the gulag or executed.

Back in the UK, we've never had a broad-based popular land reform movement, unlike in France in 1789 or in Central and South America in the twentieth century. The English Civil War, for example, was fought over religious freedom and regal over-reach: the Roundheads' agenda certainly wasn't redistributive. But this hasn't stopped today's rural radicals from searching for a founding father, for a peg hewn from English oak upon which to hang their ideas. And in doing so, they've lit upon a relatively obscure figure, Gerrard Winstanley, and a relatively shortlived collective, the Diggers.

In 1649, Winstanley & co. took over a hill in Surrey, decrying that 'some are lifted up in the chair of tyranny and others trod under the footstool of misery', planning henceforth to work the land together, sharing what they grew with anyone who joined them. Local reaction was much the same then as it would be now: total horror. Ratepayers wrecked the Diggers' planting and sent in heavies to break up their camp, and very soon they were driven out. Winstanley subsequently found work as an estate steward, before being dismissed for mismanagement. He wrote more pamphlets; he got in with the Quakers; and finally in 1657 his father-in-law gifted him some land and he turned into a solid citizen: chief constable of Elmbridge, no less.

If you're seeking the seeds of progressive British politics, those months in Surrey can be made to do a lot of heavy lifting: 'He is variously credited as the father of English communism, socialism or environmentalism, depending on which is seeking paternity,' wrote Harvard history professor Mark Kishlansky, reviewing *The Complete Works of Gerrard Winstanley*.

But the Diggers, whatever they did or didn't achieve, are necessary heroes on a barren field. Many nations, in Europe and the rest of the world, willed themselves into being by rejecting oppression, whether internal or external, which gives them a roster of underdog heroes to celebrate: Giuseppe Garibaldi and Simón Bolívar, Crazy Horse and Paul Revere. But Britain, especially England, last conquered in 1066, has been the conqueror ever since.

You can feel the Victorian writer, Charles Kingsley, wrestling with this conundrum as he's writing a romp about Hereward the Wake, the Saxon nobleman who (we tell ourselves) fought a valiant guerrilla war against the Normans in the marshlands of east England.* Kingsley, channelling the dominant, pro-colonial narrative of his day, says the Normans civilised us, globalised us, linked us to the international community – to the Pope, to Rome, to the Renaissance. But at the same time, in an impressive piece of cognitive dissonance, he denounces the Norman Conquest as 'a mighty crime' and laments the Saxons' last stand: 'Their bones lay white on every island in the fens; their corpses rotted on gallows beneath every Norman keep; their few survivors crawled into monasteries, with eyes picked out, or hands and feet cut off, or took to the wild wood as strong outlaws, like their successors—'

(Can you guess who's coming next?)

—Robin Hood, Scarlet, and John.

Hereward was more or less real. Robin Hood, sadly, is more or less made up. His theoretical peak was in the 12th–13th centuries, but the name refers not to one man, but to an archetype, a composite, to (as an old edition of

..........

* If we'd ever had a communist revolution here, you can bet Hereward would be a major national icon (with his noble background scrubbed out), much as Spartacus (cf. Spartak Moscow football club) was the acceptable face of the Roman Empire in the Soviet Union.

*The Dictionary of National Biography* puts it) any 'robber-leader who made his home in forests or moors, excelled in archery, defied the oppressive forest laws, and thus attracted popular sympathy'.

And yet, isn't Robin Hood the most conservative of rebels, ever and always loyal to his absent king? More often than not, the stories turn him into a nobleman on his uppers, an aristocrat with lovely manners who leads the Nottingham mafia a merry dance until the king shall return. He robs from the rich, sure, but only from the bad rich, the *nouveau* rich. When Richard Lionheart arrives at Sherwood Forest, Robin doesn't slit his purse: he dishes up cakes and ale and divine right on a platter.

And so the Tudor court could delight in tales of *merrie men* in the *greene woode,* while simultaneously cracking down hard on people who actually *did* live outside the bounds of towns and villages: the 'Egyptians'. This misunderstanding of the origins of Romany people, who in fact migrated out of India, is what gave us the word Gypsy.*
Successive pieces of sixteenth-century legislation targeted 'an outlandish people' who travelled 'from shire to shire, and place to place'. The state was suspicious of anyone who wasn't tied to one parish, to one craft, and retaliated by threatening them with deportation or death, offering a reprieve only if they adopted a 'normal' life. However, Romany people stayed both in Britain and on the road, and have been romanticised and vilified ever since.

The writer and adventurer George Borrow, whose books *Lavengro* (1851) and *The Romany Rye* (1857) are

..........

* In the UK today, different travelling people identify variously as Gypsies, as Romany, as Travellers or Irish Travellers, or as Roma, the word often used by more recent Romany migrants from Central and Eastern Europe. The word *Gypsy*, used as an ethnonym, is not pejorative. The word *gypsy*, used to imply a certain set of prejudicial assumptions, very much is.

both at least partly autobiographical, did a great
deal to foment settled
people's fantasies of the
travelling life, a life supposed to be full of magic,
beauty and romance. His
tales about being accepted
as a Romany rye, an hon-
orary Gypsy gentleman who
understood their language and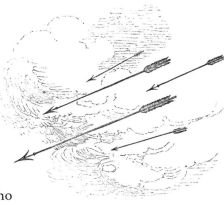
lore, became cult classics, treasured texts for the sort of
Edwardian young man who despised his clerking job and
dreamt of the wild cry of the wind on the heath, of roaming
noble and free under the sun and the moon and the stars.

But, at the same time, an equally distorted, and wholly
negative, narrative persisted. 'Our family,' writes Damian
Le Bas in *The Stopping Places* (2018), his account of a
journey around Britain, exploring his own Romany heritage, 'were the mistrusted local Gypsies, the bane of the
decent, upstanding Parish Council.' He loves his family,
loves their world, and life with them, he says, was a lot
better than being told he smelled of cowshit at school.

Their lives *were* fun, *were* free: they 'rode ponies, rode
quad bikes, poured petrol on huge stacks of wood ripped
from building jobs, and burned them as kestrels rode
currents of air high above'. He liked how his family had
different faces, different voices from other people, how
their conversations were peppered with secret words.
Later, he won a scholarship to boarding school and a place
at Oxford, but he felt he had to hide his background: 'every
time someone said "gyppo" or "pikey" within earshot,
I'd still get that terrible feeling, like a physical punch in
the gut.'

We've long been told a story – or painted a picture – about what rural living *ought* to look like: old church, big house, neat cottages, orderly fields. But Gypsies and Travellers have never fitted into that framework. In fact, whenever anyone takes up a form of country living that deviates from the approved formula, they face the same criticism: you're doing it all wrong.*

This tendency was evident in the hard, but more liberated, years between the wars, when speculators bought up abandoned farmland, parcelled it up, and sold it off to townspeople who wanted a place for the weekend, a place to retire, or a few acres where they could try to make a basic living. These informal developments, which grew up in the Thames Valley, near the Sussex holiday resorts, along the east coast, on Canvey Island, had a name: the *plotlands*.

Winifred Holtby's novel, *South Riding*, published posthumously in 1936, says that these places hummed with exuberant life: 'Young men rattled down at the week-ends on motor-bicycles from Kingsport. Young women tumbled, laughing and giggling and clutching parcels, from the buses. Urban youths with pimpled faces and curvature of the spine exposed their blotches and blisters to the sun, turning limp somersaults over the creaking gate[.]' Empty bottles, animal droppings, gramophones, revellers, sardine tins, lighted tents like 'luminous convolvulus flowers' on dark humid nights. It sounds like people were having *fun*.

Were the plotlands, as some people felt, desirably Bohemian, or were they nasty squalid eyesores? In

..........

* This dynamic also played out during peak-Covid. For years, people had been told it'd be *good for them* to get out into the countryside, but once they did, they were told they weren't doing it right. Said one national-park manager: 'We attracted more of a crowd who would usually go to Spain on holidays, and it's a different sort of culture that they have, shall I say.'

*Landscape and Englishness* (1998), David Matless explains that this question represented a clash of two pastorals: 'the ordered and systematic preservationist rural Englishness and the ragged, irregular, marginal pastoral of escape'. Touchstone thinkers like William Morris and Henry Thoreau might (in theory; both were long dead by the 1930s) have been delighted by this turn to country living – but if they rose from their graves to visit, we can imagine their complaints: no, no, too ugly, too modern, too vulgar, too many people, that's not what we meant at all.*

Come the second half of the twentieth century, however, a new sub-culture evolved, which combined life on the road with an unerring ability to have a good time.

New Age travelling grew out of the 1970s free festival circuit, back when camping in a field with strangers (plus dancing, drinking and taking drugs) was *not* a run-of-the-mill part of the summer season. New Age travellers each had their own motivations, but for some it was about wanting to reject urban life, while lacking the means to settle in the countryside. In Richard Lowe and William Shaw's *Travellers* (1993), one of their many interviewees, a woman called Shannon, sums up that view: 'rural Britain is for the rich'.

These New Age travellers were, however, very much distinct from the original English Travellers. George McKay, whose *Senseless Acts of Beauty* is a brilliant study of the late twentieth-century counterculture, meets two Gypsies on

..........

* The funniest dramatisation of this clash is Mike Leigh's *Nuts in May* (1976), a watch-through-your-fingers comedy about Keith and Candice-Marie, who've come to a Dorset campsite to soak up nature and history, to strum the banjo, to sip unpasteurised milk from the local farm. Their idyll implodes: other people just want to have a good time. Keith comprehensively loses his shit, bursts into tears and runs off into the woods.

their way to the Appleby horse fair. They despise New Age travellers, so they tell him, for 'their sponging, their laziness, their filthy lifestyles, their provocative flouting of the laws of the land, their drug taking, their music, the way they rip up hedges for firewood, their dangerous vehicles, their begging, their filth again, the length of their dreadlocks'. The men (their wagons bright, their caravan gleaming) were perfectly well aware that their (to their minds, just) criticisms of New Age travellers were very similar to some people's (to their minds, unjust) criticisms of Gypsies – but they didn't care.

The apex of the new age traveller year was the Stonehenge Free Festival, a three-week party climaxing on the night of the summer solstice. Pagans, neo-druids and mystics of various stripes had been celebrating amid the stones for decades, but their numbers had always been relatively small. By the mid-80s, however, the celebrations were turning epic. 'In our age of designated access,' writes Richard King in *The Lark Ascending* (2019), his sympathetic study of the relationship between people, music and landscape, 'it seems extraordinary that this rite could be enacted deep in the English countryside, in the presence of tens of thousands of people, without any licence, supervision or administrative control.'

It was, predictably, all a bit much for English Heritage (Stonehenge's official guardian) and the Conservative shires. A bit much, too, for some of the gentler and more idealistic celebrants, who didn't like the angry, anarchic post-punk fringe the festival was starting to attract.

In 1985, therefore, the police enforced a court injunction on the event, establishing a four-mile exclusion zone around the stones, with roadblocks, razor wire, the works. When, on the first day of June, a convoy of some 600 new age travellers set out for Stonehenge from their camp at nearby Savernake Forest, the police (numbering more than a thousand) stopped them, forcefully, in what is now known as the Battle of the Beanfield.

This is what Nick Davies, an investigative reporter for the *Observer* newspaper, saw: 'I witnessed women and children being hit with truncheons, glass from broken vehicle windows showering down on those inside and a mother dragged out of a shattered window with her child and thrown weeping to the ground.' Michael Eavis (unsurprisingly) let them into the Glastonbury festival site early. The Earl of Cardigan, who owned Savernake Forest, (perhaps more surprisingly) refused to allow the police access to his *greene woode*, where many of the travellers had retreated. Later, he even testified against the police, a class betrayal in the eyes of the Tory press.

New Age travelling was a commitment, a 24/7 lifestyle, but as the eighties became the nineties, the countryside started to play host to a new generation of *merrie folke*: ravers.

A new music (acid house) and a new drug (ecstasy) worked well in warehouses, but worked even better in big open spaces, under the stars. Some farmers could see where the smart money lay, and were more than happy to take cash in hand in exchange for the loan of a field for the night. Many thousands of young (and not-so-young) people poured out of the towns and cities to party.*

This weekly exodus, says Richard King, introduced social groups that were seldom encountered in rural Britain: people who were openly gay, people of colour. But although this was an important cultural revolution, it was,

..........

* Stream Pulp's track, 'Sorted for E's and Wizz' if you need a reminder of (or introduction to) the highs and lows of a night somewhere in a field in Hampshire. The sense of community, the vigorous exercise, the questionable legality: sounds a bit like hunting?

he stresses, resolutely unpolitical. If young people were spending their weekends tearing about the countryside off their tits, lamented rave's left-wing critics, they were unlikely to be agitating for serious social and economic change. And if the left was equivocal, the right was apoplectic.

In 1992, what was supposed to be a small festival spiralled out of control when big rave DJs turned up, resulting in 20,000 people dancing days away at Castlemorton Common, a beauty spot in the Malvern Hills. This wasn't a grubby bit of back-country; this was prime green and pleasant land, and the media loved it. Journalists pitched up, sending back reports of scandalised locals: we watched a clip of a shocked woman complaining (with justification) about a man (who'd clearly over-cooked himself) charging into her orchard, wielding a machete, chasing her lambs, yelling, 'MEAT!'

In 1994, the (much-reviled) Criminal Justice and Public Order Act made it much easier for the police to crack down on illegal raves – and so legal raves, with reliable sound and bearable loos, mushroomed across the land. The age of the commercial festival had begun.

What was once radical and rebellious has now become so much part of the establishment that *Tatler* can encourage anyone with 'a few spare ancestral acres' to 'knock up a stage, hire some fire dancers' and host their own festival. Freddie Fellowes, founder of the fantastically successful Secret Garden Party, is one such, proudly telling the magazine in 2017 (over pigeon breast and foie gras at a pub on his family's 6,000-acre estate) that people come to his festival for the hedonism: 'to dance naked and get paint-bombed and climb trees'.

But the road to revolution has many forks along the way, and a different branch, drawing inspiration from the anti-nuclear Greenham Common Women's Peace Camp, devoted itself to a green, direct-action politics of protest.

Many of today's veteran environmental activists cut their teeth on anti-road protests in the 1990s – against an extension of the M3 over Twyford Down in Hampshire; against an M11 link road through east London; against pushing the M65 through Stanworth Woods in Lancashire; and, most famously, against a bypass round Newbury in Wiltshire. Their tactics are now familiar: occupy a site you want to protect and do everything you can (climb a tree, hide in a tunnel) to stop the police (or hired security) from dislodging you.

The protesters lost every battle – the Newbury bypass opened in 1998 – but you could say they won the war. Margaret Thatcher's Roads for Prosperity scheme, launched in 1989, had been touted as the largest road-building programme since the Romans, but the determined opposition of these activists meant the political will to implement it ebbed away, until many schemes were quietly dropped.

Setting aside their concrete aims for a moment, these protesters did achieve one extraordinary thing: *they united the two pastorals.* For the first time, a mobile, youthful, radical wing (piercings, Peruvian hats, drums) joined forces with a rooted, older, more conservative wing (sensible shoes, cagoules, Thermoses) in a powerful alliance which continues to this day. Wherever the possibility of fracking (or runway expansions or giant Brexit lorry parks or high-speed rail links) rears its head, seasoned campaigners team up with furious locals to make the same forceful argument: what do you think you're doing to our land?

Today, indeed, many environmental issues, which might once have been seen as pretty far-out, are high up the national agenda, so much so that some old hands resent the movement's takeover by sustainability executives

(*greenwashers*) and the professional left (*watermelons*).*
Environmentalism, writes Paul Kingsnorth in his
*Confessions*, was 'excitingly outsiderish' when he took it up;
now it's 'almost *de rigueur* among the British bourgeoisie'.

Which rather brings us back to where we started, back to
that lingering disconnect between the progressive politics
of the town and that *something* in the countryside that's
not going to knuckle under. And it's something that fiction
writers, we've found, are best able to capture.

There's Jack, in Melissa Harrison's novel *At Hawthorn
Time*. He's quiet, almost invisible. In his life, he's passed
through every totemic site of rural resistance, but now he
lives on the margins, out of sight, in sync with the seasons,
picking daffodils in February, lambing in the spring,
mowing in summer, felling Christmas trees, fading from
view. He is itinerant by choice, 'less like a modern man and
more like the fugitive spirit of English rural rebellion. Or –
to some, at least – mad'.

Or there's Rooster Byron (played by Mark Rylance in Jez
Butterworth's play *Jerusalem*). He's brash and brazen. His
detractors call him a crap dad, a drug dealer, a corrupter of
(merrie) youth, a blot on the community, a 'gyppo'. By the
of end of the play, badly beaten up, he's about to be evicted
from his caravan in the (greene) woods, steamrollered by
the local council. And yet, like generations of rebels before
him, he remains unbowed. He feels that something deeper
– something darker, something older – is still on his side.
'Look on the map,' he says. 'This is Rooster's Wood. I'm
Rooster Byron.' Whatever any townie with a clipboard
might think, the land is still his, and he roars a rallying cry
above the pounding of drums: 'Come, you drunken spirits.

..........

* Green on the outside, red on the inside.

Come, you battalions. You fields of ghosts who walk these
green plains still. Come, you giants!'

# LOB

..........

by Edward Thomas

At hawthorn-time in Wiltshire travelling
In search of something chance would never bring,
An old man's face, by life and weather cut
And coloured,—rough, brown, sweet as any nut,—
A land face, sea-blue-eyed,—hung in my mind
When I had left him many a mile behind.
All he said was: 'Nobody can't stop 'ee. It's
A footpath, right enough. You see those bits
Of mounds—that's where they opened up the barrows
Sixty years since, while I was scaring sparrows.
They thought as there was something to find there,
But couldn't find it, by digging, anywhere.'

To turn back then and seek him, where was the use?
There were three Manningfords,—Abbots, Bohun,
    and Bruce:
And whether Alton, not Manningford, it was,
My memory could not decide, because
There was both Alton Barnes and Alton Priors.
All had their churches, graveyards, farms, and byres,
Lurking to one side up the paths and lanes,
Seldom well seen except by aeroplanes;
And when bells rang, or pigs squealed, or cocks crowed,

Then only heard. Ages ago the road
Approached. The people stood and looked and turned.
Nor asked it to come nearer, nor yet learned
To move out there and dwell in all men's dust.
And yet withal they shot the weathercock, just
Because 'twas he crowed out of tune, they said:
So now the copper weathercock is dead.
If they had reaped their dandelions and sold
Them fairly, they could have afforded gold.

Many years passed, and I went back again
Among those villages, and looked for men
Who might have known my ancient. He himself
Had long been dead or laid upon the shelf,
I thought. One man I asked about him roared
At my description: ''Tis old Bottlesford
He means, Bill.' But another said: 'Of course,
It was Jack Button up at the White Horse.
He's dead, sir, these three years.' This lasted till
A girl proposed Walker of Walker's Hill,
'Old Adam Walker. Adam's Point you'll see
Marked on the maps.'

                  'That was her roguery,'
The next man said. He was a squire's son
Who loved wild bird and beast, and dog and gun
For killing them. He had loved them from his birth,
One with another, as he loved the earth.
'The man may be like Button, or Walker, or
Like Bottlesford, that you want, but far more
He sounds like one I saw when I was a child.
I could almost swear to him. The man was wild
And wandered. His home was where he was free.
Everybody has met one such man as he.

Does he keep clear old paths that no one uses
But once a lifetime when he loves or muses?
He is English as this gate, these flowers, this mire.
And when at eight years old Lob-lie-by-the-fire
Came in my books, this was the man I saw.
He has been in England as long as dove and daw,
Calling the wild cherry tree the merry tree,
The rose campion Bridget-in-her-bravery;
And in a tender mood he, as I guess,
Christened one flower Love-in-idleness,
And while he walked from Exeter to Leeds
One April called all cuckoo-flowers Milkmaids.
From him old herbal Gerard learnt, as a boy,
To name wild clematis the Traveller's-joy.
Our blackbirds sang no English till his ear
Told him they called his Jan Toy "Pretty dear."
(She was Jan Toy the Lucky, who, having lost
A shilling, and found a penny loaf, rejoiced.)
For reasons of his own to him the wren
Is Jenny Pooter. Before all other men
'Twas he first called the Hog's Back the Hog's Back.
That Mother Dunch's Buttocks should not lack
Their name was his care. He too could explain
Totteridge and Totterdown and Juggler's Lane:
He knows, if anyone. Why Tumbling Bay,
Inland in Kent, is called so, he might say.

'But little he says compared with what he does.
If ever a sage troubles him he will buzz
Like a beehive to conclude the tedious fray:
And the sage, who knows all languages, runs away.
Yet Lob has thirteen hundred names for a fool,
And though he never could spare time for school
To unteach what the fox so well expressed,

On biting the cock's head off,—Quietness is best,—
He can talk quite as well as anyone
After his thinking is forgot and done.
He first of all told someone else's wife,
For a farthing she'd skin a flint and spoil a knife
Worth sixpence skinning it. She heard him speak:
"She had a face as long as a wet week"
Said he, telling the tale in after years.
With blue smock and with gold rings in his ears,
Sometimes he is a pedlar, not too poor
To keep his wit. This is tall Tom that bore
The logs in, and with Shakespeare in the hall
Once talked, when icicles hung by the wall.
As Herne the Hunter he has known hard times.
On sleepless nights he made up weather rhymes
Which others spoilt. And, Hob being then his name,
He kept the hog that thought the butcher came
To bring his breakfast. "You thought wrong," said Hob.
When there were kings in Kent this very Lob,
Whose sheep grew fat and he himself grew merry,
Wedded the king's daughter of Canterbury;
For he alone, unlike squire, lord, and king,
Watched a night by her without slumbering;
He kept both waking. When he was but a lad
He won a rich man's heiress, deaf, dumb, and sad,
By rousing her to laugh at him. He carried
His donkey on his back. So they were married.
And while he was a little cobbler's boy
He tricked the giant coming to destroy
Shrewsbury by flood. "And how far is it yet?"
The giant asked in passing. "I forget;
But see these shoes I've worn out on the road
And we're not there yet." He emptied out his load
Of shoes for mending. The giant let fall from his spade

The earth for damming Severn, and thus made
The Wrekin hill; and little Ercall hill
Rose where the giant scraped his boots. While still
So young, our Jack was chief of Gotham's sages.
But long before he could have been wise, ages
Earlier than this, while he grew thick and strong
And ate his bacon, or, at times, sang a song
And merely smelt it, as Jack the giant-killer
He made a name. He too ground up the miller,
The Yorkshireman who ground men's bones for flour.

'Do you believe Jack dead before his hour?
Or that his name is Walker, or Bottlesford,
Or Button, a mere clown, or squire, or lord?
The man you saw,—Lob-lie-by-the-fire, Jack Cade,
Jack Smith, Jack Moon, poor Jack of every trade,
Young Jack, or old Jack, or Jack What-d'ye-call,
Jack-in-the-hedge, or Robin-run-by-the-wall,
Robin Hood, Ragged Robin, lazy Bob,
One of the lords of No Man's Land, good Lob,—
Although he was seen dying at Waterloo,
Hastings, Agincourt, and Sedgemoor too,—
Lives yet. He never will admit he is dead
Till millers cease to grind men's bones for bread,
Not till our weathercock crows once again
And I remove my house out of the lane
On to the road.' With this he disappeared
In hazel and thorn tangled with old-man's-beard.
But one glimpse of his back, as there he stood,
Choosing his way, proved him of old Jack's blood,
Young Jack perhaps, and now a Wiltshireman
As he has oft been since his days began.

# FISHING

.....................

*Is fishing a sport or a ceremony? Both, I think.*
John Lahr, 'Goldfish are my homies' (2020)

Unlike the countryside's other bloodsports, fishing has broad social appeal and no massive anti lobby, which means, by and large, anyone can enjoy it undisturbed. As a sport (/hobby?), fishing has many attractively modern qualities: it's mindful, it's meditative. It could even become the sort of thing doctors prescribe, along with walking or gardening, as a potentially effective way to knock mild-to-moderate depression on the head without meds. And as an activity that's perfectly normal to do on your own (or with other people, but without having to talk too much), it's ideal if you have social anxiety. In fact for men* struggling with tricky childhoods, or problems with drugs or alcohol, or bad experiences serving in the army, fishing has time and again proved to be incredibly helpful. As England footballer Phil Foden says: 'If there's a few problems you're having, you just go fishing and clear your head.'

The don of fishing writers, Izaak Walton, acknowledged the truth of this back in 1653, when he published *The Compleat Angler* during a century of political turmoil, which included the English Civil War and the beheading of a king. Fishing, so the provost of Eton (the 'chair of governors' in any other school) tells him, is 'a rest to his mind,

..........

* Fishing – with apologies to all the exceptions who prove the rule – has long been a male preoccupation. Official stats show that of fishing licences bought, 96 per cent go to men and 4 per cent to women. Unless there is an epidemic of women fishing illegally, that's pretty conclusive.

a cheerer of his spirits, a diverter of sadness, a calmer of unquiet thoughts, a moderator of passions, a procurer of contentedness.'

Three hundred years later, one angry young man felt exactly the same way. 'No one bothered you,' explains Arthur in Alan Sillitoe's *Saturday Night and Sunday Morning* (1958), 'you were a hunter, a dreamer, your own boss, away from it all for a few hours on any day that the weather did not throw down its rain.'

In *Coming Up for Air*, George Orwell's affecting account of a middle-aged man returning to the country town of his childhood, fishing is *the* symbol of the happy days of his youth, a lost time he is trying desperately to recapture.*

> You'll think it damned silly, no doubt, but I've actually half a wish to go fishing even now, when I'm fat and forty-five and got two kids and a house in the suburbs. Why? Because in a manner of speaking I am sentimental about my childhood – not my own particular childhood, but the civilisation which I grew up in and which is now, I suppose, just about at its last kick. And fishing is somehow typical of that civilisation. As soon as you think of fishing you think of things that don't belong to the modern world. The very idea of sitting all day under a willow tree beside a quiet pool – and being able to find a quiet pool to sit beside – belongs to the time before the war, before the radio, before aeroplanes, before Hitler.

And, to be honest, post-Hitler, things only got worse.

Pesticides and fertilisers, leaching into our pools and ponds, our little tributaries and great rivers, killed fish without discrimination, either poisoning them or triggering

..........
* In vain, as it turns out. Imagine Proust having to eat a pack of shrink-wrapped madeleines in the Carrefour carpark outside Caen.

devastating algal blooms. Even the Atlantic salmon, which you might have thought would do better in relatively remote Scottish waters, was driven towards extinction at every stage of its life cycle.

Having beaten Mother Nature so comprehensively into retreat, people have, however, been coming up with

workarounds. It's still possible to be a passionate fisherman, whether you catch the bus to the edge of town or the overnight sleeper to Inverness.

**On a canal.** This is only going to cost you tens of pounds for an annual licence. Plus, a seemingly grubby canal can offer fish every bit as wild as those caught on a picture-perfect bend in the Thames. We once watched a fisherman pluck a pike ('the tyrant of fresh water'; thanks, Walton) from a canal bang in the middle of London; he was treated like a king by dozens of passing hipsters. That pike, however, was a lucky strike. You're more likely to be catching other *coarse fish*: perch, roach or rudd, barbel or bream.

**On a purpose-built carp pond.** Here you might be looking at £50 for an annual membership, plus £20–25 for each 24-hour visit: but at least you can be sure the fish are really there. The fun lies in setting up your brilliantly complicated rig, your gizmos and creature comforts, and spending many happy hours waiting for your bait alarm to sound. Remember: carp are not amphibious. Keep their time on the bank for your photo sessions to an absolute minimum.

**On a chalk stream in Hampshire.** If you want twenty-four trout-fishing days on a stretch of the River Itchen, then that's going to push you up to £3,000 a year. Ironically, for a pastime that looks so *au naturel*, you're likely to be fishing not for native Brown trout, but for Rainbow trout, introduced from North America and released annually.

Trout, along with salmon, is a so-called *game fish*. To catch one, you stand on a riverbank (or in a river in waders) and cast a pretend fly. This can be a *wet-fly* or a *dry-fly*, depending on whether you trawl your fly underwater or flick it precisely over the head of a fish which you've seen rising. For what it's worth, dry-fly fishing has traditionally been seen as much posher than wet-fly fishing.*

**On a Scottish salmon run.** If you've a fancy to fish for salmon at the height of the season on one of the best beats on the River Tweed, you could be looking at upwards of £1,000 for the day. On the plus side, you might get the services of a *ghillie* thrown in; a bit like a gamekeeper, but in this instance for salmon. Horses, as they say, for courses.

..........

* The dry-fly man, according to the cartoonist Norman Thelwell, on the money as ever, 'likes to study the river from his Bentley and is interested only in water as clear as gin and twice as expensive'.

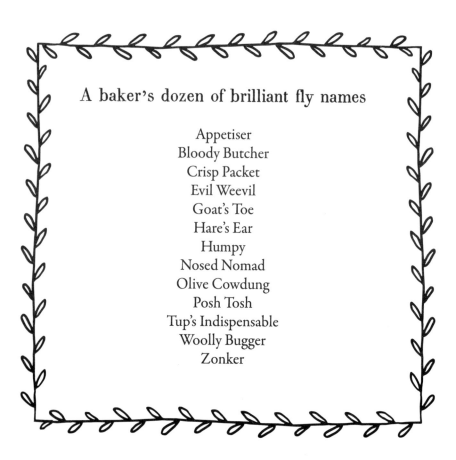

## A baker's dozen of brilliant fly names

Appetiser
Bloody Butcher
Crisp Packet
Evil Weevil
Goat's Toe
Hare's Ear
Humpy
Nosed Nomad
Olive Cowdung
Posh Tosh
Tup's Indispensable
Woolly Bugger
Zonker

# EELS

............

*PLAIN FAMILY DINNERS FOR NOVEMBER.*
*Monday – 1. Stewed eels.*
Isabella Beeton, *Mrs. Beeton's Book of*
*Household Management* (1861)

Eels were once everywhere. The remotest lakes, the most secluded pools, the channels of the greatest rivers, the wayside ditch, the marshlands of Avalon, the fens of Ely, wherever a watery living was to be made, eels were making it. Now? Not so much. Eels have been making out as badly as water-meadows: populations are barely 5 per cent of what they were even in the 1980s.

Why? Reduced habitats. Rivers blocked by flood defences and hydro schemes. Parasites and pathogens introduced from other parts of the world. Shifting ocean currents. Smuggling—

But, enough, enough! Let's not bring ourselves down. Let's talk about something *fun*. Let's talk about eel sex, that most slippery of subjects, that conundrum which stumped philosophers and scientists for centuries. A German microscopic anatomist even groaned on his deathbed (in our favourite apocryphal *cri de coeur*) that everything was known to science ... except the answer to the eel question. And the question was this: how did they breed?

Aristotle laid out the issue in his *Historia Animalium*: 'Eels are not produced by copulation, nor are they oviparous. No eel has ever been caught which had either milt* or eggs; nor when cut open are they found to possess passages for milt or a uterine passage.'

So far, so good. But his conclusion was a bit off: 'They are formed out of the so-called "earth-guts", which take shape spontaneously in mud and soggy soil.'**

Yet for a long time, nobody could come up with a better idea, although not for want of trying. Pliny the Elder, the David Attenborough of the ancient world, had a theory that sounds rather like reproduction via frotting. Izaak Walton, the Civil War-era fishing guru, said they were formed from dew. But everyone clung on to Aristotle, because – Aristotle.

And then, in the late eighteenth century, an Italian professor was sitting down to lunch. Delicately (he was a professor of anatomy), he cut up a piece of eel. As he brought it towards his lips, he paused. Something had caught his eye. He gasped. Reeled. Called for more light – a sharper knife. For he was, indubitably, the first man in recorded history to gaze upon the sex organs of a female eel. Aristotle's spontaneous-genesis theory was ditched.

Next stop: eel balls.

Gloriously, it was Sigmund Freud who rose to the challenge. Aged nineteen, he was dispatched to a research station in Trieste, where he set about collecting eels from the fish market, dissecting them and squinting at their bits under a microscope. Four hundred fat Adriatic eels later, not one paltry ball.

It was only some twenty years later that a sexually mature male eel was brought to book off the coast of Sicily. The penny dropped: eels only grow sex organs when they need

..........

* A special word for *fish sperm*.
** Still, a better effort than most of his theories about women.

them. But answering this question, only threw up others. So, eels definitely do reproduce like other fish – but where?

Enter a very persistent Dane. For the first two decades of the twentieth century (with a brief hiatus because of the war), Johannes Schmidt trawled the western Atlantic seaboard, from the Faroes to the Canaries, and on into the Mediterranean, as far as Egypt, looking for clues. He did find eel larvae, but they were all pretty much the same size – relatively big – which meant he was no closer to finding their spawning grounds. They must, he concluded, be further afield. And so he begged the bemused skippers of Danish cargo ships to drag nets for him, and the data they sent in was conclusive. The further west you went, the smaller the larvae became, until you got to the Sargasso Sea, a gyre, east of Florida, north of the Caribbean, full of eponymous Sargassum weed.

Problem solved. Well, everyone said solved, but there was still no definitive proof that those tiny eel larvae were connected to our adult eels. And then, in 2018–2019, researchers tagged twenty-six eels in rivers in the Azores, tracked them by satellite for up to a year, and *yes*, they did wind up in the Sargasso Sea. But no-one has ever found adult eels courting in the weeds, nor a clutch of eggs bobbing midst the fronds, so there's still work to do.

But at least now the eel's life cycle is clear:

1. Be born in Sargasso Sea.
2. Drift across Atlantic, in larval form, taking your time.
3. Metamorphosis one. Cross the continental shelf and change into a transparent glass eel, about 3 inches long. Head into an inviting estuary, e.g. the Bristol Channel.*
4. Metamorphosis two. Hit freshwater and change into an elver. Before eel stocks crashed, this could be quite a sight. Sir Herbert Maxwell, author of *British Fresh-Water Fishes* (1904), said that 'in May and June, [elvers] appear in such prodigious numbers that I have seen a Scottish trout-stream slate-coloured from bank to bank with the throng for a distance of twenty or thirty yards'.
5. Metamorphosis three. Elvers mature into yellow eels (which also look brown) and can stay that way for decades. These are what you'd jelly or stick in a pie, back when eels were cheap as chips.
6. Metamorphosis four. Head back to salt water.** Skin turns silver, snub nose turns sharp, eyes grow big. Lose stomach and intestines, put on a lot of weight, develop sexual organs, set back off across the Atlantic, a long, food-less journey. Breed, die.
7. This obviously makes the eel a reverse salmon. Salmon are anadromous (Greek, *up-run*): they go up-river to breed. Eels are katadromous (Greek, *down-run*): they go down-river to breed.

..........

* These little glass eels are smuggled in huge numbers. You can't breed eels in captivity, but you can grow them on, until they become incredibly valuable silver eels. The money's as good as cocaine, but the penalties are much lower. One smuggler, found guilty of making sixteen illegal shipments worth £53 million, got a suspended sentence and 240 hours of community service.
** If an eel's path to the sea is blocked, it can walk, or least work its way across semi-solid ground, for several hours.

# How to catch an eel the old-fashioned way

The Bristol Channel is like a big net, a jaw of land, scooping up eels, and so the river Parrett, which gurgles muddily from Bridgwater Bay to the Somerset Levels, was always a place where you stood an excellent chance of catching one. You could coppice an osier (a basket willow) to make a wicker trap, but all you really needed was:

**Perfect weather.** Heavy late-summer rain.

**Perfect time.** The deadest dark of night.

**Perfect kit.** Two poles, a ball of wool, a bucket of worms, a galvanised wash-tub painted white on the inside.

**Perfect method.** Insert one pole through the handles of the tub and float it on the river. Tie a length of wool on to the end of the other pole. Tie a worm on to the wool. Dip the worm into the water. Wait (not for long; eels were legion back then) until you felt an eel's teeth snag on the wool. Hoist the pole out of the water. Tap the pole on the edge of the tub. Watch the eel drop, obligingly, into the bottom.

# POOHSTICKS

......................

*Work and play are alike to him; his plays are his occupations, and*
*he sees no difference between the two.*
Jean-Jacques Rousseau, *Emile, or On Education* (1762)

Reading *Winnie-the-Pooh* or *The House at Pooh Corner* is a
queasy experience. A. A. Milne's syrupy prose lands uneas-
ily on the stomach, like an Italian pastry which you think is
going to be delicious, but is just *too sweet*. One thing worth
salvaging, though (along with the poems; some of them are
good), is the game *Poohsticks*.

You know the drill? Bridge, big stream or small river,
one stick per person, drop stick up-river, race to other side
of bridge, sticks emerge, announce winner. Repeat ... and
repeat ... and repeat. Why *do* small children like this game
so much? Factors there are three:*

**Liberté.** The choice of stick – the exercise of autonomy.
Other games adults choose to (re)play with children are
prescriptive: the numbered dice, the numbered squares, the
numbered cards, but here – the child's freedom to choose
the stick; the stick's freedom to leave the child. The teddy
(the *ursine avatar*) remains domestic and em-pillowed, but
the stick (the *ligneous avatar*) is granted and re-granted
its embarkment, whereby the child can rehearse its own
one-day departure from the home.

**Egalité.** When the child accepts the provocation of
Poohsticks, be it howsoever young, it intuits that it thereby

..........

* We acknowledge this chapter's debt to Frederick C. Crews, who pioneered
(over-)readings of the Pooh corpus, aka *The Pooh Perplex*.

enters the fray on an equal footing with its parent(-figure). In other provocations, the child knows that if it wins, it is being suffered to win, and so victory signifies defeat. But here, on the bridge, no advantage accrues with size: the littlest goat can stick it to the troll.

**Fraternité.** As each stick descends into the darkness, there is no way of controlling which will survive its katabasis. The large stick can be embayed. The small stick overborne. All sticks are potentially forfeit. But in sympathising with the Other's loss, and in accepting the Other's sympathy for one's own losses in turn, the child accepts the possibility of fellowship with the Other; the existence of a comrade who will console one amidst life's darkest tunnels, who cheer one when those tunnels do finally come to an end.

# HEAVEN

....................

## by Rupert Brooke

Fish (fly-replete, in depth of June,
Dawdling away their wat'ry noon)
Ponder deep wisdom, dark or clear,
Each secret fishy hope or fear.
Fish say, they have their Stream and Pond;
But is there anything Beyond?
This life cannot be All, they swear,
For how unpleasant, if it were!
One may not doubt that, somehow, Good
Shall come of Water and of Mud;

And, sure, the reverent eye must see
A Purpose in Liquidity.
We darkly know, by Faith we cry,
The future is not Wholly Dry.
Mud unto mud! – Death eddies near –
Not here the appointed End, not here!
But somewhere, beyond Space and Time
Is wetter water, slimier slime!
And there (they trust) there swimmeth One
Who swam ere rivers were begun,
Immense, of fishy form and mind,
Squamous, omnipotent, and kind;
And under that Almighty Fin,
The littlest fish may enter in.
Oh! never fly conceals a hook,
Fish say, in the Eternal Brook,
But more than mundane weeds are there,
And mud, celestially fair;
Fat caterpillars drift around,
And Paradisal grubs are found;
Unfading moths, immortal flies,
And the worm that never dies.
And in that Heaven of all their wish,
There shall be no more land, say fish.

# METAPHORICALLY SPEAKING

UNTIL THE COWS COME HOME

... FOR A VERY LONG TIME

Cows really do move at their own splendid, stately pace; until they decide to attack, that is.


A HARD ROW TO HOE

... A BAD SITUATION

Hoeing raised beds when it hasn't rained for months is the pits.


MAKE HAY WHILE THE SUN SHINES

... SEIZE AN OPPORTUNITY

Making hay while it's raining is even worse.


PLUCK THE LOW-HANGING FRUIT

... DO THE EASY STUFF

Nobody enjoys teetering at the top of an orchard ladder being dive-bombed by hornets.


DON'T LOOK A GIFT HORSE IN THE MOUTH

... DON'T BE UNGRATEFUL

You can work out a horse's age by looking at its teeth, but that's rude if somebody's offering you a free horse.


TAKE THE BIT BETWEEN YOUR TEETH

... TAKE BACK CONTROL

A bad horse bites down on its bit so it can ignore you sawing on the reins.

**SEPARATE THE WHEAT FROM THE CHAFF**
**... SORT THE GOOD FROM THE BAD**
The chaff is the dry, scaly husk around the bit of wheat
we can actually eat, so obviously you want to get rid of it.
(You'll also want to get rid of that rubbish free horse.)

**BUY A PIG IN A POKE**
**... FAIL TO GET PROPER VALUE**
A poke was once a small bag (cf. pocket), and buying a pig
in any sort of bag, large or small, was a really stupid thing
to do, because why would anyone put a pig in a bag, unless
there was something seriously wrong with the pig?

**GO TO GROUND**
**... DISAPPEAR, PROBABLY FOR SOME TIME**
What con-men do after they've sold you a pig in a poke.

# A VERY BIG HOUSE IN THE COUNTRY

.................................

*And, these grudged at, art reverenced the while.*
Ben Jonson, *'To Penshurst'* (1616)

Once upon a time, the upper classes went to big country
houses to party or to politick, the working classes went to
work, and the middle classes (such as they were) went to
be patronised at annual garden parties. Nowadays, we visit
such houses for all sorts of reasons: the café, the adventure playground, the farm-park, the Halloween and Easter
trails, the craft markets and second-hand bookshops; the

Christmas grotto and the ice-skating rink; the exhibitions, talks and concerts. And when we're back home, we spend another couple of hours imagining what it might have been like to live there.

The vernacular of big houses, via hundreds of books, films and TV shows, is so familiar: the cigarette holders, the cricket whites, the stiff butler, the flirty footman, nanny in the nursery, the housemaid sobbing under the stairs. And if imagining isn't enough, we can even cosplay for the day (wedding reception; best frock, champagne on the lawn) or the whole weekend (boutique hotel; tea, croquet, solitaire). Each generation has a new version of this big-house fantasy. In the eighties, we had Brideshead and Sebastian's teddy bear. In the nineties, Mr Darcy's wet shirt and Pemberley. In the noughties, Downton Abbey and Maggie Smith's eyebrows. And now – Bridgerton.

But what's most remarkable is how we've been encouraged, by some sleight of hand, to think they're in some way *ours*, that we, the nation, saved them from wrack and ruin. For throughout the first half of the twentieth century, it looked as if the big houses were well and truly done for.

Jacquetta Hawkes, in *A Land*, draws a direct comparison between the fate of grand Roman villas after the legions left and that of the large country estates in her lifetime:

> The forces of disintegration were too strong for them. Leaking roofs were not mended and each winter more tiles split and slipped; the waters came in and loosened the mosaic floors, tesserae came up and were not reset. Then a gale, a heavy fall of snow, and there was a collapse that could never be made good; the tiny citadel of civilised living contracted still further. At last the owner might abandon the struggle with his derelict home and go

to the nearest town where some form of civic organisation was tenuously maintained. Sometimes a villa was brought to an end by the pillage, fire and murder of a barbarian raid, but more often it was by these quiet, sadder processes of decay.

People really did think this was going to happen in England. Depression, war, taxes, depression, war: nobody thought the aristocracy would weather it. Was land, one's ancestral acres, now for chumps? As early as 1895, Lady Bracknell, sneering her way through *The Importance of Being Earnest*, thought it was: 'It gives one position, and prevents one from keeping it.' One by one, writes D. H. Lawrence in *Lady Chatterley's Lover* in the 1920s, the stately homes and handsome halls of England were being abandoned: 'smuts fall and blacken on the drab stucco, that has long ceased to be golden'. And during the Second World War, a book giving tips about moving to the countryside was equally sure the game was up: 'Taxation and death duties have turned pleasure acres into poultry farms. Hunter has become hunted. Tax-collectors press at the door of the wealthy with ever-increasing insistence. There are weeds in the drive and the lodge is let to strangers. The Lord of the Manor keeps pigs.'

But everyone got it wrong. Evelyn Waugh, writing a new preface to *Brideshead Revisited* in 1959, admitted that his novel, written during the war, was 'a panegyric preached over an empty coffin'. In his defence, he writes:

> It was impossible to foresee, in the spring of 1944, the present cult of the English country house. It seemed then that the ancestral seats which were our chief national artistic achievement were doomed to decay and spoliation like the monasteries in the sixteenth century. So I piled it on rather, with passionate sincerity. Brideshead today would be open to trippers, its treasures

rearranged by expert hands and the fabric better maintained than it was by Lord Marchmain.

So what happened? Let's rewind a little.

Drawing inspiration from commons preservation societies, the National Trust was founded in 1895 by three people (Octavia Hill, Robert Hunter and Hardwicke Rawnsley) who wanted to protect open spaces and historic buildings from the creep of modernity. Mark Cocker, in *Our Place* (2018), calls the trust 'patrician in both make-up and ethos', and certainly it has never been redistributive. Nevertheless, the founders were committed social reformers, who genuinely wanted (in their words) 'our poorer brethren' to have a share of beauty.

At first, the trust acquired land and houses via legacies and fundraising, but in the 1930s it came up with a new scheme. When owners could no longer afford to run their estates, they could cut a deal with the trust, including hefty tax breaks, which allowed them to go on living where they always had done, so long as they opened their houses and gardens to the public. After the war, Hugh Dalton, the Labour chancellor who ushered in the welfare state, backed the creation of a National Land Fund, which could use cash raised by flogging surplus military stores to take on big houses in lieu of death duties. The socialists, in other words, thought the aristocratic beast was slain, and so saw no harm in turning its corpse into a rug and sticking its horns on the wall for us to admire.

And perhaps, after the horror and upheaval of two world wars, people did find the sense of continuity comforting. There is, after all, a very persistent seam in conservative English sensibility, which feels not only that the beauty of our country houses is one of our greatest achievements, but also that a sort of enlightened feudalism is somehow quite nice, quite natural – almost soothing. This, too, probably dates back to the whirlwind of industrialisation, when uprooted and disorientated people consoled themselves with fables of a happier past, when the kindly squire swapped racing tips with his groom, when his bountiful lady schemed with her gardener, when it all just *worked*.

Even the radical William Cobbett bought into it, up to a point. In a famous passage from *Rural Rides*, published in the 1820s, he wrote that 'a resident native gentry, attached to the soil, known to every farmer and labourer from their childhood, frequently mixing with them in those pursuits where all artificial distinctions are lost, practising hospitality without ceremony, from habit and not on calculation' is better than a 'distant and haughty' rentier owner, who buys land only to speculate, who has no interest in country pursuits, who despises his neighbours and their ways.

Such thinking, however, could be pushed even further, pushed to mean that this socio-economic order was somehow as preordained as all things bright and beautiful, all creatures great and small, as the now often omitted third verse of Cecil Frances Alexander's hymn puts it:

> The rich man in his castle,
> the poor man at his gate,
> God made them high and lowly,
> and ordered their estate.

Jane Wells Webb Loudon, or Mrs Loudon as she was known when she wrote gardening books rather than science fiction, exemplifies this (self-interested) nineteenth-century paternalism in *The Lady's Country Companion* (1845):

> The proprietor of a large estate ought to be regarded by the labouring cottagers in the light of a protector, to whom they can look up for advice and assistance in their troubles; and as a friend upon whose kindness they may confidently rely, and who they know will be interested in their welfare. When this is the case, the tenantry of a country gentleman will form his best body-guard; and, instead of ever attempting to injure his property, they will do all in their power to protect it.

She does, at least, admit that 'the poor' do not like to be interfered with, to be spied upon, to be told what to eat and wear, something which Thomas Hardy, who came from a working-class family, also understood well. In an article titled 'The Dorsetshire Labourer', published in 1883, he describes how one villager liked to hoodwink the condescending squire and/or his lady.

> 'I always kip a white apron behind the door to slip on when the gentlefolk knock, for if so be they see a white apron they think ye be clane,' said an honest woman one day, whose bedroom floors could have been scraped with as much advantage as a pigeon-loft; but who, by a judicious use of high lights, shone as a pattern of neatness in her patrons' eyes.

Even the vast social and political changes of the twentieth century have failed to eradicate some people's affection for those times. The novelist John Fowles, for example, claimed to prefer the 'antiquated class-system of village life' to the suburban streets of his childhood. And in *England: An Elegy*, published in 2000, the conservative thinker Roger Scruton says: 'It was not snobbery but a kind of decorum that motivated the English people to seek out their separate spheres of belonging.' The country house, he believes, did once dispense 'kindness and hospitality' and provide 'in wise measure for all its many dependants'.

This, then, has been the get-out for generations of major landowners: they are the natural custodians of the countryside, practising *noblesse oblige* in the grand old manner, shored up by a notion that lots of aristocrats are actually quite scruffy, actually quite down to earth, as likely to have a leaky bucket catching drips in the hallway as a Rolls Royce parked out front.

In *Red Rag to a Bull*, Jamie Blackett, owner of the Arbigland estate in Scotland, is happy to mount a full-throttle defence.

To some people, he says, an estate (or the *e-word*) implies land acquired on the back of some historical crime (he references the Norman Conquest, the enclosures and the Reformation) then passed down through a male-orientated system of primogeniture; to some people, he says, it smacks of a privileged rentier life and the exploitation of tenants and labour. But to him, an estate is far more than the sum of its parts. In his eyes, it is a community of people living and working together; a balanced portfolio of businesses; a balanced landscape of tourism, forestry and farming; a place where heritage and habitats are preserved; where the traditions of field sports are honoured; where long-range planning is prioritised; where trees are planted for one's great-grandchildren.

Admittedly, even he has experienced major change: he now lives in the estate's smaller dower house,* the big house having been sold off after the family fortune was

.........

* The dower house was traditionally where you parked your widowed mother. Freed of the cares of running the big house, she could then devote herself to tormenting your wife, much as your father's mother had once tormented her.

bludgeoned by the Lloyds insurance meltdown and the early-90s recession.*

But however hard you spin it – and people do try – it's difficult to outrun the fact that a very small number of people own very large houses on very large tracts of the British countryside, thanks solely to being descended from a very small number of people, hundreds and hundreds of years ago. Gerald Grosvenor, the sixth Duke of Westminster (who left the public school Harrow with two O-levels), was once asked what advice he would give to a young entrepreneur hoping to rival his billion-pound business portfolio. His (very disarming; cf. that leaky bucket) reply: make sure you have an ancestor who was a very close friend of William the Conqueror.

And so, even as some people have been keen to foster a sense of the rightness, the inevitability, almost the inviolability, of British landownership, others have long been asking questions about who owns what and how and why.

Considering a grand house and park in *The South Country* (1909), the poet Edward Thomas asks what is the price of such beauty: 'Only a thousand years of settled continuous government, of far-reaching laws, of armies and police, of road making, of bloody tyranny and tyranny that poisons quietly without blows, could have wrought earth and sky into such a harmony.' A few decades later, George Orwell, in his 1941 essay 'The Lion and the Unicorn', compares the British country house to a family with skeletons bursting out of its cupboards; there is, he says, 'a deep conspiracy of silence about the source of the family income'. And

..........

* Blackett compares seeing the big house redecorated by its new occupiers to 'coming downstairs and seeing one's mother dressed up to go to a vicars and tarts party in fishnet stockings and suspenders', an observation which this footnote lacks the courage to unpack.

Raymond Williams, writing in the 1970s, called country houses 'visible triumphs over the ruin and labour of others'.

We've quoted liberally to make the point that when today's progressive writers criticise 'a tourist-board narrative of a great empire, a proud history, steam engines, top hats and globally acclaimed costume dramas' and call big houses 'treasure chests stuffed to the eaves with violent plunder' and 'radiant monoliths to the myth of white supremacy' (Nick Hayes), they're not saying anything that revolutionary. Interrogating our past is categorically *not* some new-fangled wokery dreamt up last Thursday.

Building a country house has always been a form of money-laundering. Quick – get away from the docks, the mines, the factories, from where you made your money, and settle down somewhere you can pretend your family are as old as the hills, somewhere you can spend your money without having to watch it being made.

We can trace this unease far back into the nineteenth century. In Charlotte Brontë's *Jane Eyre*, Mr Rochester has locked up his 'bad, mad, and embruted' first wife, a woman he'd like to forget, in the attic of his house. Bertha Mason is the daughter of a planter in the West Indies and his Creole wife, and some people have speculated that means she has both Black and white heritage. It's possible – and indeed tempting – to read Rochester's decision to hide her at the heart of Thornfield Hall as a stand-in for wider British society's need to conceal from itself just how much of its national wealth derived from the trade in enslaved Africans.

Go back a few decades, and we read in Jane Austen how the forced labour of African people in the Caribbean underpins the 'elegancies and luxuries' of Mansfield Park: everything is funded by Sir Thomas Bertram's Antiguan plantation wealth. Fanny mentions this to his son, her cousin, the man she will marry:

'Did not you hear me ask him about the slave-trade last night?'

'I did – and was in hopes the question would be followed up by others. It would have pleased your uncle to be inquired of farther.'

'And I longed to do it – but there was such a dead silence!'

What can we not read into that silence?

And today, it seems, some people think it would be a lot easier if the silence continued. In 2020, the National Trust published an interim report on 'Connections between colonialism and properties now in the care of the National Trust, including links with historic slavery'. Superficially, at least, its findings were incontrovertible. Some people grew rich on empire; some people grew rich on the trans-Atlantic trade in enslaved people. Some people used their money to build new houses or remodel old ones. Some of those houses have since been acquired by the National Trust. The trust now wished to be candid about any such connections.*

Simple? No. A lot of people were furious.

They thought the National Trust was 'patronising, preaching and posturing' (Tory MP Sir John Hayes); it was breaking faith with the families who had donated their houses (a *Telegraph* leader); it should 'conserve, not comment' and 'pass things on to future generations in a spirit of intelligent affection' (same leader); it would do well to remember that people visit big houses for 'a recreational experience culminating in a cream tea, not to be lectured by a cultural thought police' (conservative commentator Simon Heffer); after all 'history is history' (one of the trust's five million members).

..........

* The report put the number of its houses with connections to colonialism and slavery at 93, including Winston Churchill's, which was factually accurate, but strategically unhelpful.

And yet, to divorce houses from their historical context is actually crazily post-modern. *Il n'y a pas de hors-maison.* Is there really nothing outside the house? But we don't think that's what the critics meant. We think they meant look at *this* history, not *that* history.

The academic Corinne Fowler, one of the report's co-editors, is also the author of *Green Unpleasant Land* (2020), which poses a number of questions, which might illuminate any walk around the stunning innards of a big country house. She invites us, for example, to reflect on what it might mean, then and now, for oil paintings to hang on the walls in which Black servant boys appear as status symbols. And, she reminds us, doesn't a table made from mahogany harvested in a Caribbean forest have a very different history, signify something very different, to one made from a cherry tree down the road? And doesn't that ivory figurine, fashioned from the tusk of an Indian elephant, tell a very different story to one moulded out of Staffordshire clay?

We'd suggest that she's not saying, *I hope you choke on your scone*; rather, she's giving us more information, more knowledge, more insight. After all, shouldn't it always be possible to ask such questions, and to reflect upon whatever answers we might find? And if the answers are sometimes difficult, perhaps we should ask ourselves *why* we find them so.

That is, in the end, the very least we can do.

# CARIBBEAN EYE OVER YORKSHIRE

*(for John Lyons)*

by John Agard

Eye
perched over
adopted Yorkshire.

Eye christened
in Caribbean blue
and Trinidad sunfire.

Eye tuned in
to the flame
tree's decibels

and the red
stereophonic bloom of immortelles.

Eye once a stranger
to silver birch and conifer
now on first-name terms

with beech and elm and alder.
Eye making an ally
of heather and lavender.

Eye of painter
eye of poet
eye of prankster

eye looking into linden
for ghost-traces
of silk-cotton

eye of crow
in carnival cape
seeing inward

eye of blackbird
casting
humming-bird shadow.

# OH, DO GROW UP!

...................................

*We'll be children seventy years instead of seven*
Rupert Brooke, a letter*

The fantasy of the countryside (green grass, green fields, green trees, green hills) and the fantasy of childhood (innocent, natural, simple, green) are the top and bottom layers of a Victoria sponge cake, stuck together with the cream and jam of some of Britain's most successful cultural artefacts: our books for children.

These books, populated with lost boys, naughty toads and gnomic bears, with brave rabbits and braver hobbits, with hedgehogs and kittens in bibs and bonnets, work very hard to keep us safe in their fictional paradises. Beyond the Wild Wood lies the Wide World and that, as Ratty warns Mole, is something that *doesn't matter*: he's never been there, he's never going there, and Mole, if he's got any sense, won't go there either.

The writer J. R. R Tolkien had a lot in common with both creatures: he hated traffic, factories and what he called 'the rawness and ugliness of modern European life', channelling his love of the Midlands countryside into his writing by way of compensation. 'It is a work written to keep the modern world at bay that the modern world adores,' the journalist and novelist Jenny Turner wrote of *The Lord of the Rings* – although a less sympathetic critic said it was simply a children's book which had got out of hand.

..........

* Quoted by Paul Delany in *The Neo-Pagans: Friendship and Love in the Rupert Brooke Circle* (1987).

Bookshop gifting shelves still groan with the same stories, but Pooh and Pippin and Peter (Rabbit, Pan and Pevensie) have kicked over the sentence's traces, spat out the book's bit, and galloped off into a sunset of massive film franchises and small-screen spin-offs, of pyjamas and pants, of fast food tie-ins, trading cards and all the other merch (we think) we and our children need. These stories, then, are now commodities, the rights to them bought and sold by companies worth billions, their intellectual property value rising and falling, like the spot price for *mithril* on the London Metal Exchange. And yet despite this – or do we mean because of it? – these old stories, and the new versions built on their foundations, remain incredibly important to us.

They remind us of our childhood, or the childhood we wished we'd had. And when we read them to our own sons and daughters, they function like incantations, like summoning spells for happiness. For the books conjure up a succession of perfect places, Ratty's river, Bilbo's Shire, places we ourselves look back at with longing from the thornier topography of adulthood.

Indeed Jean-Jacques Rousseau's advice, that the young Emile should breathe 'the fresh air of the country' rather than 'the foul air of the town', has long straddled the fence between the literal and the metaphorical. This conflation of childhood with the countryside, explains the academic Jacqueline Rose in *The Case of Peter Pan, or the Impossibility of Children's Fiction* (1992), 'places on the child's shoulders the responsibility for saving humankind from the degeneracy of modern society'. We imagine 'a primitive or lost state' to which children have special access, crediting them with a store of natural wisdom, the same sort of wisdom we seek from wise old countrymen, whom we see as equally untouched by the corruptions of culture.

'The child,' she says, 'is innocent and can restore innocence to us.'*

Many people have theorised that this tendency became entrenched by the shock and rupture of the First World War. There was, or we have encouraged ourselves to *think* there was, one last golden Edwardian summer, and then it was all over: the weasels fixed bayonets, the warren was gassed, the Black Riders advanced. Frodo, after all, dreams of the Shire with the same intensity that Charles Ryder dreams of Brideshead, the one fated to be ravaged by Saruman's ruffians, the other by uncouth squaddies.

'To look upon the maps of Middle Earth, or of the Willows, or of the Hundred Acre Wood, is now, after decades of war rooms and map rooms, to see the cartographies of nostalgia,' explains Seth Lerer in *Children's Literature* (2008). And yet, he acknowledges, what pleasure those generations must have taken in abandoning the didactic pieties of Victorian writing for children (even their fairies were rubbish; so *deedy*) to play instead with the occult, the fantastical, the spiritual, the speculative.

You don't, however, need to look far to find people who loathe these susceptibilities. Partly, such critics dislike the books themselves, but they mightn't dislike them quite so intensely if the books had stayed in the nursery. What they can't bear is how Nanny brings them downstairs and parades them about the drawing room, expecting the grown-ups to take them seriously. Here, for example, is Germaine Greer throwing up her hands in horror when she discovered that *The Lord of the Rings* had topped a popular BBC book poll:

..........

* There's a possible corollary here in how we lionise young climate activists today. Isn't it wonderful, we say, that they have this instinctive grasp of the need for climate justice? The children will save us! This allows us, conveniently, to forget that we are the grown-up, and that if there's going to be any saving, it's got to be done by us.

Ever since I arrived at Cambridge as a student in 1964 and encountered a tribe of full-grown women wearing puffed sleeves, clutching teddies, and babbling excitedly about the doings of hobbits, it has been my nightmare that Tolkien would turn out to be the most influential writer of the twentieth century. The bad dream has materialised.

And if Greer was horrified, Michael Moorcock, a writer's writer if ever there was one, was incandescent: 'all these books,' he says, taking (very effective) aim in his essay 'Epic Pooh' at the entire canon, 'seem to have been written with a slight lisp.' Witheringly, he calls the Shire 'that Surrey of the mind'. Firmly, he tells us we must do better.

'This refusal to face or derive any pleasure from the realities of urban industrial life, this longing to possess, again, the infant's eye view of the countryside, is a fundamental theme in popular English literature,' he says. 'I sometimes think that as Britain declines, dreaming of a sweeter past, entertaining few hopes for a finer future, her middle classes turn increasingly to the fantasy of rural life and talking animals, the safety of the woods that are the pattern of the paper on the nursery room wall.'

Moorcock wrote that back in the late seventies; today, with the inexorable rise of glamping, his nightmare has turned into reality. We can spend whole weekends in teepees and shepherds' huts, in treehouses and Gypsy caravans, making believe we're Moley or Pooh, Fiver in his warren, Bilbo in his Hole, all tucked up together like so many Lost Boys.

And yet you can bet your first editions that the children out there right now, toasting marshmallows on firepits across the land, they aren't going to put up with Kenneth Grahame or J. M. Barrie. No way! Too wordy, too slow. Even if we haven't moved on, they certainly have. No, if they're reading an animal story, it'll hopefully be something from the mighty pen of Erin Hunter.*

The *Warrior Cats* series (across dozens of books) tells the tale of a number of feral feline clans, who live culturally rich but violent lives in an unnamed British forest; they despise domestic kittypets; they are, in fact, postercats for rewilding. *Survivors*, meanwhile, gives us packs of dogs weathering a civilisation-ending natural disaster, and *Seekers* tracks an implausible collective of bears contending with habitat destruction and climate change.**

In and amongst the tension, the cliffhangers, the fiendishly complicated inter-animal relationships, our children are being introduced to a lexicon of ideas, which should stand them in good stead in their adult lives: nature vs culture, courage in the face of catastrophe, the importance of environmental stewardship.

Perhaps they'll save us after all.

..........

* In reality, a crack team of master wordsmiths.
** Trigger warning: bedtime-ruining mummy-bear death.

# EXTRACT FROM 'GOBLIN MARKET'

by Christina Rossetti

Morning and evening
Maids heard the goblins cry:
'Come buy our orchard fruits,
Come buy, come buy:
Apples and quinces,
Lemons and oranges,
Plump unpeck'd cherries,
Melons and raspberries,
Bloom-down-cheek'd peaches,
Swart-headed mulberries,
Wild free-born cranberries,
Crab-apples, dewberries,
Pine-apples, blackberries,
Apricots, strawberries;—
All ripe together
In summer weather,—
Morns that pass by,
Fair eves that fly;
Come buy, come buy:
Our grapes fresh from the vine,
Pomegranates full and fine,
Dates and sharp bullaces,
Rare pears and greengages,
Damsons and bilberries,
Taste them and try:
Currants and gooseberries,

Bright-fire-like barberries,
Figs to fill your mouth,
Citrons from the South,
Sweet to tongue and sound to eye;
Come buy, come buy.'

# AND IS THERE JAM
# STILL FOR TEA?

Hell, yes!

## THE THEORY

**The pectin.** When you cook fruit, it releases *pectin*, a starch found in the cell walls of most fruit and vegetables. Pectin acts a bit like a plant glue, turning your fruit juices into a gel, which sets as it cools. Fruits high in pectin (crab apples, currants, gooseberries, plums) set easily. Fruits lower in pectin (apricots, blackberries, blueberries, cherries, pears, raspberries, strawberries) need some help, either from jam sugar (sugar fortified with pectin) or from straight-up pectin powder.

**The sugar.** Remember, it's much more than a sweetener: it's the key to the jam lasting. Add too much and your jam will crystallise. Add too little and it'll go mouldy.

**The acid.** This helps fruit release its pectin, brightens the colour of the jam and improves the flavour. Pectin-rich fruit comes with plenty of acid of its own. Pectin-poor fruit needs extra – usually lemon juice.

239

**The fruit.** Slightly under-ripe fruit releases more pectin, so don't think you can make jam with the dregs of your fruit crop.

## THE PRACTICE

From the above, you'll realise that making gooseberry or blackcurrant jam is a doddle, but we'd suggest (from bitter experience) that neither is a crowd-pleaser. Raspberry jam, on the other hand, is pretty reliable if you use proper jam sugar. The real challenge, though, is strawberry jam.

The standard jam recipe: equal weights of fruit and sugar, plus lemon juice, leaves you with runny strawberry gloop. Delicious, but not what we're after. You need jam sugar, lots of lemon juice, plus pectin powder. (If you want to go #cottagecore, eschew powder in favour of redcurrant or gooseberry juice like they did in yore.)

## THE KIT

**Jars.** Don't buy them specially, but hoard pleasing shapes and sizes throughout the year. (Note: jam in a peanut butter jar is a grievous category error.) Soak off the labels and run them through the dishwasher. When you're ready, put the jars in the oven at 120°C to sterilise them.

**Waxed circles.** Once you've filled the jars, you put the circles on top, waxed/shiny side down, and press them on to the surface, pushing out air bubbles. The wax melts slightly on the hot jam, helping to seal it and keep out mould.

**Cellophane circles.** You dampen the cellophane with a sponge, fit it over the jar and fix with an elastic band. As it dries, it shrinks and clings tightly. If you want to smash the jam section at the fete, you'll have to do it this way, but we reckon you're actually better off using the (sterilised) lid the jar came with. It keeps better, plus you can stack them.

**Jam pan.** Use something relatively wide and relatively shallow so the water boils off fast. Don't fill it beyond halfway because the jam bubbles up as it boils.

THE RECIPE
- 2 kg strawberries, not too ripe, halved or quartered if fat. Wipe off any dirt, but don't wash.
- 2 kg jam sugar
- Juice of two lemons
- 8 g pectin

1. Put the strawberries into the pan and add the lemon juice. Heat gently to soften the fruit and extract the pectin. If you want to end up with large chunks of fruit, stir carefully. Chunks look classy, but it's easier if you just mash it all up. Remember: once you add the sugar, the fruit won't soften any more.

2. Add the sugar and pectin. Continue heating and stirring until all the sugar is dissolved. You'll feel the crunch of any undissolved sugar at the bottom of the pan.

3. Turn your ring up to max and bring to a rolling boil. You'll be glad you didn't overfill the pan. Stop stirring.

4. After about 10 minutes, start to test the set. There are lots of ways of doing this.

You can fork out for a jam thermometer, but they do have a habit of breaking. You can put a saucer in the freezer, drip a spoon of jam on it, put it back in the freezer for a minute, remove and poke to see if it has set, but that is a total faff. We find it easiest to dip a wooden spoon into the mix and hold it up high over the jam. You will see it begin to form a sort of flake along the bottom of the spoon. When one drop hangs off this flake, you're set.

5.  You'll see a ring of foam round the edge of the pan. That's scum. Some people stir in butter to disperse it, but you can just skim it off with a spoon. If you don't get it all off, it's a bit unsightly, but it won't spoil the jam.

6.  Take your jars out of the oven and leave them to cool for 10 minutes or so. If you pour jam into very hot jars, it will bubble up and continue cooking. Allowing the jam to cool slightly also means the fruit is less likely to rise to the top, which would lose you marks if you're trying to win prizes.

7.  Remind yourself that the jam is still extremely hot. Fill the jars right to the top, which'll be easier if you have a jam funnel. The jam sinks as it cools and too much air is an opportunity for bugs. Add the wax circles and cover. Label when cool.

8.  If you've cocked up and it hasn't set, don't try to reboil it. You've made delicious strawberry sauce to pour over ice-cream.

9.  Spend ages de-sticking the kitchen.

10. Next year, you might find a bit of mould on the jam. Just scoop it off and don't tell anyone.

# HORSES AND PONIES, 1

What to do if your child asks for a pony:

CHILD          Please can I have a pony?

YOU            No.

# HORSES AND PONIES, 2

Here's a rundown of our native horses and ponies. which you are under no obligation to buy, feed, exercise, muck out, take to the vet, furnish with insanely expensive kit or sob over when dead.

Listed roughly north to south, heights in hands (hh):

**Shetland.** Can be any colour other than spotted. The smallest native breed. Browses on sparse grazing. Pulled carts and ploughed. Now favoured as a first ride for children. Up to 10.2 hh.

**Eriskay.** Usually grey but can be black. Comes from the Outer Hebrides and was a working breed, but is now in favour as a patient mount for children. 12–13.2 hh.

**Highland.** Can be dun, grey, black or bay. Lives up to its name as a sure-footed mount or load bearer in tough terrain. 13–14.2 hh.

**Clydesdale.** Bay or brown, usually with shaggy white socks. A native of Lanarkshire. The Scottish heavy-lifting breed competing with the Shire and Suffolk Punch down south for honours on the battlefield. 16–18 hh.

**Cleveland Bay.*** Ancient Yorkshire native. Originally a fine working horse. Now, with the addition of some Thoroughbred blood, the Cleveland is in demand as a

..........

* Back around 1700, three stallions from the Middle East were brought to England and introduced to our native mares, particularly the Cleveland. Their progeny laid the foundations for the Thoroughbred horses we see racing today. In 1793, James Weatherby, then the secretary of the Jockey Club, issued the General Stud Book in which the pedigree of every foal born to a Thoroughbred horse has been recorded ever since. If it's not in the book, it's not a Thoroughbred.

showjumper or hunter. Often pulls the carriages in royal processions. 16–16.2 hh.

**Fell.** Black, grey, brown or bay. Originated in Cumbria but was widely adopted across the Pennines. The classic sure-footed packhorse. Would later become one of several smaller breeds sent down the coal mines. Up to 14 hh.

**Dales.** Usually black, but can be brown, grey or bay. Another very hardy upland working breed from the Pennines, where it was used in lead mining. Nearly extinct after the Second World War, it is still at risk. 14–14.2 hh.

**Shire.** Black, brown, grey or roan. The Shire originated in Leicestershire and Lincolnshire. Very strong and powerful, it was used for hauling and ploughing. Horses were enlisted in time of war. 17+ hh.

**Hackney horse.** Black, brown, bay or chestnut. Bred by crossing Yorkshire and Norfolk roadsters in the eighteenth century. Very distinctive high-stepping trot, which led to its adoption for carriage driving. 14.2–16.2 hh.

**Suffolk Punch.** Can only be chestnut. (Yes, no T.) Another big powerful beast, ideal for farm working and hauling heavy artillery. 15.3–17 hh.

**New Forest.** Bay, chestnut or grey. Working heritage. Now a tourist attraction. Up to 14.2 hh.

**Exmoor.** Usually dun, bay or brown, with oatmeal or 'mealy' markings around the muzzle and eyes. Once a great all-rounder for the hill farmer, now a friendly family mount. Thrives on rough forage, so making a comeback as a conservation grazer. 11.2–12.3 hh.

**Dartmoor.** Usually bay but can be any colour. Historically used for pit work, now an ideal child's pony. The ones you see roaming the moor may well have had unsanctioned liaisons, so wouldn't necessarily pass muster with the purist. Up to 12.2 hh.

**Welsh ponies and cobs.** These natives of the Welsh mountains are divided into four *sections*. Cobs are typically chunkier than ponies and capable of carrying heavier loads. All make good riding mounts. 12–13.2+ hh.

- Section A. 12.0 hh max. The typical Welsh pony is grey, but any colour other than piebald and skewbald is permitted.
- Section B. 13.2 hh max. A bigger pony.
- Section C. 13.2 hh max. A more thickset pony with cob characteristics.
- Section D. 13.2 hh and over. The true Welsh cob.

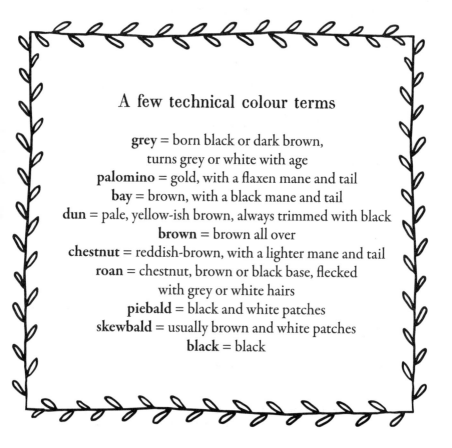

## A few technical colour terms

**grey** = born black or dark brown,
turns grey or white with age
**palomino** = gold, with a flaxen mane and tail
**bay** = brown, with a black mane and tail
**dun** = pale, yellow-ish brown, always trimmed with black
**brown** = brown all over
**chestnut** = reddish-brown, with a lighter mane and tail
**roan** = chestnut, brown or black base, flecked
with grey or white hairs
**piebald** = black and white patches
**skewbald** = usually brown and white patches
**black** = black

# GARDENS, GARDENERS, GARDENING

........................................................................

*So also gardening, as far as gardening is an art, or entitled to that
appellation, is a deviation from nature; for if the true taste con-
sists, as many hold, in banishing every appearance of art, or any
traces of the footsteps of man, it would then be no longer a garden.*
Sir Joshua Reynolds, *Discourses on Art* (1797)

England's fortunes might, at times, feel a little precarious, but we don't think we'd be speaking out of turn to say
that *we've still got gardening.*\*

George Orwell, in his essay 'The Lion and the Unicorn',
lists any number of things the English are no earthly good
at (being artistic, being intellectual, being philosophical,
being practical), before allowing, approvingly, that we do
love flowers. 'This is,' he says, 'one of the first things that
one notices when one reaches England from abroad', and it
is, he explains, perfectly possible to be an excellent gardener
in the absence of any 'aesthetic feeling' whatsoever.

And yet, the *jardin anglais*, the English landscape
garden, is, in the words of the essayist Rebecca Solnit, 'one
of the great English contributions to Western culture'.
There *is* something radical about considering gardens as
art: you can neither mass-produce them, nor collect them,
nor display them. You have to *do* them. If you buy a painting, you do not become a painter. But if you buy a garden,
you have to become a gardener, or what you have bought
will quickly cease to be a garden.

..........

\* Fact for you. The ornamental plant trade contributes around nine times
more to the economy than the entire fishing industry.

Gardens have also given us an artful frame through which we can look at nature itself; they are proving grounds between the domestic and the wild. The different philosophies, moreover, of the (very rich, very powerful) people practising large-scale gardening have been so influential that they still affect how we look at the countryside today. In fact, what we might think of as *natural* or *English* is often anything but. As works of art go, gardens have really got under our skin.*

The words *garden* and *paradise* derive from very old Germanic and Iranian words meaning *enclosed*. From the Garden of Eden right up until the Tudors, this was the dream: a *hortus conclusus*, a sanctuary, your own little piece of civilisation, shut off, shut away. On that, the grandest of lords and the humblest of nuns would have agreed: gardens needed walls. There, safe and hidden from view, you might think upon your God, or perhaps your Love, but one thing you definitely wouldn't have been thinking about was Nature. You were trying to forget *that*; that's what the walls were for.

During the Enlightenment, when humanity started to reckon it stood a fighting chance against nature, gardeners became more confident. Nature was no longer something to fear: it could be licked into shape, marshalled into straight lines, into acres of dauntless geometry. (Picture the gardens at Versailles, the style's apotheosis.) Plants were to be displayed like statues or jewels, and topiary – nature imitating culture – was all the rage. 'Any Ladies that please may have their own Effigies in Myrtle, or their Husbands in Hornbeam,' scoffed the satirist Alexander Pope. Nobody

..........

* Witness how the meaning of the word *landscape* has changed over time: a painting of some land → a view of some land → the land itself.

wanted movement or flow or subtlety, and there was certainly no notion of doing anything so outlandish as mimicking the wilderness.

But Horace Walpole, the classic eighteenth-century man of letters, all snuff and powdered hair, was having none of it. He said we needed to abandon such childish attachment to novelty, such displays of bad taste. We should do away with 'barbarism, formality, and seclusion' and instead focus on a style 'at once more grand and more natural'. In other words, instead of trying to force nature into a straitjacket, we should follow its lead.

This new style, in Walpole's famous phrase, 'leaped the fence, and saw that all nature was a garden'. The hills and valleys, the groves of trees, the winding stream, the distant view, suddenly everything the eye could see was conceived of as an extension of the garden; the hard border between the domestic and the wild, that was gone. This radical departure, delivered by men such as William Kent and Lancelot 'Capability' Brown, is what English gardening is most famous for, and it only worked because, at that period, England was a secure and self-confident country; a country untouched by war or revolution; a country in which a certain insouciant informality (the Victorian era is still a long way off) was in vogue.

Tom Stoppard, in his play *Arcadia* (1993), dramatises the shift impeccably. Hannah, an academic, rigorous and unsentimental, calls it the decline *from thinking to feeling*:

> There's an engraving of Sidley Park in 1730 that makes you want to weep. Paradise in the age of reason. By 1760 everything had gone – the topiary, pools and terraces, fountains, an avenue of limes – the whole sublime geometry was ploughed under by Capability Brown. The grass went from the doorstep to the horizon and the best box hedge in Derbyshire was dug up for

the ha-ha so that the fools could pretend they were living in God's countryside.*

And God's countryside had a distinctly Mediterranean edge. Back then, Italy and Greece were the exotic places for a smart young man to visit on his gap year (or his grand tour, as it was known in those days). It was there that he learned to admire landscape paintings, especially those by Nicolas Poussin, Salvator Rosa and Claude.** These pictures, whether rugged or serene, celebrated NATURE in a way nobody had really done before, and it was a look which smart young men (once they inherited) were keen to recreate at home. Or as Stoppard's Hannah puts it: 'English landscape was invented by gardeners imitating foreign painters who were evoking classical authors. The whole thing was brought home in the luggage from the grand tour. Here look – Capability Brown doing Claude, who was doing Virgil.'

But, as you imagine, it was hard to create a fantasy of rolling hills if there were peasants, and not the quaint kind, spoiling the view. Landowners had to separate the two. Furrows and hedges for *them*. Serpentine rills for *us*. Busy productivity *there*. Prelapsarian idyll *here*.

'With the cult of the park,' explains Marion Shoard in *A Right to Roam* (1999), 'the idea of excluding others from attractive landscape became an end in itself. Enclosure had meant removing people from fields and woods. To create parks, landowners were quite ready to remove people from

..........

* If you're wondering about all that grass, you'd be right. Before the invention of lawnmowers it took a small army to keep it short. Scythes don't work very well on uneven ground so lumps, bumps and molehills had to be removed. And it's easier when there's still dew on the grass, so the workforce had to be up at cock-crow, cutting and raking while everyone else was still in bed.
** He does have a surname (Lorrain), but he's always plain Claude.

their homes as well.' In other words, a great deal more than aesthetics was at stake. Sometimes entire villages were demolished to make way for rich men's improvements, which the Anglo-Irish writer, Oliver Goldsmith, denounced in his poem, 'The Deserted Village' (1770):

> The man of wealth and pride
> Takes up a space that many poor supplied;
> Space for his lake, his park's extended bounds,
> Space for his horses, equipage, and hounds.

The next twist was to make the Brownian vision more rugged: to rough it up a bit; to create a look that was more decline and fall, less pomp and circumstance. William Gilpin, artist, curate and teacher, was an early advocate of this trend, known as the picturesque, which is basically shabby chic *avant la lettre*.

A piece of classical architecture, he wrote in 'Essay on Prints', is obviously elegant (those lovely proportions, that pleasing symmetry), but if you put it in a picture, it looks too formal. 'Should we wish to give it picturesque beauty, we must use the mallet, instead of the chisel: we must beat down one half of it, deface the other, and throw the mutilated members around in heaps. In short, from a smooth building we must turn it into a rough ruin.' And what was fashionable in a landscape painting – roughness – duly became fashionable in landscape itself.

Back in *Arcadia*, Lady Croom isn't buying it. This is what she has to say to her garden designer (a riff on a real man called Humphry Repton; *the* big designer of this period), who's showing her before-and-after pictures suggesting how she might update her garden:

> Where there is the familiar pastoral refinement of an Englishman's garden [i.e. now old-school Brown], here is an eruption of gloomy forest and towering crag, of ruins where there was never a house, of water dashing against rocks where there was neither spring nor a stone I could throw the length of a cricket pitch. My hyacinth dell is become a haunt for hobgoblins, my Chinese bridge [...] is usurped by a fallen obelisk overgrow with briars—

Cutting-edge gardening, therefore, was now supposed to be Gothic-meets-Romantic, and the younger generation went mad for it. Jane Austen has a lot of fun at the expense of her heroine Catherine Morland who, tutored in the picturesque by her beau, arrives at Northanger Abbey hoping for *atmosphere*: groves of ancient oaks, the last beams of the dying sun playing on high windows, that sort of thing, only to find modern furniture, disappointingly pretty English china and a sad lack of cobwebs.

It turned out that Lady Croom had a point; the Gothic garden was a challenge. Nice to read about in novels; not so much to live in. The owners of Hawkstone Park in Shropshire had a good stab at it: dark and eerie caves, a tolerably conversant hermit, a rocky ledge above a 700-foot drop, but it only really worked because their land came with ready-made sandstone crags.

Unsurprisingly then, once the nineteenth century was underway, we see a shift to the very Victorian themes of order and progress, of technology and empire, whether manifested in huge advances in greenhouse design or a huge boom in plant collecting – which saw callow young under-gardeners dispatched to far-flung imperial outposts, charged with bringing back 'exotic' specimens.

The spirit of the age also lent itself to a return to formality. In Mrs Loudon's *The Lady's Country Companion* you can read blissfully clear instructions on how to arrange twelve geometric beds, each to be planted in succession with one thing and one thing only, making sure flowers do not spread and intermingle. Written as a series of letters to a young friend called Annie, you can feel the full force of the Victorian era reverberating down the decades: there is a *right and proper* way to do things. (You were supposed to practise more complex patterns on 'Berlin paper' to make sure you didn't screw up.) Luckily for the middle classes, who were keen to copy big-house fashions, this style of bedding, unlike ha-has and hermits, was possible to recreate on a small scale. And so, people dutifully planted out their white alyssums, their blue lobelias, their yellow marigolds, all in neat patterns, in orderly rows.

Nowadays, of course, this look is very much looked down upon, confined to roundabouts on the edge of town and the most un-hip of city parks. Because: revolution.

The new broom was William Robinson, an Irish gardener and journalist who poured disdain on the Victorian lack

of imagination: 'I saw the flower-gardener meanly trying to rival the tile or wall-paper man,' he wrote in *The English Flower Garden* (1896). As well as the indignities of bedding plants, he railed against fountains, vases and statues, balustrades, stucco and useless walls. Instead, he drew his inspiration from orchid-flecked meadows, from undercliffs 'untroubled by the plough', and if that sounds sort of familiar, it's because the style he ushered in – known as the *cottage garden* – is still very much with us today.

'Those who look at sea or sky or wood see beauty that no art can show,' Robinson declared, 'but among the things made by man nothing is prettier than an English cottage garden [...] They often teach lessons that "great" gardeners should learn, and are pretty from Violet and Snowdrop time till the Fuchsia bushes bloom nearly into winter.'

Cottage gardens (shut your eyes: little white gate, thatched roof, foxgloves, climbing roses) were once tended by the sorts of people Thomas Hardy called the backbone of village life, the carpenter, the blacksmith, the shoemaker, the shopkeeper, the seamstress, the curate, the mason. These people had been gardening, oblivious to fashion, for centuries, and so their gardens were full of old plants, old flowers, columbines and pinks, larkspur and wallflowers. Everything was native, wild, simple: the new buzzwords – and a rare example of taste travelling sharply *up* the socio-economic ladder.*

But the artless 'oh-me-and-my-little-cottage' look was, in fact, incredibly hard work, and Gertrude Jekyll** (the biggest turn-of-the-century designer) was very wry about how people failed to appreciate this. Here she is, walking

..........

* It's worth noting that the original cottage gardens were most common in Surrey, Kent and the south of England. It was, therefore, a localised style that got turned into *the* style.
** It's a long *e*. Not a short *e* as in Jekyll and Hyde.

an acquaintance, who wants in on this new fashion, around her garden:

> We were passing along my flower-border, just then in one of its best moods of summer beauty, and when its main occupants, three years planted, had come to their full strength, when, speaking of a large flower-border he had lately had made, he said, 'I told my fellow last autumn to get anything he liked, and yet it is perfectly wretched. It is not as if I wanted anything out of the way; I only want a lot of common things like that,' waving a hand airily at my precious border, while scarcely taking the trouble to look at it.

As Vita Sackville-West, herself the creator of the famous gardens at Sissinghurst, wrote about Jekyll's art: 'there is a kind of haphazard luxuriance, which of course comes neither by hap nor hazard at all'.

Up until now, garden design had tracked broader cultural and political movements, but when modernism swept across Europe it struggled to bring the garden on board. Christopher Tunnard, writes Alexandra Harris in *Romantic Moderns* (2010), was about as close as gardens got to a Le Corbusier; you could, she says, call his designs 'machines for relaxing in', since they were long on hard landscaping and interesting chairs, but rather short on actual plants and flowers. But once a garden becomes functional and sleek and universal, doesn't it stop being a garden?

Plus, once the National Trust started to take over big houses, they preserved the gardens, freezing them in time, rather than experimenting with radical redesigns. It would be a brave head gardener who bulldozed Jekyll's planting in favour of provocatively painted dead shrubs and meaningfully sculpted sand.

In fact, if anything, we now want to push the cottage garden even further: it may have been natural compared with Victorian geometry, but today it's not nearly natural enough. If the eighteenth-century trailblazers pushed the garden out into the wild, today we're inviting the wild back. Says Pam Lewis, whose book *Sticky Wicket: Gardening in Tune with Nature* (2007) details her move from painterly borders to cultivated chaos, 'I don't call it a garden.'

And, as we've seen before, it's about so much more than aesthetics. Not mowing, not dead-heading, not tidying up fallen trees, becomes a sort of creed, a moral imperative. Your lawn is short: you hate bees. Mine is a riot of dandelions: I love the bees and the bees love me! Is it because we've busted nature that we now long for wilderness? Or did we read too much post-apocalyptic fiction in the 1970s and 1980s? Or does a hands-off approach simply suit the Gen-X slacker down to the ground?

For the time being, an army of mothers-in-law sallies forth each winter, armed with secateurs, to prune the hydrangeas, but when they pass on to a better world, what then? The seedheads will droop and rot, the leaves will pile up, layer upon layer, every freakishly mild winter, a rhapsody of resignation, an offering to the climate gods.

# TEN COMMANDMENTS

I. There's no such thing as a low-maintenance garden. It's like a low-maintenance child. Or spouse. Doesn't exist.

II. Wait. Don't move in and *do things*. Wait – a year. If you're not patient enough to do that, you're not going to make much of a gardener.

III. Ask advice. Nobody wants to read the first draft of your novel, but they will poke around the first draft of your garden.

IV. If your neighbours try to give you a plant, be careful. It's probably a *thug* and will spread everywhere. And don't buy unusual plants. They're unusual for a reason.

V. Don't be seduced by photographs of the frosted stems of last summer's herbaceous border against a pale winter sky. Yours won't look like that. Yours will be a sad dead wet mush. Same with prairie planting. Looks wonderful in the summer. In the winter? Dead stalks.

VI. Ruthlessly remove anything that does not bring you joy. It won't look any better next year. And don't mourn dead plants. A corpse is an opportunity.

VII. It's easier to do smart gardening on acid soil. You can grow rhododendrons and camellias. Your hydrangeas will be blue. Your magnolias will thrive.

VIII. A truly great gardener can break all the rules. Until then, no pampas grass, no heathers, no dwarf conifers and no stag's horn sumach.

IX. Whoever you are, a monkey puzzle will always be a brave statement,

X. Water when it's raining.

# GOOD FENCES MAKE GOOD NEIGHBOURS: THE HA-HA

If you're an eighteenth-century gent, standing in front of your house, looking out over your lawn and parkland, you don't want your vibe ruined by a barrier, be it a hedge, a hurdle or a drystone wall. But you need something, because you've got cows grazing down in the park, and you don't want them wandering up into the garden and crapping on the immaculate grass. And you can't just get rid of them because a) they're part of the vibe which you've spent a dashed fortune on and b) without cows your parkland will revert to scrub.

**Solution.** Build a ha-ha.

**Method.** Decide where garden becomes park. Dig a vertical drop, about 4 feet high, on the garden side. Brace it with bricks or stone. Dig a sloping bank on the parkland side; sloping so the cows don't fall in, break their legs and die. You now have what's basically a very posh ditch.

# FROM *SENSE AND SENSIBILITY*

by Jane Austen

Edward returned to them with fresh admiration of the surrounding country; in his walk to the village, he had seen many parts of the valley to advantage; and the village itself, in a much higher situation than the cottage, afforded a general view of the whole, which had exceedingly pleased him. This was a subject which ensured Marianne's attention, and she was beginning to describe her own admiration of these scenes, and to question him more minutely on the objects that had particularly struck him, when Edward interrupted her by saying, 'You must not enquire too far, Marianne: remember I have no knowledge in the picturesque, and I shall offend you by my ignorance and want of taste if we come to particulars. I shall call hills steep, which ought to be bold; surfaces strange and uncouth, which ought to be irregular and rugged; and distant objects out of sight, which ought only to be indistinct through the soft medium of a hazy atmosphere. You must be satisfied with such admiration as I can honestly give. I call it a very fine country, – the hills are steep, the woods seem full of fine timber, and the valley looks comfortable and snug, – with rich meadows and several neat farm houses scattered here and there. It exactly answers my idea of a fine country, because it unites beauty with utility – and I dare say it is a picturesque one too, because you admire it; I can easily believe it to be full of rocks and promontories, grey moss and brush wood, but these are all lost on me. I know nothing of the picturesque.'

'I am afraid it is but too true,' said Marianne; 'but why should you boast of it?'

'I suspect,' said Elinor, 'that to avoid one kind of affectation, Edward here falls into another. Because he believes many people pretend to more admiration of the beauties of nature than they really feel, and is disgusted with such pretensions, he affects greater indifference and less discrimination in viewing them himself than he possesses. He is fastidious and will have an affectation of his own.'

'It is very true,' said Marianne, 'that admiration of landscape scenery is become a mere jargon. Every body pretends to feel and tries to describe with the taste and elegance of him who first defined what picturesque beauty was. I detest jargon of every kind, and sometimes I have kept my feelings to myself, because I could find no language to describe them in but what was worn and hackneyed out of all sense and meaning.'

'I am convinced,' said Edward, 'that you really feel all the delight in a fine prospect which you profess to feel. But, in return, your sister must allow me to feel no more than I profess. I like a fine prospect, but not on picturesque principles. I do not like crooked, twisted, blasted trees. I admire them much more if they are tall, straight, and flourishing. I do not like ruined, tattered cottages. I am not fond of nettles or thistles, or heath blossoms. I have more pleasure in a snug farm-house than a watch-tower, – and a troop of tidy, happy villages please me better than the finest banditti in the world.'

Marianne looked with amazement at Edward, with compassion at her sister. Elinor only laughed.

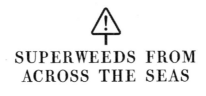

# SUPERWEEDS FROM
# ACROSS THE SEAS

Japanese Knotweed (*Fallopia japonica*) is perhaps Britain's most notorious alien, literally jeopardising its foundations. Its questing roots specialise in exploiting any cracks or weaknesses in a building, giving mortgage lenders the willies. A herbaceous perennial, it retreats during the winter, only to erupt every spring, growing 10 cm a day, crowding out everything in its path. Knotweed first arrived in the nineteenth century, courtesy of the plant-hunter Philipp von Siebold, who sent a sample to Kew. Back then, people thought the flowers were pretty.

*Rhododendron ponticum,* mostly from the Iberian peninsula, has spread extensively in the wild, covering spring hillsides in a purple haze. It was originally used as a rootstock for more select rhododendrons, which then died, allowing the original to proliferate. Pointing and saying *oooh pretty* is one of the most townie things a person can do. It's not pretty. It's a nightmare. Once it takes hold, it suppresses all other species, as well as playing host to two pathogens, *Phytophthora ramorum* and *Phytophthora kernoviae,* both of which can cause terrible tree damage. Clearing *ponticum*, which somehow always manages to take hold in really impractical places, costs a fortune, and you have to keep on spraying the stumps or it just grows back.

**Himalayan balsam** (*Impatiens glandulifera*) arrived shortly after knotweed, escaped from its garden home, and now (thanks to its explosive seed pods) romps along ditches and riverbanks, outgrowing everything in its path.

It's an annual, so it dies in the winter, leaving the banks bare, which makes them much more likely to wash away in heavy rain. One laborious solution is to cut off its stems before they set seed, but access can be a problem. People are experimenting with introducing the rust diseases which control it naturally in its mountain homeland. (Will this end well, we ask?)

**Giant hogweed** (*Heracleum mantegazzianum*) is a monster. An umbellifer, i.e. kin to parsley, parsnip, carrot, cumin and coriander, but *pure evil*. Its sap burns. Even brushing against it with a bare arm is enough.

**But, lest we forget, it's a two-way street.** British ships took our plants and pests *there*, long before their plants and pests came *here*. Bracken, chickweed, knotgrass, curled dock, stinging nettles, bindweed, those familiar British natives now crop up on five other continents. In fact, most international weeds are European – make of that what you will.

## OF MOLES AND MOLE-MEN

*But what makes a mole fight death?*
William Horwood, *Duncton Wood* (1980)

The old sympathetic magic says the closer we work with an animal, the more akin to it we become, gifting us such archetypes as the creamy milkmaid, the stolid plough-man, the ferrety ferreter, an affinity that runs especially strongly between the solitary, shy mole and the shy, solitary mole-catcher.

One of the lonelier figures that haunts the rural landscape, the mole-catcher might seem a fitting match for amiable Moley, so meek, so mild. And yet in reality the mole is no nervy herbivore, and the mole-man deals in death as surely as any of the countryside's flashier hunters. Mary Russell Mitford, the one who was so very keen on her poacher, cautions us that her local mole-man had 'the stalk of a ghost':

> The little round traps which hang behind him over one shoulder, as well as the strings of dead moles which embellish the other, are incrusted with dirt like a tombstone, and the staff which he plunges into the little hillocks by which he traces the course of his small quarry, returns a hollow sound as if tapping on the lid of a coffin.

Perhaps unsurprisingly, her mole-catcher moonlighted as helper to the village sexton, and even today tales proliferate of grieving families startled by moles beetling over coffins in pursuit of the worms which we must assume live long and prosper in our graveyards.

A mole, you understand, needs to eat six fat worms a day, at least half its body weight, and it is this appetite which sets it on a collision course with humanity. When the mole digs tunnels, its network of underground worm-traps, it shovels earth above the surface, fly-tipping our lawns and fields, our cricket greens and churchyards, creating the contested intersection between man and mole – the mole-hill.

Farmers have two reasons to kill moles. 1) Soil from mole-hills can get into silage. That soil can contain either listeria or clostridium. Those bacteria can kill sheep, cattle or horses. 2) Soil from mole-hills ruins grass. Sheep, cattle or horses could – at a pinch? – go hungry.

Non-farmers have a different reason. People call the mole-catcher when moles destroy their lawns, although usually, writes Marc Hamer, author, gardener, one-time mole-man, 'they don't want to see the dead enemy, just the lawn, the bright shiny lawn, just grass all neat and flat and stripy, under control, safe, forever'.

For a long stretch of the last century, the mole-catcher's skills were redundant, because to keep your lawn neat, all you needed to do was drop a few worms laced with strychnine into a tunnel and assume the mole would gorge, convulse, asphyxiate and die. Strychnine was banned in 2006, and although professionals can still gas moles with something called phosphine, it's so toxic that you can't use it near homes, children or pets. And so a new generation of mole-men and -women are learning the old tricks, with no small degree of pride. Says the British Mole Catchers Register: 'To call a mole catcher a pest controller is akin to labelling a traditional thatcher a roofing contractor.'

The mole fashions its traps out of earth. Worms fall into the tunnels and thrash around, alerting the vigilant mole. The mole-catcher buys his traps, grateful he no longer has to fiddle about with horse hair and willow. (Live traps don't work. Released above ground, far from its worm larder, the 'freed' mole faces almost certain death.) Moles patrol their tunnels. The mole-catcher patrols his traps, marked with flags, sticks, stones, or dots on his smartphone's camera. Moles eat the worms. 'With fastidious care, a mole will squeeze the gritty gut contents out of a worm before eating it, holding the head in its sharp teeth and pulling the slimy body through its nails,' writes Rob Atkinson, author of the authoritative *Moles* (2013). Nobody, so far as we can judge, has ever made a convincing case for eating any part of a mole – although once upon a time a dandy might sport a moleskin waistcoat.

But even though our tepid winters should be boom-time for the mole population (a severe frost kills off worms), no-one's pretending mole-catching is an easy living, if indeed it ever was. The poet John Clare wrote about a mole-catcher supplementing his income by selling mushrooms and leeches, eggs and eels, and it's not so very different today. A mole-man of our acquaintance, his forearms as strong as his quarry's thanks to eight-egg omelettes, hunts moles across three counties, a patch the mole-men of old could only have dreamt of. But even he needs other strings to his bow.

He tackles hornets' nests in village attics. *Hornets are happy drunks when they're away from their nests. 'Alright, mate?' Close to, they're angry. 'Oi, what you looking at?'* He shoots rats in chicken-sheds. *Best problem-solvers going, rats.* He deals with rabbits, discreetly. *It's not a good look having bleeding animals staggering around a National Trust property.* He eliminates mink. *Nobody likes mink.* He rears orphaned crows. *'Mate,' the bloke said, 'your pocket's cheeping.'* His wife is vegetarian. *Works in an animal shelter.*

People have long been fascinated by those amongst us who can 'read' wild animals, although sometimes we're tempted to see them as separate from us. Workaday farmers, women at their weeding, all of them marvel at John's Clare mole-man, considering him a walking almanack. Mary Russell Mitford's mole-catcher is 'the wise man of the village, the oracle of the village-inn, he foresees the weather, charms away agues, tells fortunes by the stars'. Marc Hamer has lived rough, outside settled life, closer to nature, further from people. Says our mole-man, 'If you work a lot alone, you can become socially awkward. You miss cues.'

Let's take a closer look at those moles. Improvise a probe to find a tunnel leading away from a fresh hill. Use a fat knife or a thin trowel to open up the tunnel's roof. Admire the neatness, the littleness, the intricacy – the paw marks along the edges. And then, if you decide you must kill it, why not do it yourself?

A set of decent traps needn't cost more than £30, and they're yours for life. A mole-catcher, on the other hand, might charge you £50 a mole, and let's be realistic, no decent mole-tunnel will stay empty for long. Prime your trap. Lower it into the tunnel. Replace the soil to block out any light. Moles aren't stupid and will back-fill a tunnel if they sense anything suspicious. Mark your trap and return to it often. If you catch a mole, have a good look at it. It will probably be smaller than you expected, *cuter*, its giant paws appealingly out of proportion.

Once upon a time, a mole-catcher would have hung his dead moles on a boundary fence, 'sweeing in their chains' in Clare's unforgettable phrase, rudimentary but effective advertising. But all you need do is drop it into a hedgerow, perhaps returning with a shovel to scoop up the soil of the mole-hill. It has a fine tilth, friable, aerated, clump-free, like damp old flour shaken through a sieve. It'll do very nicely on your raised beds.

# THE KITCHEN GARDEN

There are many sound reasons to grow your own fruit and veg. Save money. Save the planet. Save your gut biome, save face, save your soul. But it's more motivating by far if you just really, *really* enjoying eating them.

Forget about micronutrients, about food miles, about supermarket waste. Forget about *Good Life*-ery and the relentless pickling of runner beans. Dream instead of larding your harvest, however large or small, with butter and oil, with salt, sugar and spice, tucking it under pastry, dousing it with cream – kitchen gardening should waltz hand-in-glove with greed.*

Let's assume it's January 1st. Let's assume it has been a dry (optimistic), but not excessively cold (more realistic) Christmas. Let's get started. You don't need much. A seed catalogue. A big spade. A little fork.

## DIG RAISED BEDS

These not only look nice, but after the initial burst of hard work they're easy to look after. (Plus, it's the best sort of hard work. Only plunging into an icy brook feels more new-year-new-you than leaning on a spade chatting to a robin.) The soil will now drain better. Both weeding and harvesting will be easier. And raised beds are also, let's not forget, very fashionable.

Aim for rows a yard across with a foot-wide path in between. Some people border their beds with interlocking planks, which is of course lovely but in no way essential.

Next, round up all the cardboard from your Christmas shopping and lay it flat over the beds, a DIY weed suppressant. Stick some compost on top. Your soil now has five long lovely wet months to ready itself.

## SOW UNDER COVER. PLANT OUT

Don't get over-excited. Don't skip round your garden scattering seed willy-nilly on the first sunny day after Easter.

..........

* We have, thank goodness, moved on from Mrs Beeton: 'The time vegetables take to boil depends on their age. Young vegetables with tender fibres will, as a rule, cook in about 20 minutes, whereas those fully matured, and consequently containing a relatively larger amount of fibrous substance, will average no less than 40 minutes.'

Instead, hold off until the ground is so warm that you would happily sit upon it bare-bottomed. This will be later than you think.

If you want to get ahead, you can start planting stuff in pots from February onwards, following the instructions on your seed packets. Apart from root vegetables, which don't like being moved, most things can be started off in the warmth of your windowsill / conservatory / improvised polytunnel / greenhouse. Keep them indoors until the risk of night frosts is past, probably from mid-May onwards. If your seedlings grow fast, you might have to pot them on, i.e. transfer them from little pots to medium ones, before you plant them out in your beds.

## STARTER FRUIT AND VEG

**Chard, especially Bright Lights.** Prolific. Grows back rampantly after each cutting. A 2-for-1 deal because you can fry the stems as you would celery. Very friendly with eggs. Slugs snack on the droopier leaves if you don't keep them tidy.

**Kale, especially Nero di Toscana.** Sturdy plants soldier on well into winter, doggedly sprouting new leaves however many batches of kale crisps (oil, soy sauce, miso paste, maple syrup, sesame seeds, hot oven) you make. Prone to white-fly. Give the plant a good kick and watch the flies shimmy into the air like a snow globe before you scissor your leaves. Wise to net against pigeons.

**Herbs.** Thyme, rosemary, sage. Easy all year round. Chives. Amazing in the spring. Mint. Beware: it's highly ambitious and will try to take over your garden. Parsley. Sow in succession over the summer. Coriander. Bolts in the summer. Better sown under cover in the winter to eat with dhal when all your fresh veg has run out. Basil. Split a supermarket pot across four of your own and keep indoors.

**Beans, green.** Grow dwarf French beans (the skinny ones that are imported from Kenya out of season) rather than trying to climb anything up bamboo. Need assiduous watering when they're new in the ground, but once established, they're very self-reliant. Pick well and often to generate more pods. Blanch and freeze any surplus.

**Sweetcorn.** Can be grown like scarecrows amongst other crops with a lower profile. Resist peeking until the cobs feel really firm. Tickle unwary members of your household with the hairy bits under the husk. Corn on the cob is all very well, but try corn off the cob too. Mix with as much salt and spice as you can stand and fry in hot oil until carbonised.

**Courgettes, especially Romanesco.** These ribbed beauties are so delicious you won't find yourself trying to palm them off on all and sundry. They keep for days on end. Oil, salt, griddle pan. Hazelnuts, basil, feta. (Don't get suckered in by the pretty yellow ones. Flaccid and watery.)

**Autumn raspberries.** The summer ones land when you're already busy and cheerful, whereas these leaven the good-times-are-over, back-to-school season. Shaggy nodding bushes. No need to fiddle around tying in new growth. Robust as a weed. Wasps will nibble their noses, but there's normally enough to go round. Hack down to the ground when the season's over.

INTERMEDIATE FRUIT AND VEG
**Leeks.** Shop leeks are relatively expensive, so a satisfying monetary win. You can fit a lot into a small space. You can stagger your planting so you have leeks all through the winter. Leekaroni cheese, leek rarebit, leekarbonara, leek samosas. Long live the leek.

**Squash.** Triffids. Once the fruits have set, cut away the suckers that are trying to take over your veg patch. You have to play chicken with the first frost. Leave on the vine as long as possible to ripen, but don't get busted by a cold snap. Harvest en masse and store. When roast squash palls, try grating and grilling with Lebanese seven spice.

**Beans, borlotti.** England is relatively behindhand in growing its own protein, but borlotti beans are a good option. They grow like green beans, but you eat the seeds rather than the pods. Fresh, they're delicious with anything Italian. Dry, they look smug and rustic in Kilner jars in your kitchen. Great with your squash in veggie chillis.

**Purple-sprouting broccoli.** Bide your time. Sow in pots in May and plant out in July so you can crop in the late winter or early spring. Net against pigeons. Roast with the leaves still on. Or go Italian again: chop and fry; add wine, stock, parmesan, pasta, cheese; cook until the pasta's done; add parsley, lemon, more cheese.

**Redcurrants.** Genuinely liking redcurrants is a marker of a mature palate. Too delicate for most supermarkets, they grow cheerfully and prettily against even north-facing walls. They freeze extremely well, delivering pops of tartness throughout the winter. Good with tahini, better with lemon shortbread, best of all with white chocolate ice-cream. Or all three.

**Apples.** Watching spring embroider the sleeves of an apple tree in pink and white is one of April's hottest tickets. Your fruit will set in May. Once the June drop (when the tree sheds surplus fruit) is in full swing, give nature a helping hand, thinning the apples until there's only one per twig, otherwise they'll grow small and measly. You also need to prune back new growth to stop your tree turning gangly and unproductive. Locate each new shoot, count along two buds, sever.

Different varieties are ready for harvest from September to November. Watch for the first windfalls and then apply the lift-and-twist test. If ripe, the apple will succumb to a gentle touch. If you have to tug, stop and wait a few days. Be gentle. Bruised apples do not keep. Store somewhere dark and cool, adhering to the advice in Maggie O'Farrell's beguiling novel *Hamnet* (2020) for absolute perfection: 'The fruit has been placed with care, just so: the woody stem down and the star of the calyx up. The skin mustn't touch that of its neighbour. They must sit like this, lightly held by the wooden groove, a finger width from each other, over the winter or they will spoil.'

### ADVANCED FRUIT AND VEG

**Tomatoes.** Freshly picked, sun-warmed home-grown tomatoes do taste really special but beware ... you have to be prepared to do a lot of staking, tying in, pinching out and watering. If you take long summer holidays, and don't have either an expensive watering system or kindly neighbours, forget it.

**Lettuces.** Success depends on succession: if you want a regular supply you have to be prepared to sow every two or three weeks. Lettuces are not patient. They are raring to set seed and will bolt the moment your back is turned.

**Padron peppers.** Mini green tapas peppers. Grow under cover or somewhere very sunny and sheltered. One in ten is killer hot and the rest are merely tasty. Fry them until they're blistered and eat with salt and pink wine. Perfect for presents and/or showing off.

**Beans, broad.** 'Broad beans are heartbreakers; blackfly will devour them more quickly than I can, which is no small feat,' writes Charlotte Mendelson, the author of the very lovely *Rhapsody in Green* (2016).

Blackfly are indubitably the most sinister of garden pests because they are *farmed* by ants, who love their sticky honeydew (aka poo). Ants go so far as to carry baby blackfly to new plants to found new blackfly colonies, which makes you feel you're perpetuating a dystopian horrorverse rather than being wholesomely rural. And yet broad beans, picked ever so tiny, are worth fighting for.

Step one is to give your beans a headstart by overwintering them. Plant them on the first nice day after Bonfire Night and you should see green shoots by Boxing Day. Step two is to water them fanatically come spring. Blackfly and their ant masters are drawn to weakness. Step three is to visit them daily, pinching away fly-infested tips.

You can of course spray blackfly into submission, but at the risk of turning your nice plot into a bio-hazard exclusion zone. At the end of the day, if your broad beans fail, you're not going to starve.

**Asparagus.** The downside of asparagus is that it takes up a bed which can't ever be used for anything else. The upside is ... asparagus, arriving exactly when you thought winter would never end. Roast or griddle rather than steam, and make like Robert Louis Stevenson: 'And I, being provided thus/ Shall, with superb asparagus,/ A book, a taper, and a cup/ Of country wine, divinely sup.'

You can enjoy your asparagus for six happy weeks, but then you must let it grow out and recuperate, turning into an enormous bushy forest which is heaven for bees, cats and toddlers. Cut the forest down in autumn (great ballast for your compost heap) and tuck the bed in for winter with wood-chips and a layer of salt to keep weeds at bay.

Asparagus is preyed upon by its own special beetle, very pretty and very rapacious. We advise ambush and hand-to-hand combat. Creep up on your asparagus, soft-foot or the beetle will scarper, wearing gloves unless you're very butch, and squish them.

**Figs.** Braving an ebullience of wasps gorging on figs is a great gardening adrenaline rush, but the thrill of fear makes the eating all the sweeter. If you're starting from scratch you need a hot wall and patience. Once you have a fig tree established you'll never move house.

**Mulberries.** Hairy bloated raspberries. If you plant a tree, it'll be ages until it fruits. If it does fruit, the birds might get the lot. And if they don't, harvesting is hard work. But they taste extraordinary, fat and sweet and winey and intense.

### EXERCISE CAUTION

**Carrots, onions, potatoes.** A cost-benefit analysis says these offer poor returns, unless you have acres of space.

**Cauliflower.** Delicious, but sulky. If you manage to coax them to maturity, they do have a tendency to arrive all at once. And slugs *love* them. Drop the heads in water to force the slugs to abandon ship; up to you whether to save them or let them drown.

**Peas.** Over-rated. Stevenson, evidently expert in more than the life piratical, is right when he says, 'the bean/ That gathered innocent and green/ Outsavours the belauded pea'. Toss a pack of Birds Eye petit pois in your freezer and have done.

**Spinach.** Another committed bolter. People will try to recommend perpetual spinach instead, but don't be fooled. It's not spinach. It's chard pretending to be spinach. (Although it does make a decent base for eggs Florentine.)

**Cabbage.** Roast cabbage and sauerkraut are both super-modish and yet ... and yet ...

**Beans, runner.** Skip, unless you're after the Longest Bean rosette at the village show. They do have beautiful red flowers and they do look lovely growing up their wigwams, but you have to string them after you pick them and they taste only OK. The mature beans, on the other hand, are the most beguiling pink colour. Makes you realise why Jack handed over his cow.*

## NEXT STOP: THE VILLAGE SHOW

It will take place in the village hall. There will be tea. There will be games and jumble. If there isn't a bottle stall something is seriously awry. But the showing and judging of flowers, of fruit and vegetables, of jams and jellies, that is its *raison d'être*.

Normally, growing your own **fruit and veg** means you can embrace the knobbly, the wonky, the manky, the skanky, but the show demands perfection.

No green shoulders on your **carrots**. No lumps and bumps. Tie them up with raffia.

No eyes on your **potatoes**.

Sit your **onions** upright. Fold the tops over and tie with raffia.**

You're after a straight barrel on your **leeks**, and a base that is neither swollen nor bulbous.***

Remember, you will also be judged on the *snap* of your **peas and beans**.

Keep the tap-root on your **parsnips**.

Peel back the husk of your **sweetcorn** and tuck it neatly under itself to show off the ear.

A small big **tomato** is not a cherry tomato.

..........

* The desirability of the runner bean caused our only serious creative difference. Jonny loves them, but I was the last one to see the proofs of this book so the runner bean is where it belongs *mwa-HA-haaaaaaa*.
** We nailed First Prize, Onions, 2021 *sans* raffia. But our onions were, frankly, flipping ginormous.
*** We overwinter our leeks so never have any to show, which is lucky because we *love* a bulbous base.

A bloated courgette is not a **marrow.**

In the **any-other-vegetable** category, we find that the more phallic your entry, the greater your chance of success. (Try the squash cultivar called Tahiti melon.)

Don't irritate the judges with sub-standard entries in **every single category** just because you're chasing the points cup. It might backfire.

A hairdryer will open your **dahlias.** Wire the blooms in place overnight to encourage them to **peep up** at the judges (but make sure you de-wire before showing).

For **flower arrangements**, you're allowed to buy in. (That'd be cheating if you did it for the dahlias.)

**Jam** and **marmalade** is a mine-field. You'll get marked down for grubby jars, sticky jars, jars that have commercial markings on them, jars without cellophane, wonky labels, labels lacking a full date, for dullness, for scum, for sugar crystals, for mould, for runniness, for stickiness, for poor distribution of fruit.

**Don't get caught out.** In *Memoirs of a Fox-Hunting Man*, one villager is found to have bought vegetables in town: 'The judges suspected him, so they went to his garden in a pony trap and found that he has no glass – not even a cucumber frame.'

# Weeding

*I passed by the field of the sluggard, and by the vineyard of the man
lacking sense, and behold, it was completely overgrown with thistles; its
surface was covered with nettles, and its stone wall was broken down.*

Proverbs, 24:30–31

Thanks to the deep penetration of biblical metaphor-making, a weedy garden is more than a practical problem. A weedy garden makes you feel that a) you are a sinner and b) judgement is nigh. Here's how to maintain your serenity in the teeth of centuries of cultural opprobrium.

1. You cannot win. You must accept their existence as you accept all the blots on your life. Your lawn will sprout mole-hills. Your roof will spring leaks. Your dog will try to eat the neighbour's spaniel. You will grow old and die. Weeds will grow.

2. Name them. Learn their ways. The tufty sprigs that spring up in April, airy as candy floss. The dastardly spikes that sacrifice their upper limbs to protect their intransigent roots. The innocent shape-shifter that camouflages itself midst your raspberries. The malevolent clover which fights its way through 6 inches of wood-chip.

3. Destroy them, knowing you can only win skirmishes, never the war itself. Never the present perfect tense, I *have* weeded. Always the continuous past, present or future, I *was* weeding, I *am* weeding, I *will be* weeding.

4. Embrace them. Weeding is an example of what the philosopher Kieran Setiya terms an *atelic* activity. No finishing line, no prizes, no *telos*. Drawing on Schopenhauer's observation that we swing between pain when we don't have what we want and boredom when we do, weeding allows us to *do* something which can never be *done*, a radical gift, freeing us from the pursuit of empty goals.

## The hungry gap

This isn't the bit of the day when you ache for a fourth meal, be that second breakfast or tea-and-cake or kids-tea-leftovers. No, it's the time of year when, according to John Seymour, 'people used to go down like flies from scurvy, and become like skin and bone'. Perhaps confusingly, it arrives with the daffodils.

You've eaten your roots, emptied your clamps, and everyone's so sick of roast squash somebody's thrown the last two in a ditch. Your potatoes have grown weird eyes and your apples are pap. The chard you coaxed through winter is as appetising as a pair of laddered tights and your last four leeks have bolted.

But it's still weeks until the wild garlic, until the radishes and rocket you've planted undercover, until the asparagus and the first baby broad beans.

The hungry gap, then, is why pickling (and the freezer; your friend at harvest time) was invented. (Not to mention the supermarket.)

# THE DESCENT OF VEG; OR WHAT DOES F1 ACTUALLY MEAN?

When you're browsing fruit and veg seed packets, the first thing you'll notice is that an awful lot of them are marked: F1. Squished inside that terse little tag is the history of how we improve on evolution, how we take a God-given plant and bend it to our will.

You start with one wild species, say *Brassica oleracea*, or wild cabbage.

Some people really liked the leafy parts, so they kept the seed of the plants which grew the biggest leaves, replanting them year after year, until they got *kale*.

Some people liked it when the leaves were bunched up, so they kept the seed of the plants with the bunchiest leaves, replanting them year after year, until they got *cabbage*.

Some people really liked fat stems, so they kept the seed of the plants with the fattest stems, replanting them year after year, until they had *kohlrabi*.

Some people thought the flower heads were really tasty, so they kept the seeds of the ones with the floweriest heads, replanting them year after year until they got *broccoli*.

Some people thought there was something missing at Christmas, so they chose the Christmas-iest plants, replanting them year after year, until they had *Brussels sprouts*.

All those vegetables seem really different to us, but they all remain members of the same species. (Think Irish wolfhound vs French bulldog.)

You can play the same game with *Beta vulgaris*, or sea beat, which over thousands of years has become beetroot, sugar beet, chard and mangelwurzel. *Daucus carota* is a species of flowering plant of which only one sub-species is the carrot. We eat the edible seeds or unripe pods of *Phaseolus vulgaris* in the form of (to name but a few) the kidney bean, the haricot bean, the pinto bean and the French bean. Proto-maize had drab little ears, perhaps the size of your finger: compare that with today's big fat shiny yellow corn on the cob.

All this obviously happened very slowly over a very long period of time. But today, plant breeders can make better plants more quickly, more efficiently and more profitably, by developing first generation (or F1) hybrids.

You do this by controlling how plants interbreed or cross. By crossing selected plants with different but desirable features, you're aiming to produce child-plants with the best features of both parents. Perhaps you think yellow courgettes are pretty, but are disappointed by how pappy they are? Perhaps you dream of creating the SupaYellaCourgetta™ which will make your fortune? Here's how.

1. Choose the brightest yellowest courgette and the crunchiest tastiest courgette.
2. Inbreed each type for about ten generations, until they are 90 per cent homozygous (i.e. they have 90 per cent the same DNA) and possess a uniform phenotype (i.e. they always come out looking exactly the same). In human terms, you're making the courgettes mate only with their brothers and sisters. Don't think about it too hard.
3. Each inbred batch, as you can imagine, will now be really feeble.* But here comes the really clever bit: when you take one inbred line and cross it with another inbred line, the first generation is (unsurprisingly) uniform

..........

* Remember the Hapsburgs? Imperial inbreeding did for them.

and (surprisingly) vigorous. This is down to something called heterosis or hybrid vigour.

4. When you're crossing your two lines, you have to make sure that all the action is yellow-on-crunchy or crunchy-on-yellow, not yellow-on-yellow or crunchy-on-crunchy. That's called a self, and a self is no good. What you do, therefore, is castrate the yellows (or the crunchies) by removing all the male flowers. Either that, or you cross by hand, dabbing yellow's pollen on crunchy's pistil.

5. Victory. Your SupaYellaCourgetta™ is a triumph. You now wait a year, tapping your fingers Mr Burns-style, because if your customers want more of the same, they'll have to buy the seeds *from you*. They cannot save the seed because F2s, the next generation, do not breed true.

6. Not all plants will put up with this. Corn, sugar beet, spinach, broccoli and onions are amenable. Lettuce is very resistant. Beans and peas, no: they release their pollen before their flowers open which makes hand pollination too tricky and expensive.

What's the difference between F1 and genetically modified seeds? Simple. With F1, you're selecting for a yellow-allele, a yellow variant of a gene that already exists. If, however, you decide that the next big thing is going to be an Even-BettaPinkaCourgetta™, but you can't isolate a pink allele, and so instead you get some raspberry DNA and poke it (stop us if we're getting too technical) into a courgette, that would be genetic modification.

# FORAGING

........................

*A good hobby flatters its practitioners by making them feel skilful.*
*The best hobbies make them feel virtuous too.*
Richard Mabey, 'Healing force' (2005)

Foraging (aka gathering) was once the dull tails to hunting's shiny heads, but today it gets great press. Nobody's going to shake their fist in your face and call you a bloodthirsty, murdering ***t. You might hear the odd mutter of *middle-class*, but rise above it. Bask in the numinous glow of your inconvenience food. Let them eat Deliveroo.

## SOME GROUND RULES
If you're foraging, trespass is still trespass.

But the law is otherwise quite encouraging: 'A person who picks mushrooms growing wild on any land, or who picks flowers, fruit or foliage from a plant growing wild on any land, does not (although not in possession of the land) steal what he picks, unless he does it for reward or for sale or other commercial purpose.'

This means: 1) you can forage around footpaths and on common land, 2) even if you're trespassing your Tupperware of blackberries isn't going to be an aggravating factor. But it does also mean: 3) the flowers, fruit, foliage or fungus (the four Fs!) have got to be genuinely wild, otherwise it's stealing.

Some landowners, such as nature reserves, explicitly ban foraging altogether; others only ban it if you're intending to make money. And, technically, you can't forage on the vast tracts of land that were opened up by the Countryside and Rights of Way Act, which scuppers your embryonic whortleberry-jam empire right there.

Some plants are protected, wherever they're growing.

You can't uproot plants (as opposed to picking the four Fs) unless you're an authorised person, i.e. unless you have permission from the landowner.

And seriously, be careful with knives. To be legal, a knife needs to be really small, less than 3 inches, and foldable. If it locks open, it's not within the law. So, a kitchen knife, in theory, is a *bladed article*, and carrying one of those in public could get you in trouble. The answer? Pack a crap pen-knife, scissors and secateurs.

And for God's sake make sure you know what you're eating. You need either a friend who's done it before – or a proper foraging book. This is not a proper foraging book; John Wright's *The Forager's Calendar* (2019), on the other hand, is. Basically, don't get sick. Definitely don't die. Not on our watch. Please.

GREENS

The Balkans, Greece and points further east, are good at wrapping greens in pastry to make spanakopitas and böreks, which makes the excessively wholesome exquisitely palatable. Just gather what you can from our suggestions below, supplement with garden / supermarket stuff as needed, cook down, squeeeeeeeeze out all the water, add salt, pepper, herbs, lemon zest, eggs, cheese, smush together, enfold in pastry, scatter sesame and/or nigella seeds, bake.

**Wild garlic.** The sign that spring really is at hand. It's easy to find a patch in woodland. Just follow your nose. Once you've got it home, if you don't fancy börek, round up all the random nuts lurking in your cupboards. Blend wild garlic, nuts, olive oil, salt, pepper. It'll make that last squash taste a lot nicer.

**Chickweed.** A revelation. You get to weed and forage at the same time – and if that doesn't make you freaking high, you need to rebalance your dopamine levels.

**Nettle leaves.** You're after the babiest of the baby leaves. (We're less keen on this tidbit from Ralph Whitlock's *The Lost Village*: 'For hygienic reasons lambs had their tails docked a few days after birth, and the tails were regarded as a culinary delicacy – a spring-time treat much as peewit eggs or nettle-top soup'.)

**Dandelion.** We did try to blanch (or force) the leaves to make them less bitter by sticking a bucket over the top, but people kept on stealing the damn bucket.

**Watercress.** Wild watercress is the dog's whiskers. But you've got to run the gauntlet of a nasty fluke called *Fasciola hepatica*. We're not brave enough.

**Fennel.** We've never been able to find any in the wild, but it does make all those other greens taste a lot better, so we've planted some under our washing line where it and the mint grow like ninepins.

TREES AND FLOWERS

**Birch.** You can tap a silver birch when its sweet sap rises in the spring: you just stick the point of your knife into the trunk and wait. If the sap's rising, it'll trickle down your knife. You'll probably feel like you're making a tree cry, and go and buy a bag of caster sugar instead.

**Elder.** As a tree, elder doesn't get good press. Too scrubby, too edgy, too hedgy. Bad-smelling. Opportunistic. But elderflower cordial a) totally works and b) makes you feel like the GOD OF THE WOODS when you drink it. Just don't call it the Englishman's grape. That's delusional.

Pick 15 heads of elderflower. Remove creepy-crawlies. Tip 500 g caster sugar, 3 tbsp runny honey in a pan with a litre of water. Bring to boil, stir until sugar dissolved, remove from heat. Add zest and juice of two lemons. Add the elderflowers. Lid on and leave. A day later, strain and store in sterilised bottles. Kids mix it with water. You mix it with cheap fizz.

(You can totally make elderberry cordial out of the fruits later in the year, but not if you've picked all the flowers.)

**Primrose.** We've probably passed peak flowers on food, but these guys work if you're having a retro 2010s night, drinking kombucha out of a Kilner jar, playing with your fidget spinner, dabbing, etc.

**Lime.** Pick lime flowers, dry lime flowers, dunk lime flowers in boiling water. You now have lime-flower tea, or *tilleul*. It's French, so it won't date.

FRUIT

**Blackberries.** We'll assume you know how to pick blackberries, but don't eat them after September 29th (old Michaelmas day, the feast of the Archangel Michael) because that's when Satan comes and spits on them, because Michael cast him into hell.

Obviously eat them on their own, obviously in apple crumble, obviously smushed on to griddle cakes with clotted cream. Perhaps less obviously but nonetheless essentially with feta and tahini. The best thing, though, is this blackberry crumble cake. Basically, instead of sticking crumble on top of fruit, you stick crumble on top of cake. Devilishly good.

**Cake bottom:**
- 125 g butter, 250 g soft brown sugar, 2 eggs, 250 g plain flour
- 1 tsp baking powder, 1 tsp mixed spice, 1 tsp ground all-spice, good pinch salt, very good grind of pepper

- 200 g sour cream
- 300 g blackberries

**Crumble top:**
- 120 g brown sugar, 60 g plain flour, 60 g cold butter

**Method:**
Heat oven to 180°C. Grease a deep 22-cm cake tin.
Cream butter and sugar. Add eggs.
Sift dry ingredients.
Fold half of the dry mix into the wet mix. Fold in sour cream. Fold in rest of the dry mix.
Pour half the batter into tin. Scatter blackberries. Pour rest of batter on top.
Rub crumble ingredients together until breadcrumb-y. Scatter over top.
Bake for 50–60 minutes.

To drink with it, please can we recommend that three weeks before you make this cake (i.e. at the very start of the blackberry season) you also make blackberry whisky. Put 600g of blackberries in a large, sterilised Kilner jar. Add 300g of caster sugar and a bottle of cheap whisky. Seal, shake, store in a dark place, shaking again every couple of days. When you want to drink it, you can filter out the berries, or not, as you choose.

**Apples.** We don't mean scrumping, which is a fancy name for apple poaching. Nor do we mean crab apples. They're gross. We mean finding a tree with edible apples in the wild. Apples, you see, grow very happily from the seed of a tossed core but, because they are extreme heterozygotes, they don't breed true, i.e. the child tree will be nothing like the parent tree. That means it's a total lottery how tasty the fruit of any individual tree will be. You never know, you might get lucky and chance upon an ambrosial cultivar that's destined to bear your name down the ages.*

**Sloes.** Pick sloes. Freeze to split the skins. Stick in a bottle with a load of gin and sugar. Wait a few months. Strain. Drink.

**Cherries.** Good in puddings or in booze. They're a bit tart. If only you had some birch syrup.

**Whortleberry.** Chalky downs: wildflowers. Acid moors: whortleberries! Sparse, fiddly, basically a total bastard to pick. Immensely pleasing to eat. There are heroic people who make amazing whortleberry jam. We can only suggest you search online and order some the next time you need cheering up.

## NUTS

**Hazel.** You obviously don't gather nuts in May. You gather them in the autumn, especially after a hot climate-changed sort of summer, but unless you've shot all your squirrels there probably won't be any left.

**Sweet chestnuts.** Score a cross on them. Put them in a big metal basin on the fringes of your judicial bonfire. When the witch starts screaming, they're done. Peel. Enjoy in lieu of popcorn.

## MUSHROOMS

Mushrooms are the fruiting bodies of certain fungi. Most of the time, a fungus looks nothing like a mushroom: it looks like lots of threads called *hyphae*, which tangle up together into a web called *mycelium*. When some underground fungi are ready to reproduce (not all of them do it

..........

* How do you grow apples commercially, then? Good question. The answer is by *grafting*. Take a sturdy, generic apple tree root. Take a branch from your tasty new cultivar. Splice the branch on to the root and tape it up. Rather miraculously, a tree bearing the fruit you want will grow from there.

like this), they poke a mushroom up into the open air. Beneath the mushroom's cap are gills, and in the gills are spores, and these spores help the fungus reproduce. Or, you can go with a nice Baltic account (courtesy of Helen Macdonald): 'mushrooms were thought to be the fingers of the god of the dead bursting through the ground to feed the poor.'

We admit that we, like many British people, are scaredy-cats when it comes to fungus. We do, however, stretch to field mushrooms and parasol mushrooms, and you could too, although we'd strongly advise you to talk to a serious human being who knows their mushrooms, backed up by a serious mushroom book, before you even *think* about embarking on your mushroom journey.

**Field mushrooms.** Found in ... fields. They look exactly as you'd expect a mushroom to look: sensible shape, white cap, pink-to-brown gills.

The only trouble is that the younger ones can be mistaken for a death-cap (common) or a destroying-angel (rare), whose names are very much *not* false advertising. Eating just one will kill you. Things that should immediately scream danger: it's growing under a tree; it has properly white gills; the cap and rim are really smooth; there's a ring at the top of the stem; and (the biggie) there's a *volva*. This is the remains of the mushroom's veil, a bit like an amniotic sac, which the cap originally burst out of; it's hard to spot because it's often partially buried in the ground.

You could always start out by finding a death-cap, and then you'll know what to avoid. (Children, also, are much keener on looking for a mushroom that might kill them, rather than one they might be compelled to eat.) But if you find one, please don't eat it. Please don't even *pretend* to eat it. Deaths caps are really, really good at their job, and we don't want your agonising death on our consciences.

**Parasol mushrooms.** There are, in theory, poisonous mushrooms you could confuse these with, but only if you're really not paying attention.

They make an extraordinary base for a vegan chilli. Roast a kilo of them with a kilo of red onions until most of their liquid is gone. Whizz up a tube of tomato purée, a big jar of roasted peppers, a tbsp cumin, a tbsp coriander, a tbsp paprika, a tbsp cinnamon, two tsp chipotle paste, a head of peeled, crushed garlic, salt, pepper. Add to the vegetables, along with two tins of drained black beans. Turn the oven right down and roast for as long as you dare.

**Magic mushrooms.** These are obviously illegal, so we won't direct you towards books and/or websites and/or YouTube videos because you're not going to be picking them.

It was back in the 1950s that US researchers cottoned on to the psychoactive properties of a Central American mushroom called *Psilocybe mexicana*, of which the indigenous people were already well aware. It didn't take long for people in Britain to discover (or rediscover?) that a reliable version of the 'food of the gods', the liberty cap or *Psilocybe semilanceata*, already grew very happily here. Using magic mushrooms (drying, cooking, eating; brewing, drinking) was quickly criminalised, although possession of fresh mushrooms was fine as late as 2005.

Pyschonauts have been coming up with their own theories about the startling effects of magic mushrooms for decades ('I'll not forget the dancing lights, the rippling and the merriment, the halos and the melting trails that followed anything that moved'*), but it's only recently that scientists have pinned down how *psilocybin*, the active ingredient, actually works. Apparently, it reduces activity in our default mode network. If our thoughts resemble a pack of hounds, careering about willy-nilly, then the default mode network is the brain's whipper-in, keeping you on task, on track, not rioting off into the bushes. But if you take a carefully calibrated magic-mushroom derivative, as part of a carefully controlled research experiment, the default mode network is shown the door and your brain is off the leash.

This produces an effect very different to other Class As. Not mad dog (meth), cuddly dog (MDMA) or bad dog (coke), but a dog lying on its back, eye whites showing, tongue lolling, balls to the four winds. Research subjects report a mystical sense of interconnectedness, a loss of ego, a profound feeling of love, of peace, of joy, which can help people struggling with severe depression and intractable addiction achieve startling breakthroughs. Unfortunately, when mushrooms are taken by intemperate youth with a cocktail of booze and big feelings, the effects reported aren't always so positive.

This is how you spot magic mushrooms in the wild.

1. Moist and acid soil. Grassland or pasture, perhaps where sheep have been lightly grazing. Probably not parks or gardens. Definitely not woodland. Nor in wood-chips, dung or bare soil.

2. From August in higher, colder, rainier places. From September elsewhere. Until the first hard frosts.

3. Rarely all alone; but not tightly clumped.

4. Tall and thin stems. Often wonky and wiggly. Smooth not grainy.

..........

* A pre-enclosure farmer having a good time in Jim Crace's novel, *Harvest*.

5. Cap about the size of a thumbnail, normally taller than it is wide. Often with a little nipple on top, but don't rely on it; a double nipple is a positive sign; nipple often a slightly different colour from the rest of the cap.

6. Shiny, almost oily, caramel colour when wet; turns opaque and creamy-white when dry. Vertical gill-lines (not ridges or grooves) visible through the skin when wet; gill-lines only visible as a dark rim around the bottom edge when dry. Bottom edge tucks in slightly.

7. When wet, a jellyish membrane peels away from the cap.

8. The gills are dark brown and attach at the top of the stem; i.e. they slant diagonally upwards (not horizontally) from the rim.

If you ignore points 1–8, there are plenty of lookalikes which could do you an awful lot of damage, up to and including death. You might get over-excited about a deadly webcap (grows in woods), or a *Conocybe coprophila* (grows in dung) or a funeral bell / deadly skullcap / autumn skullcap / deadly galerina (many scary names for same species which grows on decaying conifers). But there's no risk of you poisoning yourself – is there? – because you're not going to be picking magic mushrooms in the first place, are you???

**Magic mushroom hunters.** Some are really easy to recognise, closely resembling the pictures in any good field guide. Hair dreadlocked or concealed beneath an interesting hat. Boots large or feet bare. Flapping coat. Eclectic dog. Smell of weed in the damp autumn air. But there is a sub-species that is harder to spot, and therefore all the more satisfying when you make a positive identification. The external markings (Finisterre jacket, merino beanie, cockapoo) will be distracting. The secret is to focus on the gait. Walk, stop, stoop, peer. Walk, stop, stoop, peer. You'll quickly get the hang of it.

# THE COLD EARTH SLEPT BELOW

by Percy Bysshe Shelley

The cold earth slept below;
  Above the cold sky shone;
    And all around,
    With a chilling sound,
From caves of ice and fields of snow
The breath of night like death did flow
    Beneath the sinking moon.

The wintry hedge was black;
  The green grass was not seen;
    The birds did rest
    On the bare thorn's breast,
Whose roots, beside the pathway track,
Had bound their folds o'er many a crack
    Which the frost had made between.

Thine eyes glow'd in the glare
  Of the moon's dying light;
    As a fen-fire's beam
    On a sluggish stream
Gleams dimly—so the moon shone there,
And it yellow'd the strings of thy tangled hair,
    That shook in the wind of night.

The moon made thy lips pale, beloved;
  The wind made thy bosom chill;
    The night did shed
    On thy dear head
Its frozen dew, and thou didst lie
Where the bitter breath of the naked sky
    Might visit thee at will.

# O COME ALL YE PAGANS

*we heard the bells chime but the fields was our church*
John Clare*

When we began this section, we thought we knew what we were going to tell you. We were going to explain how British folk customs are built on (rural, rooted, timeless) pagan traditions; how those traditions went underground during the (alien, unfamiliar, oppressive) heyday of Christianity; how maypoles and pumpkins are actually pagan artefacts, which have been hiding in plain sight for generations. It turns out, however, that we were *totally* wrong.**

We hadn't been long at our books before everything went topsy-turvy. There is, we discovered, a gulf between our popular understanding of folk imagery, folk celebrations and a more historical, more academic analysis. If you

..........

* A fragment from *John Clare's Autobiographical Writings* (1983), edited by Eric Robinson.
** The word *pagan* comes from the Latin *paganus*, which means nothing more or less than *of the countryside*, the religion of the woods and fields.

take a turn around Twitter, you can even find historians rolling their eyes at our collective naivety. Here are three of them (we've cut their @s – we don't want a pagan pile-on!), exasperated by the public's fondness for finding paganism under every rock and stone:

BuT tHe GrEeN mAn

But, BUT sheela na gig!!!!

but what about the witch-cult?!?

No, they say, the foliate heads you find in some churches *aren't* representations of an ancient nature spirit carved by wily pagans right under God's nose.

No, they say, the vulva-waving carvings of women *aren't* evidence of a secret cult of the Mother goddess.

No, they say, the witch-hunts had *nothing* to do with the suppression of an actual underground pagan religion.

No *no*.

But it is, perhaps, a little unfair for the professionals to tease the amateurs. Because this idea – call it the pagan underbelly – wasn't something the amateurs came up with all by themselves. On the contrary, the idea took seed amongst antiquarians in the nineteenth century, before being propagated with immense enthusiasm by professional (or at least semi-professional) folklorists until the latter half of the twentieth century, by which time serious scholarship caught up and set about hacking apart everything we thought we knew. But, by then, the pagan underbelly idea had been repeated so many times, in so many popular books and films, that it had burrowed deep into our cultural psyche – and we were in no rush to abandon it.

But how did the idea arise in the first place?

The academic Ronald Hutton (who is to pagans what Oliver Rackham is to trees, a master of detail and a generous guide) suggests a number of overlapping answers.

**Geology.** In the nineteenth century, we began to grasp the great age of the earth, and it became, by association, both plausible and pleasing to think of folk customs as cultural fossils, prehistoric bones poking up through civilisation's soil.

**God.** Early modern evangelical Protestants spent a lot of time condemning fun, noisy, messy communal customs, and what better way to ruin a custom's reputation than to call it godless. But just because joy-sucking Puritans said a maypole was heathen, didn't mean it actually was. Nevertheless, late-Victorian intellectuals were delighted to run with this idea, because it helped frame Christianity as just another silly primitive superstition, which was very appealing if you were keen to detach yourself from the established church.

**Grief.** Industrialisation, urbanisation and modernity scared people. Anchoring the fast-changing present in a distant past was strangely reassuring, especially for people who were ill at ease with modernity, but had no desire to hark back to a rich-man-in-his-castle quasi-feudalism. An attachment to a pagan past, therefore, met a young socialist's (otherwise slightly shameful) need for nostalgia, but in a politically acceptable way.

The upshot was an orgy of misattribution. Folklorists flocked to the countryside to forage for customs. As soon as they found one, they admired it, minutely described it, and then, on the flimsiest evidence, or on no evidence at all, ascribed an origin story. This would then become so widespread that the villagers themselves started to repeat these stories back to the next generation of researchers.

Subsequent academics might delve deeper, and discover that a supposedly ancient custom was actually Tudor or even Victorian, and was nothing to do with some amorphous pagan ritual and everything to do with a far more complex (and interesting) set of social and economic factors.

To see this in action, let's trace the evolution of the maypole, remembering that the same dynamic could apply, for example, to Morris dancing, sword dancing or Mummers' plays; the list is long. If you'd asked us about maypoles a couple of months ago, we'd probably have offered you something about *tree worship* and *fertility rites*, but the answer is a whole lot more nuanced. 'The impulse to celebrate the arrival of summer in Europe's northlands, by bringing home blooms and leaves, is probably ageless,' says Ronald Hutton in *The Stations of the Sun* (1996), but that's about as far as you can go.

Maypoles, it turns out, only appear in the historical record around 1350–1400, and then very much in English areas, not in Ireland or Scotland, i.e. they were a new custom, not something which survived from pre-Roman times. These original poles, it seems, were simply a handy focal point for a seasonal party, something to hang greenery and flowers on, a place to dance, to have fun – and as such they were inevitably banned by Oliver Cromwell. The political philosopher Thomas Hobbes, in *Leviathan*, written during the Civil War, claimed maypoles honoured Priapus, the Roman phallic god, but this, we stress, was based on zero evidence: he just didn't like parties. Maypoles returned with the Restoration of (party person) Charles II, only to fall out of fashion in the eighteenth century.

Our conception of the maypole, then, dates not to some pagan past, nor even to the medieval or early modern period, but to a self-conscious, elite-driven revival during the Victorian era. Its renewed popularity, explains Hutton, was a response to the emotional needs of the age, bound up with the politics of nostalgia.

Two hundred years ago, in the wake of the French Revolution and the Napoleonic Wars, with industrialisation kicking in and radical politics starting to simmer, British society – if you were a landowner – felt distinctly wobbly. In this context, maypoles were catnip to the gentry. The squire could invite the village to a wholesome party that promoted strong community ties, soundtracked by

Alfred Tennyson at his most sentimental: 'And I'm to be Queen o' the May, mother, I'm to be Queen o' the May.' And the ribbons? The interweaving dancing? That dates to a London stage show in 1836, but it looked so good that the practice swiftly spread to the provinces, all the better to prettify this orgy of high-Victorian paternalism.

But then along came Sir James Frazer, guru of the pagan underbelly movement, to tell us in *The Golden Bough* (1890) that:

> In spring or early summer or even on Midsummer Day, it was and still is in many parts of Europe the custom to go out to the woods, cut down a tree and bring it into the village, where it is set up amid general rejoicings [...] The intention of these customs is to bring home to the village, and to each house, the blessings which the tree-spirit has in its power to bestow.

He cites, approvingly, examples of British country people decorating their houses with greenery but, crucially, he didn't ask them why they did it; because he was such a grandmaster of comparative religion, he thought he knew (or rather, he *knew* he knew) better than they did. If he had asked them, they might have said something (to his mind) daft and rustic, like, 'Oh, we do it because it's pretty, because it's spring.' But Frazer would always have known the *real* reason: tree-spirits! 'Many collectors and commentators,' says Hutton, who's not sparing anyone's blushes, 'managed to combine a powerful affection for the countryside and rural life with a crushing condescension towards ordinary people who carried on that life.'

Nevertheless, that theory of Frazer's, and others like it, have seeped inexorably into our collective consciousness. But why on earth should 'pagans' get all the credit? When it comes to how we celebrate, how we commiserate, how we party, how we commune, we're actually far more nimble, far more imaginative than we might think.

This was very apparent during the Covid lockdowns, with brand-new rituals (clapping, purification), foods (banana bread, sourdough), heroes (Joe Wicks, key workers), villains (lockdown breakers, viz. Dominic Cummings, Matt Hancock) appearing in only a few short months. We've always been tweaking and updating our festivals to suit the time and place, to suit our changing needs.

In *England on Fire* (2022), Stephen Ellcock and Mat Osman's breath-taking visual journey through 'Albion's psychic landscape', the authors tell us that we should see our ability to be flexible, to be ready to change, to be happy to conjure up 'fresh mongrel traditions' as a mark of strength. 'All traditions were new once,' they write, 'no family is truly young. England will grind every story beneath the harrow, back into the soil, and let strange wild blooms burst forth.'

# Future folk

Let's play a fun game, and turn the clock forwards, instead of backwards, and see how this might work in the future.

It's Britain, 2400. Why, a researcher wonders, is it popular for pre-pubescent girls to wear shimmering sapphire dresses to mid-winter parties? Perhaps, she thinks, it's some ancient folk custom.

Next, this lucky researcher uncovers a cracked and grainy clip of girls in the early 2000s, wearing similar dresses, dancing in a village hall decorated with snowman balloons, singing a song of which only one line is audible: 'The cold never bothered me anyway.'

This, the researcher realises, is incontrovertible evidence that the late Elizabethans attempted to prevent the climate catastrophe which engulfed their civilisation by entreating the snow to return.

And if her academic rivals subsequently say, no, you've got it all wrong, it had dick all to do with that, it was just a performance of normative femininity at the peak of the consumer boom, nobody will want to listen to them. They'll just keep saying, isn't it really cool how they had this amazing folk ritual to save the polar bears?

# HOW TO GROW THE BIGGEST AND BEST AND SCARIEST PUMPKINS

..................................................................................

*Monsters ... We make them ourselves.*
Derek Walcott, *The Odyssey* (1993)

Select your pumpkin patch. You're going to have to slash and burn new ground or sacrifice something else. Pumpkins spreeeeeeeeeeeeead. For eight decent fruit, you need about 15 square metres. Dig a hole for each plant. Fill the hole with the rotted poo of a friendly herbivore. Mound the soil. Mark with a cane.

Put your feet up with the seed catalogue. Jack of All Trades is for the beginner. Dill's Atlantic Giant is for the ambitious. If you're new to veg, admire how pumpkin seeds do, in fact, look like pumpkin seeds. Who knew?

Sow in late April or early May, either indoors or in a greenhouse where the temperature doesn't drop below 16°C, about 2–3 inches deep, in ¼-litre pots. They should germinate pretty quickly. Once the roots are starting to poke out, pot them on into 1-litre pots.

Come the end of May, harden them off, i.e. move them outside to a sheltered spot, but bring them inside or cover them up if the nights are unseasonably cold.

It should be safe to plant them out by mid-June, but it's worth staking each plant with a small cane to stop them flailing around in gusty winds.

The plants develop long tendrils, and then the flowers will appear. The perfectionist will use a fine paintbrush to dust the female flowers (the ones with a mini-pumpkin at the base) with pollen from a freshly opened male flower.

The laid-back gardener will leave it to the birds and bees.

Once fruits are firmly set, hopefully around mid-July, select the best on each plant and cull the remainder. As the season progresses, prune the side shoots once they're a couple of metres long.

Water well in dry spells.

Pumpkins need to sit comfortably, with their stems perpendicular to the vine. They like a smart platform, too. An upturned seed tray should do – or a wooden pallet if you've got delusions of grandeur.*

Leave them on the vine until the skin has set hard, which more or less coincides with Halloween, which is *infinitely* more scary in the proper darkness of a village lane.

BOO!**

..........

* As we go to press, the British record is 1,205 kg: yes, more than a tonne. Basically, you'd need a forklift truck to shift it.
** Feel under absolutely no obligation to make pumpkin pie. Toss them on your compost heap once they've served their spooky purpose.

# STONES, STILL STANDING

..................................................................

*You may put a hundred questions to these rough-hewn giants as*
*they bend in grim contemplation of their fallen companions.*
Henry James, *Transatlantic Sketches* (1875)

We know next to nothing about the details of prehistoric
pagan rituals, and are frankly kidding ourselves if we think
we do, but that doesn't mean they didn't happen. 'The
history of paganism in Britain,' Tom Shippey, medieval-
ist (and Tolkien expert), reminds us, 'spanned more than
30,000 years, almost the whole time that humans have
inhabited these islands, bar a few state-enforced Christian
centuries, in the medieval and early modern periods.'

Walking through the countryside, therefore, you meet
any number of pagan relics: stone circles and henges,* long
barrows and burial chambers, man-made mounds and hill-
top forts, some world famous, signposted for miles around,
others tucked on out-of-the-way farms. We, for example,
love Cow Castle, an Iron-Age rampart on a triangle of
high land, up on Exmoor where two rivers meet, but wherever you live, wherever you like to visit, you can find your
own. In fact, if there's someone you're especially fond of,
track down for them a copy of Julian Cope's *The Modern
Antiquarian* (1998), an odyssey through megalithic Britain,
a beautiful labour of love.

..........

* When archaeologists needed a word for prehistoric earthworks, they
borrowed the word *henge* from Stonehenge. But Stonehenge isn't a henge and
henges aren't made of stone. (Aaargh.)

Despite this proliferation of sites, each with its own peculiarities, its own bone-dry datasets, its own shaggy legends, it is, perhaps inevitably, to Stonehenge that we return, again and again. And yet Stonehenge, which can appear so definitive, was in fact a relative latecomer. Nor is it the work of a single, singular lost culture, but the climax of centuries of work on the Wiltshire plains, which also included Silbury Hill, the Avebury stone circle and the West Kennet long barrow. Stonehenge is only one site in a vast Neolithic Mecca, and it was itself adapted and refined over 1,500 years – over dozens of generations.

But even as our technical knowledge of Stonehenge improves, we're still only groping towards an understanding of the people who created it. Who were they? Why did they build it? How did they think and feel? 'It is like some very ancient and corrupt text, of which one can decipher just enough to be sure it is very important, but never enough to establish exactly what it is saying,' writes the novelist John Fowles in *The Enigma of Stonehenge* (1980).

Instead, Stonehenge has long been a lithic screen on to which we've projected our anxieties and our ambitions, our preoccupations and our prejudices. Remember when Luke has to go into that spooky tunnel in *The Empire Strikes Back*? 'What's in there?' he asks Master Yoda. 'Only what you take with you,' comes the gnomic reply. Allow us, then, to share a thousand years of our subjectivity.

**Merlin did it.** Geoffrey of Monmouth's *The History of the Kings of Britain* was a runaway bestseller in twelfth-century Europe. He wrote about the founding of Britain by Brutus, Aeneas's great-grandson; his is the earliest version we have of King Lear; the first major retelling of the King Arthur myths is also his. So good was his book, in fact, that for centuries people took it as gospel, and it's still very readable today.

In the fifth century, according to Geoffrey, King Aurelius Ambrosius (Arthur's uncle) wanted to build a monument to commemorate the men who had been massacred by a Saxon warlord in a Dark Ages version of the Red Wedding episode in *Game of Thrones*. He told the best carpenters and stonemasons in the land to come up with something worthy, but they confessed they were stumped.

It then occurred to Aurelius to ask Merlin, who obviously knew exactly what was wanted: the Ring of Giants, a stone circle in Ireland. The king was keen and so Merlin, with the ease you'd expect from a seasoned wizard, dismantled them and shipped them back to Salisbury Plain where he arranged them perfectly, 'thus proving that his artistry was worth more than any brute strength'.

This story was the frontrunner for a surprisingly long time, and shows how desperate we were to give ourselves a really good back-story, a Matter of Britain to match anything the French might have to offer.

**The Romans did it.** Geoffrey's *History* connected Britain to the great classical civilisations of Greece and Rome. Inigo Jones, who introduced the principles of classical architecture to Britain in the seventeenth century (search for an image of St Paul's Church in Covent Garden), tried to achieve the same effect. He wrote reams of notes (collated and published after his death by his son-in-law) attempting to prove (despite all evidence to the contrary) that Stonehenge was a proud example of vintage Roman architecture on home soil.

**The druids did it, part one.** Inigo Jones was right about one thing: the skill involved in the construction of Stonehenge is obviously mind-blowing. The finely dressed stones. The cunning adaptation of woodwork techniques. The accuracy: the outer ring deviates from a mathematically true circle by less than 4 inches. It was all so amazing,

thought the antiquarian William Stukeley, that there was no way primitive woad-y Britons could have built it.

And so, in *A Temple Restor'd to the British Druids* (1740), he confected an extraordinary tale of philosopher-priests, contemporaries of Abraham who, he said, travelled here from the east, bringing with them a patriarchal religion, which was Christianity in all but name. He compares these British druids to the magi of the Persians, to the gymnosophists* of the Indians, to the hierophants** of the Egyptians, before straining his theorising even further to suggest that Britain was, in fact, God's chosen nation and the Church of England was, in fact, God's chosen church.

**The druids did it, part two.** Stukeley's notion had legs but, in general, the public preferred their druids to be more homespun: sickle-wielding Getafixes, rather than oriental Wise Men. The rise of Romanticism at the end of the eighteenth century helped cement a neo-druid revival along these lines, with both Williams Blake ('the druid's golden knife/ Rioted in human gore') and Wordsworth ('long-bearded teachers, with white wands/ Uplifted, pointing to the starry sky') very much on board.

..........

* Literally: *naked wise men*. The name given by the ancient Greeks to ascetic Indian philosophers.
** Literally: *holy-show*. The name given by the ancient Greeks to priests who could interpret sacred or arcane mysteries.

Edward Williams, born in 1747, went so far as to refashion himself as Iolo Morganwg, claiming that he was the last in a long line of Welsh bards-cum-druids. He wrote fake medieval Welsh poetry, created a secret druid society, invented a whole raft of druid ritual, and generally paved the way for bulwarks of the establishment (e.g. William Thackeray and Winston Churchill) to become members of the Ancient Order of Druids, which had its first meeting not on Salisbury Plain, but in Soho.

The crushing voice of science eventually confirmed that Stonehenge was built not two or three *hundred*, but two or three *thousand* years before the arrival of the Romans, which should have ended the connection between the monument and the druids who feature, albeit hazily, in classical sources. And yet this movement – which John Fowles, with characteristic asperity, calls 'the farce of white-robed cranks dressing up suburban Christianity in oak-leaves and mistletoe, the silly notions of blood-stained knives over the Slaughter Stone' – persists to this day.

**Aliens did it.** Once we grasped the amazing precision with which the stones line up at summer solstice sunrise and winter solstice sunset, some people couldn't believe Stonehenge was the work of regular human beings. Aliens, howsoever conceptualised, must have lent a helping hand.

In the 1960s and 1970s, boom-time for both space exploration and UFOs, the Earth mysteries and/or alternative archaeology movement started to build on the earlier (comparatively conservative) theory of ley-lines. Alfred Watkins, in the *Old Straight Track* (1925), had originally conceived of these as ancient pathways or sight-lines between significant mounds and beacons: numinous, perhaps, but not extra-terrestrial. His inheritors at the dawning of the Age of Aquarius argued that ley-lines were, in fact, energy corridors criss-crossing the world, which had once acted as navigation or landing lights for spaceships containing divine beings, who no longer wanted anything to do with us because we'd become so greedy and materialistic.

John Michell, the esotericist, wrote in his introduction to *The View Over Atlantis* (1969), which did much to popularise this line of thinking, that: 'The important discoveries about the past have been made not so much through the present refined techniques of treasure hunting and grave robbery, but through the intuition of those whose faith in poetry led them to a scientific truth.'

**The Bronze Age (misogynists) did it.** By the twentieth century, feminism had made a very welcome crash landing, with one of its wings attracted to the theory that matriarchy flourished during the Neolithic, before being toppled by toxic Bronze Age masculinity. It's possible to argue that a shift in burial customs, from communal graves to the celebration of high-status individuals, marked the replacement of peaceful farmers who worshipped a Mother goddess by quasi-Homeric pastoralists who worshipped a patriarchal pantheon.

The long years during which Stonehenge was built spans this population shift, encouraging Julian Cope (who is a post-punk musician as well as an impressive megalith researcher) to call Stonehenge a 'Bronze Age power statement'. He doesn't wish to deny its 'glorious cosmic achievement' or its 'brazen uniqueness', but he sees temple-building as part of a dangerous separation from Mother Earth, the starting point for our current sense of 'cultural dispossession and hopeless guilt'.

**Never mind who did it.** In *The Lark Ascending*, Richard King muses that to have taken part in the Stonehenge Free Festival in the 1980s, when space-rockers Hawkwind piped up the dawn, when the rising midsummer sun aligned with the Heel Stone, when shadowy druids performed their mysterious rituals, when you were coming up on LSD, was clearly one hell of an experience. 'The audience,' he writes, 'clearly believes a transmission is occurring between the stage and the standing stones, and whatever the form of this imperceptible exchange, it is one that draws its energy from an ancient source.'

Why ruin the fun by pointing out that solstice parties only date back to seventeenth-century midsummer fairs?

**The right tools and hard work did it.** Professional archaeologists tear their hair out when confronted by some elements of what – for them – is a lunatic fringe. However, while a purely empirical approach (dig, sift, sort, count, measure, etc.) obviously remains at the forefront of archaeology, the discipline now toys with *phenomenology*, which permits the researcher to use their own senses when considering a site; in other words it's no longer academically taboo to wonder how a prehistoric person might have felt watching the sun rise on midsummer's day.

**They did it, but what do we do now?** Stonehenge is a tourist attraction. As Jacquetta Hawkes was already lamenting in the 1950s: 'Cafés and chewing gum, car parks and conducted excursions, a sense of the hackneyed induced by postcards, calendars and cheap guide books has done more to damage Stonehenge than the plundering of some of its stones.' We made it, she says, and now we've destroyed it by handing it over to a heritage industry which deals in soft patriotism and the sentimental repackaging of the nation's past.

But thankfully, as it turns out, the patriotic package isn't all that neat. Precisely because, as we've seen, Stonehenge has meant so many things to so many people, it is a wonderfully bad conductor of nationalism: it is not a lightning rod. In fact, Ronald Hutton, in his inspiring conclusion to

*Pagan Britain* (2013), says this very profusion of interpretations of our past could help foster a Britain which *doesn't* define itself as one people, one culture, one nation. We could, he suggests, simply think of ourselves as a land, 'with historic and prehistoric resources which are open to those whose families have been here for fourteen thousand years and those whose families have been here for four'.

Simply – a land.

## CROP CIRCLES

*All that time the Martians must have been getting ready.*
H. G. Wells, *The War of the Worlds* (1898)

Since the devil first mowed a field in Hartford-fhire we've been trying to figure out what power, what force on or off earth could possibly have created the magical mystical mysterious phenomenon that is the crop circle. After a rash of them appeared in charismatic locations in the 1980s, with peak-circle coinciding with peak-rave, speculation reached a feverish pitch. Was it—?

*weather voooooortices*

electromagnetic fields

## experimental aircraft

U   F   O   s

LEY-L I  N  E          S

—or was it two blokes called Doug and Dave?

For in 1991, Doug Bower and Dave Chorley popped up to say it'd been them all along actually, and what's more they could prove it. True *croppies* refused to believe them; believers, after all, love to debunk the debunkers. But most people nodded sagely and said, there you go – a hoax, we'd always suspected as much.

But is hoax the right word?

There might be no sun god, but Stonehenge isn't a hoax. Yahweh might not be real, but the parish church isn't a con. You wouldn't barge into a Neolithic solstice ceremony, yelling *it's just a big ball of gas.* You wouldn't barge into a church, yelling *it's just stale rice paper and lousy wine.* We don't know what people felt about the sun 4,000 years ago, but we do know that for some people, holy communion is the body and blood of Christ. And we also know that crop circles, for other people, aren't just a fun story. They are evidence of other worlds, of other beings, in which it's possible to believe with the same enthusiasm and commitment as the village vicar (you'd hope) believes in God the Father, God the Son and God the Holy Ghost.

And if you show a believer footage of Doug, Dave & co.? Oh, they'll say, maybe those ones are fakes, but let us tell you about the *real* ones ...

Perhaps we can compromise, and think of crop circles as a form of land art, where the witnesses collaborate with the makers, willingly suspending their disbelief, just as they might in the theatre.* Justin Hopper, in his beguiling travelogue *The Old Weird Albion*, a journey through the South Downs on the trail of the 'everywhen', tries to honour people's faith that the visible world isn't the half of it. 'The stories people told, the lights they saw in the sky and the experiences they had in the field – those narratives were the artwork.' But that process, he says, relies on anonymity: a circle loses its power if people know it's man-made. No cerealogist gives credence to circles commissioned by Extinction Rebellion (brand synergy: 10/10), Shredded Wheat (7/10), QI quiz show (5/10), or Tesco Mobile (0/10).

## A BASIC HOW-TO GUIDE

**Location.** Think visibility. A field rising up from the road, or a natural amphitheatre in full view of the road, make perfect circle sites. And it obviously helps to choose a place with good existing energy. Chalk figures, yes. Ley-lines a bonus. A nice pub to wait in until it gets dark is another plus.

**Arrival.** Drive your stuff (a measuring tape, a plank with a rope attached to each end to form a loop, a garden roller) to your field. Better still, get somebody to drop you off: random cars look suspicious.

**Creation.** Sneak along a pre-existing path or tractor tramline to where the centre's going to be. It's not going to look very magical and mysterious if you leave an obvious trail where you've schlepped your stuff.

**Step 1.** Flatten your centre, but don't trample it willy-nilly. Make sure the crop all lies one way.

**Step 2.** Plant a stick in the middle of the centre (as if it

..........

* If you're an arable farmer in Wiltshire, you probably feel very differently. One farmer said each circle costs him a grand.

was the pin of a compass) and tie your tape to it. Or, if you've got a friend with you, get them to stand in the middle and hold the tape. Walk in a neat line to wherever you want the perimeter to be. Keeping the tape taut, walk in a neat circle (as if you were the pencil of your compass), trailing one foot behind you, flattening the crop, until you get back to where you began.

**Step 3.** Now you've got a guide line, you can use your plank or roller to flatten the rest.

**Aftermath.** Some people say the crops pop back up again. Farmers say that's bollocks.

## A word on chalk figures

All bar one are pretty recent (in the grand scheme of things), and could (as with crop circles) be viewed as land art, rather than as ritually or spiritually significant.

The only really old one is the **Uffington Horse**: late Bronze Age or early Iron Age. The rest of the horses (e.g. **Westbury, Malborough, Pewsey, Devizes, etc.**) date from the late eighteenth century or later.

The two chalk giants – **Cerne Abbas**, phallus; **Long Man of Wilmington**, no phallus – aren't prehistoric either. Neither, therefore, has anything to do with any fertility god – but don't let that ruin any alfresco fun you had in mind.

# ⚠
# WHICH SNAKE AM I?

*Why couldn't the viper vipe 'er nose?*
*Because the adder 'ad 'er 'ankerchief!*
Dad joke

We are short on snakes, which gives them extra glamour.*

Whenever you discover a snake, everyone will want it to be an adder, because adder = DANGER!!! Sadly, it's nearly always a grass snake.

The books will tell you that the adder (*Vipera berus*) has a very distinctive zig-zag pattern down its back, which seems like a good tip, until you meet a grass snake (*Natrix helvetica*), which *also* has a distinctive pattern down its back. This allows you to obfuscate. Is it a zig-zag? It could be a zig-zag? It's certainly zig-zaggy enough for adder hopefuls. This, though, is the difference.

The adder has a thick black line drawn down the centre of its back, with dabs either side.

The grass snake just has dabs.

The adder, if you will, looks more like a ladder. The grass snake looks more like a climbing wall.

The adder has sinister red eyes. The grass snake has a handsome yellow and black collar.

The adder is not all that big: no longer than a toddler. The grass snake is more impressive: it can be as long as a four year old.

..........

* Terminally short, thanks to St Patrick, on the island of Ireland.

Grass snakes pop up in compost heaps, near your veg patch, around your lawn, ordinary sorts of places. So if you see a snake at home, it's probably not an adder, but there's nothing wrong with *pretending* it's one for a good half-hour, especially if you want to inject some drama into a slow afternoon with some under-sevens.

Important: make sure you reclassify well before bedtime, possibly appealing to a higher authority, or the under-sevens will be too scared to sleep (*will it crawl in through the window?*) and the whole escapade will have backfired on you. Your climb-down (*oh, my mistake, yes it was only a grass snake*) is also a really good chance to model getting things wrong with good grace which, as we all know, is a tough life skill to master.

We've only seen adders on heathland (thin-soiled, bracken-y, basking sort of places), which is where you might also see a smooth snake (*Coronella austriaca*), but honestly we doubt you will because they're very, very rare.

You might, however, come across a slow worm (*Anguis fragilis*), which looks like snake, is called a worm, but is actually a legless lizard. A slow worm is easy to identify because its head flows seamlessly into its body, whereas a snake has cheeks. If you look closely—

Sorry, sorry, you're not here for the slow worms. You're here for the adders. Back to the real snakes.

If an adder bites you (and let's be honest, it's a big if: you're really only likely to get bitten if you peer at it, poke it, pick it up, or walk slowly and quietly barefoot through bracken on a very hot day, in which case, we hate to say it, you were probably asking for it, especially if you picked it up, oh my God, don't pick up snakes, what are you, insane??) here's what to do.

Stay calm! Odds are you won't die! (Last adder death in the UK: 1975.)

Don't stay too calm. It *is* pretty serious. Call 999.

Don't try to suck or cut the venom out. You're not in a 1950s B-movie.

Don't try to capture or kill the snake. A photo, sure.

Keep the bitten part still. Watches, bracelets, tight clothes off in case it swells.

Any allergic reaction, get into the recovery position.

Paracetamol, not aspirin or ibuprofen.

If you have been bitten, you can expect immediate sharp pain (fangs!), followed by tingling, tenderness and inflammation, until your entire limb looks swollen and bruised. In a child this might spread to the whole of their body. You might also get a bad allergic reaction, which is what makes a bite more serious. This could be nausea and vomiting, stomach pain and diarrhoea, sweating and fever; or the scary feeling when your lips swell and your throat closes and you struggle to breathe; or racing pulse, light-headedness and loss of consciousness. If things are looking dicey, you might be given an anti-venom, but we're sure you'll pull through.

When you're safe back home, the first thing you need to do is ask all your friends round to celebrate your recovery with the classic British cocktail: *snakebite and black*. For the uninitiated, that's equal parts lager and cider, and a dash of Ribena. You'll feel right as rain in no time.*

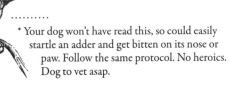

..........
\* Your dog won't have read this, so could easily startle an adder and get bitten on its nose or paw. Follow the same protocol. No heroics. Dog to vet asap.

# HORROR

.....................

*He shall find their sharpest thorns*
*In his bed at night.*
William Allingham, 'The Fairies' (1850)

Scarecrows in the dell. Intestines on the footpath. Lambs crying for their mother. The rusty lamb castrator in the ditch. Staghounds swirling around your ankles. The *boom* of pheasant guns and the *caw* of crows. Lowering mist and the sucking of bog about your feet. A man leaning on a gate who doesn't quite seem to see you. The machine whirring and grunting two fields away that you can't see. That wet and leafy walk that starts at a crossroads called Dead Woman's Ditch. The soft smile of a man leaning down to talk to you from the back of a tall hunter. Sheep feeding in a neat line at sunset like people hunting moorland for a dead child

*Hush.*

What's that noise? Is it the wind? Or is it—?

There is, to pinch journalist Joe Kennedy's reverberate phrase: 'a hard seam of terror which cuts through the terroir'. Once you're alert to it, you see it everywhere.

Sherlock Holmes, in 'The Adventure of the Copper Beeches' (1892), knows what to expect. Watson and he are riding a train west, and Watson is blithering about the spring day ... blue sky ... little fleecy white clouds ... exhilarating cold nip in the air ... foliage ... rolling hills ... peeping farms. Holmes puts him straight: 'It is my belief, Watson, founded upon my experience, that the lowest and vilest alleys in London do not present a more dreadful record of sin than does the smiling and beautiful countryside.'

The detective's take is that the loneliness, the isolation, the ignorance of country folk allow 'hellish cruelty' and 'hidden wickedness' to flourish. In the countryside, he's implying, nobody can hear you scream. And there are, after all, many and varied ways to knock off somebody you don't like: rat poison or cow stampede, man-trap or bread oven, barbed-wire garrotte or log-splitter guillotine – your choice of murder weapon is extensive. But Holmes is in the business of rational explanation (the Hound of the Baskervilles is, after all, just a big dog daubed in paint), which means he misses some of the chills the countryside has up its sleeve.

For horror, as we know, isn't just about what man can do to man, but rather about what not-man (nature?) might do to us. Such fears flicker and flare when there's darkness all around, when you're alone in a little circle of light, the campfire, the lonely inn, the farmhouse in the dell, the blue glare of your mobile phone in the middle of the woods with the battery slowly running out. That's when you start to wonder what's out there.

At the dawn of English literature, Grendel, 'that dark death shadow/ who lurked and swooped in the long nights', ravaged King Hrothgar's halls until the hero Beowulf arrived to do battle with our first demon-monster – 'a tremendous wound/ appeared on his shoulder. Sinews split/ and the bone-lapping burst' – and dispatched him for good.*

It's a story, in one way or another, that we've been telling ourselves ever since. The world outside our flame-lit mead-hall (or modern equivalent) is dark and dangerous. At any

..........

* Quotes taken from Seamus Heaney's brilliant 1999 translation.

moment, pure evil might burst through the doors and *eat us all up*. Huddle closer, friends. Cuddle the dog. Put another log on the fire and try to forget the darkness outside.

And, of course, we love these stories, because we're almost sure the evil is going to stay out there, where it belongs. In Flora Thompson's *Lark Rise to Candleford* (published in 1945 but set fifty years earlier), the village children like nothing better than to press their ears to the pub door to listen, with 'curdling blood and creeping spine' to the dark tales the men tell: the turnpike ghost and his lighted lantern; the huge black devil-dog on the lonely road with eyes of fire; the haunted gibbet where the sheep-stealers rot; the white-cloaked lady, mounted on a white horse, trotting over the bridge into town without (*gasp!*) her head.

However chilling the tales might be, the countryside itself wasn't scary for those children; the countryside was their home. But if we lose that connection, if we become estranged from the wild, then we can easily persuade ourselves that nature itself, or some personification, some spirit, might be capable of doing us harm.

And that fear goes way back.

Euripides, writing more than two thousand years ago at the peak of Athenian civilisation, was wise to this. In *The Bacchae*, something of a folk-horror trope-maker, Pentheus, the king of Thebes, makes the massive mistake of disrespecting Dionysus, the wild god. Soon enough, strange things start to happen: upright women abandon the city for the mountains, where they pillage villages, mutilate livestock, suckle baby animals, fondle snakes in their hair, all in an ecstasy of worship. The king, furious, curious, follows them into the wilds where – well, let's just say it's not a pretty ending. The take-home? Don't deny Dionysus his due.

The short-story writer Saki, hard at work during the Edwardian flood-tide of artsy middle-class nature-love, conjures an only marginally less grisly fate for Sylvia in 'The Music on the Hill'. Notwithstanding her name, he says, she was accustomed to nothing more sylvan than 'leafy Kensington'. Unlike Pentheus, she doesn't deny the wild; she does something far worse: she patronises it. She simpers about Pan (Dionysus's satyr sidekick) and, mistaking land for landscape, gazes over the Devon countryside with 'a School-of-Art appreciation'. Big mistake. The Devon countryside doesn't like it: she winds up skewered by a stag.

Film-makers in the sixties and seventies took some of these ideas and really ran with them, creating the folk-horror genre crowned by *The Wicker Man* (1973), which ends, infamously, with a policeman being burned alive as part of a pagan ceremony on a remote island.

These films often play with the same story: a naive urbanite, in his neat shoes, in his spotless car, is drawn to something in the countryside, something deep, something ancient, only to find himself in mortal danger. This danger, says Adam Scovell in *Folk Horror: Hours Dreadful and Things Strange* (2017), can come in many guises – from people who work the soil, from people who dig too deep in the soil, or simply from beneath the soil itself. Remote landscapes, backwards people, pagan religion, all the things we like to admire from the 'comfortable, lofty distance' of Romanticism, all those things, he says, come back to bite us.*

Dead Papa Toothwort, the dark creation at the heart of Max Porter's perfect novel *Lanny* (2019), is exactly the sort of pagan-spirit you'd be wise not to mess with. He's a sort of Bad Green Man, an old local legend who, neutered and defanged, might merit a mention in the county guidebook. The kids at the local primary school still draw pictures of him at Halloween, and he hates how they muddle him with the baddies they watch on TV. Wasn't I (he asks himself) much more frightening when the children drew me leafy and green?

He needn't worry. Porter breathes strange and dreadful life into him: a boy called Lanny vanishes and Dead Papa Toothwort is to blame. But, of course, nobody in the village knows that. How could they? He isn't *real*. Instead, they point the finger at Pete, a local artist, a loner, an (entirely

..........

* Some folk-horror films do, admittedly, veer towards the schlocky, which has made the genre ripe for re-invention – or pastiche. The TV comedy series *The League of Gentlemen* ('this is a local shop for local people') and the hysterical 2012 film *Sightseeing* (Candice-Marie from *Nuts in May* on a killing spree) both play the same tropes for laughs.

innocent) old man who's been giving Lanny drawing lessons. It was him, says the village. It has to be him. He's a paedophile. He's the monster.

In some ways, Sherlock Holmes is (as you'd expect) quite right. Monsters can't hurt us, but we can hurt each other; we can hurt ourselves.

In Niall Griffiths's *Sheepshagger* (2001), by far the scariest of all the scary things we read and watched, another boy, Ianto, has grown up poor and marginalised. One day, he walks up to 'the place of his odd childhood', a house on a Welsh hillside. It has new owners, a patio, a corrugated carport, a barbecue pit. His friend tries to coax him away, but Ianto stands his ground: 'I just want-a stand on-a fuckin soil, mun. That's all I want-a do. Fuck all wrong with that, is there, just standin on-a fuckin soil?' A man in aviator sunglasses warns him off, telling him he's on private land. Ianto, in his torn and dirty clothes, wavers, impotent, before these 'clean and moneyed people, occupiers of his childhood'.

There's an intimate connection between Ianto and the land, and both are in great pain. Later, he hides under a bridge, crouching troll-like, bramble-gashed, emerging to bludgeon a (wholesome rambling Romantic) boy to death, the first in a series of acts of unspeakable (although Griffiths has the skill to speak of it) violence. For the abuse Ianto once suffered (at the hands of an Englishman with a guide to Celtic Britain in his cagoule pocket) has turned him into a monster, worse than Grendel, worse than Papa Toothwort, because, in the end, he's *real*.

However much we try to divert ourselves with spooky shadow-shapes flickering on the mead-hall wall, the horrors prowling outside today are very real too. The heavy tread, the hot breath – of climate change. Waking in the Mordor swelter of a July dawn to prune the apple trees before the sun is dangerously high, watching the land turn brown, the streams run dry, the hillsides smoulder, running with sand-bags when a flash flood swoops towards the kitchen after the heatwave breaks – those, we're afraid to say, those are the true horror stories of today.

# MAD COWS AND ENGLISHMEN

*the wonderful rinderpest, rain rot and sheep scab*
Max Porter, *Lanny* (2019)

'For Britain's urban population,' writes Bella Bathurst in *Field Work*, her close-quarters account of farming lives today, 'Covid came out of the sky, a once-in-a-century event, random as a meteorite. For its rural population, Covid looked more like a continuum, a thing to add to the land's long list of adaptations.' Among those, the frontrunners are:

- **bovine tuberculosis** (leads to the slaughter of thousands of infected cows every year, plus thousands of badgers, otherwise a protected species, culled because they are thought to spread the disease)
- **foot-and-mouth** (closed the countryside in summer 2001, forcing anguished and angry farmers to slaughter six million healthy sheep, pigs and cattle to halt its spread)
- **bovine spongiform encephalopathy** (or BSE or mad cow disease, which is most famous because, as well as causing a horrible disease in cattle, it can cause a horrible disease in us).

It was December 1984 when this new disease was first detected in a herd in Sussex, and back then it was a puzzler. Nothing quite like it had been seen before, but the animals' disturbing behaviour – a strange and stumbling walk, awful trembling, a weird frenzy – helped scientists join the dots, connecting it with *scrapie*, a degenerative brain disease that infects sheep.*

Scrapie belongs to a family of diseases called transmissible spongiform encephalopathies (TSEs). *Transmissible* means it can pass from individual to individual, although luckily not very easily. *Spongiform* means the brain becomes dotted with microscopic holes (i.e. like a sponge). *Encephalopathy* means a disorder of the brain.

TSEs are caused by prions, which are misfolded proteins that somehow trigger misfolding in other proteins, although why they misfold in the first place is beyond both us and science. Crucially, though, prions are very hard to destroy. They can withstand heat, radiation and formaldehyde, things that would easily see off other infectious agents, such as TB bacteria or the Covid virus. And that, obviously, is a big problem.

Back to the cows, who were dying from something that wasn't scrapie, but was certainly awfully similar. How, then, did the first cow get infected with this new disease? One theory (and it's only a theory) is that BSE was triggered by a genetic mutation in Cow Zero, possibly triggered by Cow Zero eating a sheep with scrapie—

Hold your horses!

What?

Cows *ate* sheep?

Yes, and so when Cow A was slaughtered, it entered the

..........

* Afflicted sheep *scrape* themselves non-stop against fence posts and walls, as if plagued by intense itching, hence the name.

food chain, and so could easily have ended up being eaten by other cows—

Whoaoooooah!

What?

Cows ate *cows*?

Yes.

In the name of all that is holy, why?

Well, cows need protein (the correctly folded type), the same as we do. But a cow has to plough through a lot of grass / hay / silage to get what it needs. Much more efficient, then, to offer it proper protein (as meat fans call meat), in the form of cow biscuits, brimming with meaty goodness, made from the unwanted meaty bits of other slaughtered animals.

Waste not?

Want not.

'You could think of it,' wrote science journalist Tim Radford, 'as grass in concentrated form. In the interests of cheap food bovids with naturally coarse vegetarian tastes have been persuaded to turn not just to carnivory, but to a tasty form of cannibalism as well.'

And so, once Cows One, Two, Three, Four and Five ate the remains of Cow Zero, somehow the original mutation was passed on and on and on, until, by the time the epidemic was over, it's estimated that more than 180,000 cattle got sick, while another 1–3 million were infected but remained asymptomatic, most of whom would have been slaughtered for human consumption before developing any sign of the disease.

But, back in the 1980s, what was the government to do? Scrapie had been a problem for a while (since at least the eighteenth century), but there'd never been any sign that it could jump either from sheep to shepherd, or from sheep to sheep-eater. Initially, therefore, the government crossed its fingers and hoped the same would prove true of BSE, simply ordering a cull of infected animals. In 1988, they said we should no longer put bits of cow (or other ruminants) in cow-food. In 1989, they said, just to be on the safe side, that we should all stop eating cow offal – eyes, brain, spinal cord, thymus, tonsils, spleen and intestine, i.e. the bits that were more likely to contain the infectious agent. This came as something of a surprise to people who hadn't realised they were eating those bits in the first place. In fact, the whole thing was starting to put us right off British beef. And so, in 1990, the agriculture minister invited the press to watch his small daughter (blonde bob, pale blue Alice band) eat a beefburger. She recoiled; it was too hot. Demand for domestic beef tanked.

Much worse was to come.

In the mid-90s, young people started presenting with a degenerative brain disease, which was like Creutzfeldt–Jakob disease (CJD), a rare but fatal human TSE, but not *exactly* like it. This disease, which we now call variant-CJD (vCJD), is caused by eating cows infected with BSE. It has killed 178 people in the UK, with the last person dying in 2016. There is no cure.

Accounts of the illness, given by the families of the victims, are extremely painful to read. The disease doesn't only cause people to lose control of their limbs, it also triggers psychosis and dementia. Roger Tomkins said that by the time his daughter, Clare, died in 1998, she couldn't walk and was in constant distress: 'The most harrowing thing was when she was in bed and would howl like an injured animal. She looked at you as if you were the devil incarnate.'

Inevitably, everyone was extremely worried. In the year that Clare and nearly twenty other people died, the sober *Economist* wrote: 'It is not yet clear, nor is it likely to be clear for several years, whether those deaths are the harbinger of a plague.' Very, very thankfully, they weren't. The deaths of those 178 people were a truly terrible tragedy for the individuals and their families, but as for the rest of us – we can move on.

Right?

Well ... here's a thing.

There's another disease called *kuru*, an equally fatal TSE, which caused an epidemic amongst the Fore people of Papua New Guinea.* Their funeral rites once involved cooking and eating certain parts of their dead family members, including their brains, a custom which allowed kuru to pass from person to person. When they abandoned the practice in the 1960s, you'd have hoped that kuru would

..........

* *Kuru* means *trembling*. It's also known as *laughing sickness*.

quickly die out. Unfortunately, the long incubation period meant that the epidemic lasted throughout the second half of the twentieth century, killing as many as 200 Fore people (out of a population of only 20,000) a year, until it finally ran its course.

And so, when it comes to vCJD, the uncomfortable conclusion is that we might not be out of the woods yet. Researchers examined 32,000 samples of human tissue removed during appendix operations carried out at 41 hospitals over 12 years. The results, published in the *British Medical Journal* in 2013, suggest that one in 2,000 people have the problematic misfolded prions. And if you ate British beef in the 1980s (raising our hands here), there's unfortunately no reason why one of those people couldn't be you, even if you've never exhibited a single symptom.

Sorry. We wish we'd not written this chapter, either.

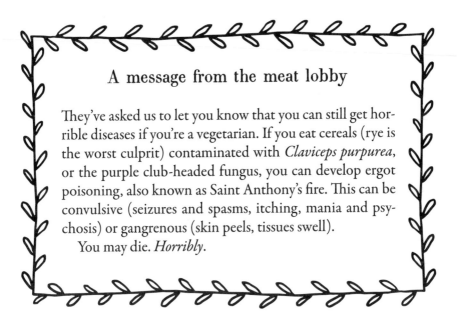

## A message from the meat lobby

They've asked us to let you know that you can still get horrible diseases if you're a vegetarian. If you eat cereals (rye is the worst culprit) contaminated with *Claviceps purpurea*, or the purple club-headed fungus, you can develop ergot poisoning, also known as Saint Anthony's fire. This can be convulsive (seizures and spasms, itching, mania and psychosis) or gangrenous (skin peels, tissues swell).

You may die. *Horribly.*

# LOUD WITHOUT THE WIND WAS ROARING

by Emily Brontë

Loud without the wind was roaring
Through th'autumnal sky;
Drenching wet, the cold rain pouring,
Spoke of winter nigh.
All too like that dreary eve,
Did my exiled spirit grieve.
Grieved at first, but grieved not long,
Sweet – how softly sweet! – it came;
Wild words of an ancient song,
Undefined, without a name.

'It was spring, and the skylark was singing:'
Those words they awakened a spell;
They unlocked a deep fountain, whose springing,
Nor absence, nor distance can quell.

In the gloom of a cloudy November
They uttered the music of May;
They kindled the perishing ember
Into fervour that could not decay.

Awaken, o'er all my dear moorland,
West-wind, in thy glory and pride!
Oh! call me from valley and lowland,
To walk by the hill-torrent's side!

It is swelled with the first snowy weather;
The rocks they are icy and hoar,
And sullenly waves the long heather,
And the fern leaves are sunny no more.

There are no yellow stars on the mountain
The bluebells have long died away
From the brink of the moss-bedded fountain –
From the side of the wintry brae.

But lovelier than corn-fields all waving
In emerald, and vermeil, and gold,
Are the heights where the north-wind is raving,
And the crags where I wandered of old.

It was morning: the bright sun was beaming;
How sweetly it brought back to me
The time when nor labour nor dreaming
Broke the sleep of the happy and free!

But blithely we rose as the dawn-heaven
Was melting to amber and blue,
And swift were the wings to our feet given,
As we traversed the meadows of dew.

For the moors! For the moors, where the short grass
Like velvet beneath us should lie!
For the moors! For the moors, where each high pass
Rose sunny against the clear sky!

For the moors, where the linnet was trilling
Its song on the old granite stone;
Where the lark, the wild sky-lark, was filling
Every breast with delight like its own!

What language can utter the feeling
Which rose, when in exile afar,
On the brow of a lonely hill kneeling,
I saw the brown heath growing there?

It was scattered and stunted, and told me
That soon even that would be gone:
It whispered, 'The grim walls enfold me,
I have bloomed in my last summer's sun.'

But not the loved music, whose waking
Makes the soul of the Swiss die away,
Has a spell more adored and heartbreaking
Than, for me, in that blighted heath lay.

The spirit which bent 'neath its power,
How it longed – how it burned to be free!
If I could have wept in that hour,
Those tears had been heaven to me.

Well – well; the sad minutes are moving,
Though loaded with trouble and pain;
And some time the loved and the loving
Shall meet on the mountains again!

# THE UPLANDS

..................................

Daniel Defoe, on his *Tour Thro' the Whole Island* in the 1720s, took against our moorlands, especially the Peak District.

> Upon the top of that mountain begins a vast extended moor or waste, which, for fifteen or sixteen miles together due north, presents you with neither hedge, house or tree, but a waste and houling wilderness, over which when strangers travel, they are obliged to take guides, or it would be next to impossible not to lose their way.

Why would he, or anyone else, leave behind the green valley, the bright shoreline, the comprehensible town and enter this other-world of lashing rain, barren soil and twisted trees? A moor was a dangerous place where a king might lose his mind or make dangerous promises to the forces of darkness, where a hero must kill or be killed, where vanquished villains vanished into the sucking bog, their screams muffled by mouthfuls of mire. Culturally, our uplands became a jumbled imaginative landscape where Heathcliff might buy a Doone clansman a drink at the Jamaica Inn after he accidentally trod on the Hound of the Baskervilles's tail.

Saddleworth Moor, on the other hand, where Myra Hindley and Ian Brady buried the bodies of the children they murdered in the 1960s, is a very real place, but those horrible crimes have been absorbed into myth, inspiring Morrissey to sing how the 'lilacked' moors could not hide the smell of death. That was 1984, but the lyrics would have made instant emotional sense to Defoe two-and-a-half centuries earlier.

### ... TO HERO ...

But for other people, the purple precocity of the heather (and the golden gorse, the red-brown bracken) triggers an entirely different set of associations: wild remote elemental empty high free trackless untouched natural open empty raw beautiful.

'There is another Britain, to many of us the better half, a land of mountains and moorland and of sun and clouds,' wrote W. H. Pearsall, an archetypal moor fan, in 1950. 'It lies now, as always, beyond the margins of our industrial and urban civilisations, fading into the western mist and washed by northern seas, its needs forgotten and its possibilities unknown.'

And it's thanks to this deeply seated love that our moors are much better protected than our lowlands, which is ironic, because the lowlands (that patchwork quilt) are actually more distinctive.* Nor are the moors an ur-landscape like Yellowstone or Yosemite; they are, in fact, only a few thousand years old, the birch, pine and alder cleared by Neolithic people, whose traces remain, marked in gothic lettering on Ordnance Survey maps. The heather and bracken? That's only there because generations of burning and grazing killed off all the tree seedlings.

Whence, then, this passion, this upland bias? Marion Shoard, in her essay 'The Lure of the Moors', explains:

..........

* The first national parks were pretty much all uplands: the Peak District, Exmoor, Dartmoor, the Yorkshire Dales and the North York Moors. The Norfolk Broads had to wait until 1989 for an official designation; the New Forest 2005; the South Downs 2010.

Since the dawn of the Romantic era [...] it is the human individual who has been venerated in the West, and we have all felt obligated to seek ourselves. Those attracted to wilderness landscape seem to be seeking a context for the pursuit of their individual identity away from the herd. To do this, they need to get away from the environment their fellow men have created for the group to a place as devoid as possible of what is obviously human handiwork. (It apparently does not matter if the landscape is in fact man-made – like a grouse moor – so long as it looks 'natural'.) A variety of other living things is also unhelpful: what is sought is a blank canvas on which individuals can commune with themselves or their Maker.

### ... TO VILLAIN AGAIN

And today, more and more people are asking whether we've got it right. Are our moors stunning, liberating, saved, or are they in fact unnatural, privileged, problematic? We're no longer invited to see them as places of great natural beauty, but as barren, sterile deserts, testament to devastation and degradation, *sheep-wrecked and grouse-trashed,* in the campaigner George Monbiot's memorable phrase. The villain is no longer the highwayman or Heathcliff, but the set-in-their-ways sheep farmer and the grouse-shooting landowner, who between them, say activists, have done to our uplands what cattle ranching is doing to Brazil's rainforests.*

Welcome to the frontline of environmental debate.

..........

* We do have an awful lot of sheep. Spain is the EU's biggest sheep player, with a headcount of roughly 15 million. We, by contrast, have 22 million, despite having far less space and far more people.

# SHEEP EXPLAINED, SOMEWHAT

Medieval England was a major exporter of wool and (later, once Flemish weavers fleeing the Hundred Years' War settled here) finished cloth. Thanks to hefty state backing, our wool dominance continued into the industrial age, when it was eclipsed first by Spanish and then by Australian sheep; and now, of course, the invention of synthetics means wool demand is a fraction of what it once was. Today, it's all about raising fat lambs for the table, which requires careful breeding.

Hill sheep, **Scottish Blackface**, **Welsh Mountain** or **Swaledale**, are robust and make good mothers, but might only bear one lamb. Less hardy breeds – **Bluefaced Leicester** is a favourite – might have two or three lambs and, what's more, have the milk to feed them, but they're a bit wet. And finally, if it's weight you're after, you need to look to the **Suffolk** (or the French **Charolais** or the **Dutch Texel**).

The trick is to cross a hill ewe with a Bluefaced Leicester ram to create a **mule** (i.e. ewes capable of producing lots of lambs, yet canny enough to look after them).* Next, cross your ewe mule, which will have a distinctive Roman nose and a speckled black-and-white face, with a meaty ram.

This should help explain the different sorts of sheep you might encounter. If you're walking the heights, you'll see sheep which have a more artisanal look: perhaps an

..........

* You might feel less enthusiastic about *lots of lambs* once you've spent a long night in a freezing lambing shed, elbow-deep in a ewe's birth canal, trying to disentangle a pair of twins who are refusing to agree which one is going to come out first.

interesting horn or a dashing black or grey coat, certainly a wry and doughty glint in their eye, definitely a regional flavour. In the Lake District, for example, this would be the rugged **Herdwick**, which are *hefted* to the hills, meaning the ewes teach their lambs where they belong, reducing the need for fencing. Elsewhere you might find the **Exmoor Horn** (curly horns; lambs have fluffy trousers), the **Welsh Mountain** (long tails), or the **Rough Fell** (white stripe on black nose).

But away from the hills, the sheep you meet are probably ewe mules. In the autumn, you'll notice that they have red or blue splotches on their bottoms, which is evidence that the meaty ram, the *terminal sire*, wearing a dye-marker block harnessed to his chest, has done his work. These rams often work in threes. Two to fight, one to *serve*. The resulting lambs will be ready for market when they're three to four months old.

# GOOD FENCES MAKE GOOD NEIGHBOURS: THE DRYSTONE WALL

The *dry* in drystone wall means you can't use mortar or cement, but instead you stack stones like pieces of mismatched Lego. They're especially good in cold places, because there's no need to worry about cement cracking; in rocky places, because there's no need to worry about driving posts into the ground; in treeless places, because there's no need to worry about how on earth you're going to grow a hedge. In other words, they're perfect on our uplands.

They also do exceptional service on North Ronaldsay, the northernmost island in Orkney, where the sheep have evolved to thrive on a diet of seaweed, feeding at low tide, ruminating at high tide. A drystane dyke (another way of saying drystone wall) confines them to the shoreline, in case they get any ideas about changing up their diet.

And so, if you're the kind of person who thinks that you and only you have the power to load a dishwasher or the boot of a car, this could be your dream job. You need:

- A large pile of local stone (flat is easiest, but you can work with anything)
- A length of string on a spool
- A spirit level
- An A-frame (to get the right taper in your wall)
- A spade, a Devon shovel, a pick-axe
- A walling hammer
- Friends and family (or other willing volunteers)

Now, let's imagine you're starting from scratch.

1. Determine dimensions. Let's say your wall will be 26 inches wide at the base, tapering to 16 inches at the top, and about 4 feet high above the ground.
2. Dig a trench 26 inches wide and about a foot deep, using your string to mark it out.
3. While you're digging, commission your friends/ family/volunteers to sort your stones into three piles: small, medium and large. Set aside the longest stones, which you'll use to hold the front and back of the wall together.
4. Line your trench with large stones, plugging any gaps with smaller ones.
5. Start building, course by course, using gradually smaller stones as you gain height. Always overlap your stones from one course to the next. Do not stack them vertically. Use smaller stones in the middle of the wall to help lock larger stones together.
6. You can use your walling hammer to knock stones into shape if you need a better fit.
7. When you hit the 40-inch mark, you can install a course of coping stones. They should be long enough (16 inches

or so) to span the width of your wall. Lay them vertically and tightly packed together.

8. Stand back and enjoy your gift to posterity.

## FARMING: FUTURE

*We must have change. We must have it! I didn't farm like my*
*father and George don't farm the same as me.*
Melissa Harrison, *All Among the Barley* (2018)

Farming is at a crossroads, or a very tricky roundabout, or a narrow bit where a tree's come down, or a dangerous dip full of murky floodwater. The old certainties, the old orthodoxies, that it was a farmer's job (morally, financially) to produce as much food as possible, as efficiently as possible, have fallen by the wayside.

'The idea that we can choose faster growth at the expense of our environment shows an inadequate understanding,' says *not* your local Green Party candidate, but William Hague, one-time Tory leader. '[We] are biological creatures that need a thriving ecosystem around us, not gods who can dispense with it if we wish,' he wrote in *The Times* in 2022.

But how to achieve this thriving ecosystem, while at the same time growing food that is both high quality and affordable?

Until we left the European Union, it was 'Brussels', that convenient whipping boy, which was largely responsible for the answers: for determining how much subsidy farmers received, and for what. When the Common Agricultural Policy paid you per head of cattle, more animals meant more money. When it paid you per hectare, more land meant more money. When it started to pay you (a bit) per hedge re-planted, more greenery meant (a bit) more money.*

And if things weren't quite working, everyone knew what do: *blame Brussels*. Now, though, we have to come up with the answers ourselves, and if we get it wrong, we're only going to have ourselves to blame.

It is, undoubtedly, a complicated issue, and farmers and environmentalists (some people are one, some are the other, a small but increasing number are both) find it immensely frustrating when shifts in the political weather obstruct their ability to plan for the longer term. Farmers need the Department for Environment Food & Rural Affairs (Defra) to offer them both expertise and stability, but that can be in short supply from ministers passing through on their way to more glamorous cabinet jobs.

In *Field Work* (2021), a sensitive and nuanced account of farming today, Bella Bathurst has a long conversation with a former senior civil servant who sums up his colleagues thus: 'The vast majority of Defra staff have never lived in or had anything to do with the countryside. They just don't get it.' More recently still, during the glory days of the Liz Truss premiership, one exasperated source told *The Times*: 'In an introductory meeting with Defra officials, one minister said they had always loved gardening, and spent half an hour talking about their favourite Beatrix Potter characters.'

Since the Brexit vote, then, there have been *seven* Defra ministers: Liz Truss, Andrea Leadsom, Michael Gove, Theresa Villiers, George Eustice, Ranil Jayawardena and Thérèse Coffey, all of whom have wrestled with varying

..........

* A bit more money for a lot more fiddly form-filling, especially if you've got an old computer, rubbish broadband and you never much liked working at a desk in the first place.

degrees of success with the job's fundamental conflict: are you on the side of E-for-environment or F-for-food?

Some farmers have taken matters into their own hands and diversified, thereby massively reducing their reliance on government policy. Around two-thirds of farms now do more than farm: they put up solar panels or wind turbines; they run campsites or glampsites; they rent barns to mail-order businesses or Pilates teachers or caravan owners; they run pheasant shoots; they open bakeries; they build natural burial sites, all while their grandfathers are turning in their old-fashioned graves. The canniest of all hire planning consultants to get their land approved by the council for the best crop of all – houses.

Some people thrive on offering this sort of complementary, experiential stuff, or on the wheeling and dealing, but it's *far* from being everyone's cup of tea. Some people just want to farm, but what *is* the right way to farm in the twenty-first century? We're going to present two of the main schools of thought, while also allowing that for some farmers the answer is *we're fine as we are, thank you.*

### THEORY A: LAND SHARING
This takes as its starting point the idea that our landscape has been created by farming co-existing with the natural world. It doesn't accept a farming vs nature, all-or-nothing binary. If we farm sensitively, the theory goes, in balance with nature, we can encourage wildlife to thrive, we can regenerate habitats – and we can grow good food.

In *English Pastoral*, James Rebanks writes enthusiastically about the possibilities of this approach, which demands that we break down the barriers between the farm and the environment and that we encourage cross-fertilisation between hard-headed agronomists and starry-eyed ecologists.

He relates how a woman called Lucy, who works for a river conservation charity without being 'lofty or know-it-all', came to talk to him about small changes (think of them as un-improvements) he could make to the streams on his land: letting them return to their natural course, fencing them off from his livestock, allowing them to become 'bustling little highways for wildlife'. This was his first step in managing his part of the Lake District 'for something other than farming', but he's very frank about the downsides: 'Farming for nature is economic suicide.' He can 'earn a crust away from the farm', he has a wife who does 'countless unheralded jobs', and so he could listen to the Lucys, take the small grants, make the small changes; others won't be able to do the same until the government ushers in a greener subsidy system, which is what – in theory – is on its way.

With land sharing, it's likely that the bits of land you do farm, you'll farm less chemically, whether that means doing away with artificial fertiliser and pesticides altogether, or working to limit their use as much as possible. You might also lean on the principles of regenerative agriculture, which goes back to basics, and says that before everything else, look to your soil. You will probably avoid monocultures; you will probably keep some livestock to manure your fields; you will probably be keen on cover crops (mustard, clover, phacelia, vetch, buckwheat) to minimise erosion and act as green manure.

'One field, just one field, made a difference,' writes John Lewis-Stempel in *The Running Hare* (2016), his account of how he undid the impact of decades of intensive farming on one small patch of land. 'If we had a thousand fields …'

It is, indeed, very tempting to dream of lovely big field margins, of wildlife corridors, of hedgerows and woodlands and ponds, of access for walkers and schools, of flocks of dormice and hedgehogs, of woodpeckers and voles, of wildflowers thrumming with hoverflies and lacewings – but there is a rub. If you farm less intensively, you need to farm more land to produce the same number of calories, which brings us to another big elephant in the field.

Rearing meat takes up more land than growing plants, and ethical meat takes up even more land than bog-standard meat. Currently, only 15 per cent of the UK is used to grow potatoes, fruit and veg, whereas beef and lamb account for 40 per cent. (And that's not even factoring in all the land overseas which is used to grow cattle feed.) 'A shift in our diets towards more plant-based content,' writes farmer Jake Fiennes (no ardent vegan) in *Land Healer* (2022), 'would use our farmland more efficiently.' However, his non-confrontational suggestion that our farming and our eating should be a lot more vegetarian is a conversation nobody's prepared to have (yet).*

And, anyway, even if we are growing and eating more vegetarian protein (beans grow well here, but lentils and chickpeas remain a relatively tough gig in the British climate), critics of land sharing say that however nice your farm is, it's still a farm – it's still not natural. Which brings us to …

THEORY B: LAND SPARING

This takes as its starting point the idea that it's better to have all your farming squished into as small a place as possible, and to grow as much food as possible, with the best technology available, on the best and most productive

..........

* There's also the possibility of lab-grown meat, warmly advocated by George Monbiot in *Regenesis* (2022). But he is aware of the drawbacks: 'There's a real danger that this revolution could be captured by big business, creating a system that replicates some of the faults and frailties of the Global Standard Farm.'

farmland. If you do this, the theory goes, you can then free up your marginal, your unproductive bits of land for – rewilding.*

Campaigners want at least 5 per cent of the countryside to be 'core' rewilding zones, where large-scale wild ecosystems can flourish, with another 25 per cent dedicated to a combination of full-on rewilding, wild-ish farming and nature-friendly farming. (As you can see, there's no hard border between land sparing and land sharing.)

What exactly rewilding is, though, depends who you talk to, but essentially it's human retreat, however managed, from the landscape. What it's not, is conservation. As George Monbiot writes in *Feral* (2013): 'Rewilding has no end points, no view about what a "right" ecosystem or a "right" assemblage of species looks like. It does not strive to produce a heath, a meadow, a rainforest, a kelp garden or a coral reef. It lets nature decide.' You might introduce absent plants and animals, you might cull intruders, but then you remove fences, remove the drains, step back, and let nature do what it does best.

As a plan, it is extremely popular. 'The fashion for rewilding has spread from a few landowners rich enough to experiment and now encompasses a broader mass of bien-pensants who regard farmers as money-grubbing vulgarians polluting the countryside,' writes Ferdinand Mount

..........

* Tom Cox, in his very clever short story collection, *Help the Witch* (2018), offers this vision of the twenty-third century: 'It was long into the time of the Self-Righteous Men, and England was divided: not by north and south, as it once had been, but by west and east. In the east, electricity remained, for the moment, and the greedy and dynastically entitled lived well, as they always had, but more so. In the rewilded west, weeds and trees burst through the tarmac, and vigilantes roamed back and forth across the wood border, picking off rich travellers with the organic arrows from their organic crossbows, then taking the spoils back to large forest communes and distributing them under the eyes of fox and badger effigies.'

(right-wing but not uber-right-wing) with reliable pithiness in the *London Review of Books*. And honestly, when has an ecological concept become so embedded, so fast? We no longer just think about rewilding farmland: we rewild *ourselves*, whether that means camping without our phones or neglecting to depilate our pubic hair.

But if the idea has been taken up joyfully in the town, there has been serious push-back in some parts of the countryside, especially where people feel 'their' land is being singled out as a possible rewilding site. A sheep farmer in the Lake District, say, or a member of the Farmers Union of Wales might complain that it all amounts to nothing but land abandonment, which is what you call rewilding if you don't like it. They might also warn that the diverse landscapes we dream of can take many lifetimes to come into being; that for decades we'd be up against the domineering species which have evolved to colonise uncultivated land.

Others complain that this is another stitch-up job, that small farmers, tenant farmers, will end up losing out (once again) to the big landowners. You can see why: to take part, for example, in a pilot rewilding project, for which the government was prepared to pay you well, you needed at least 500 hectares, which is more than 1,200 acres, which is a *lot* of land. Paul Kingsnorth, meanwhile, laments how the retreat of farming would very likely spell an end to unsentimental, everyday links between people and place: 'On the surface, it probably makes sense. Beneath, there's a sadness.' You can also, if you want to be really antagonistic, simply shrug and say, 'Oh rewilding ... isn't that just landscape gardening on an epic scale?'

All this has led wise heads to argue for a more neutral term – nature recovery – to defuse some of the tension. Others have stressed that it's not about driving people off the land their families have worked for generations, but about providing different jobs, different opportunities on the same land. Jobs in farming would become jobs in stewardship or tourism. Rewilded areas would need wardens and guides, B&Bs and whortleberry-jam shops, clay-pigeon ranges and fishing lakes, bicycle hire and riding stables, falconry, archery, the opportunities are endless, and all of which will keep shops, communities and pubs alive. If, that is, you don't mind chasing the town's pound.

As we go to print in early 2023, all parts of the UK are finally transitioning towards new subsidy regimes which are designed to reward sustainable farming, small-scale local nature recovery and large-scale landscape recovery. Farmers in the future will no longer receive a basic (area-based) payment, with optional top-up countryside stewardship (environmental) grants; henceforward, they'll get paid for the green stuff.

This will radically alter farmers' income streams. Some may thrive (the arable baron in Norfolk; the estate manager backed by a green-minded super-rich landowner), but others, those who are already on the brink, will likely be out of business. The most vulnerable are smaller, family farms, which will struggle, for example, to stump up the consultants' fees they're going to need to pay to figure out how to meet the new criteria.

There are warnings too, especially in the light of the war in Ukraine, that the (noble) goal of maximising 'the value to society of the landscape' butts up against tough questions about our food security. But, say the optimists, surely we can always import the food we need? Sure, say the pessimists, now we can, while there's food available to buy, while the pound's still got some life left in it, but who knows what the future might bring? And anyway, is it right to make *our* land as wild and beautiful and natural as we possibly can while buying (chemically farmed, low-welfare) food from poorer, producer-countries who are still degrading *theirs*?

These are exceedingly tough questions, but at least more and more people are talking about the answers. The Common Agricultural Policy was once shorthand for something too boring even to begin to think about, but how the government (our elected representatives) supports farmers (with our taxes) to grow food (for us) on the land (where we all live), that is something about which non-farmers are becoming increasingly interested.

And that can only be a good thing.

# THE TABLES TURNED

by William Wordsworth

Up! up! my Friend, and quit your books;
Or surely you'll grow double:
Up! up! my Friend, and clear your looks;
Why all this toil and trouble?

The sun above the mountain's head,
A freshening lustre mellow
Through all the long green fields has spread,
His first sweet evening yellow.

Books! 'tis a dull and endless strife:
Come, hear the woodland linnet,
How sweet his music! on my life,
There's more of wisdom in it.

And hark! how blithe the throstle sings!
He, too, is no mean preacher:
Come forth into the light of things,
Let Nature be your teacher.

She has a world of ready wealth,
Our minds and hearts to bless—
Spontaneous wisdom breathed by health,
Truth breathed by cheerfulness.

One impulse from a vernal wood
May teach you more of man,
Of moral evil and of good,
Than all the sages can.

Sweet is the lore which Nature brings;
Our meddling intellect
Mis-shapes the beauteous forms of things:—
We murder to dissect.

Enough of Science and of Art;
Close up those barren leaves;
Come forth, and bring with you a heart
That watches and receives.

# ACKNOWLEDGEMENTS

We would like to say thank you to:

**Louisa Dunnigan**. You've been an incredibly supportive and unfailingly insightful editor, cheering and chivvying us in precisely the perfect measure. It's thanks to you that *Country Matters* has mulched down to the fine tilth it is today, and we're *immensely* grateful. (That one deserved italics.)

**Cecily Gayford**. It was wonderful working with you on *Sea Fever*; we're so glad you brought us back to land.

**Victoria Hobbs**. We do hope you've enjoyed this advertorial for the Quantocks. (Jonny swears he's working on your steps.)

**Paul Forty**. It has been (and is being!) a pleasure. Never has a book felt in more capable hands.

**James Alexander.** Your remarkable skill and tenacity have turned our sprawling raw material into a truly stunning book.

**Lucy Devenish.** Any ideas what we should write next? The world needs more of your lovely pictures.

**Friends, family and neighbours.** Our conversations with you are threaded through this book like so many hyphae. We're grateful to everyone who's shared their experiences, their opinions, their expertise, their books – and their eagle eyes. We're especially indebted to: Richard Barber, Kate Best, Bernard Davis, Hugo van Dorssen, Gay Edwards, Oli Frost, Natasha Ivey, Martin Jones, the Somerset Moleman, David Montgomery, Jack Sheldrake, Chris Skelmersdale and David Wood.

But *Country Matters* is, above all, testament to the memory of **Adrian Little** and **Frank Taylor**, who introduced us to farming and gardening many years ago.

Penultimately, a massive shout-out to **Rupert** for being both Romantic and romantic, not to mention for living cheek by jowl with his in-laws with such aplomb. (Sorry we deleted the pic showing the difference between a mature spring onion and an immature leek; that one was for you.)

And last but the opposite of least: **Jane**, mightiest of matriarchs, horticultural colossus, proof-shark, jam-wizard, Latinist supreme, permissions wrangler, lamb disentangler, doughty London emigrée and all-round legend of the land. We stand on the shoulders of a giant.

# COPYRIGHT PERMISSIONS

The authors and publisher wish to thank the following for kind permission to reproduce copyright material.

The poem 'Caribbean Eye over Yorkshire' from *We Brits* (2006) by John Agard on page 231 is reproduced with the permission of Bloodaxe Books. The epigraph taken from *The Longest Journey* (1907) by E. M. Forster on page 5 is reproduced with the permission of the Provost and Scholars of King's College, Cambridge, and The Society of Authors as the Literary Representative of the Estate of E. M. Forster. The epigraph taken from *Being a Beast* (2016) by Charles Foster on page 186 is reproduced with the permission of Profile Books. The epigraph taken from *All Among the Barley* (2018) by Melissa Harrison on page 338 is reproduced with the permission of Bloomsbury Publishing. The epigraph taken from *Meadows* (2004) by Christopher Lloyd on page 75 is reproduced by kind permission of the Great Dixter Charitable Trust. The epigraph taken from *Lanny* (2019) by Max Porter on page 322 is reproduced with the permission of Faber and Faber. The epigraph taken from *The Odyssey: A Stage*

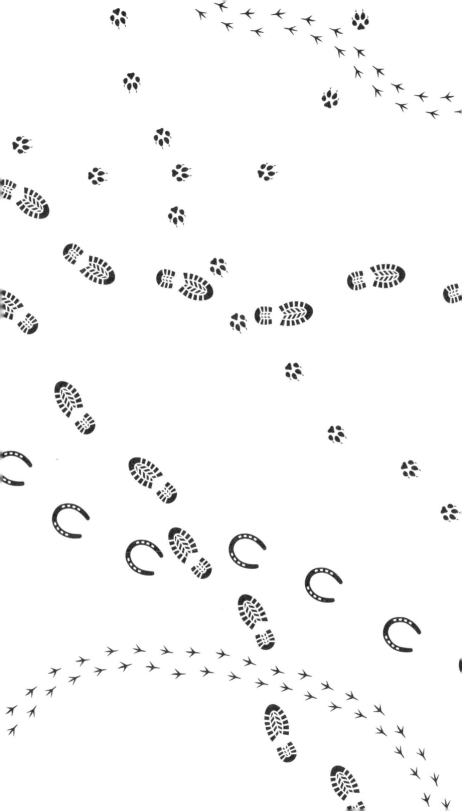

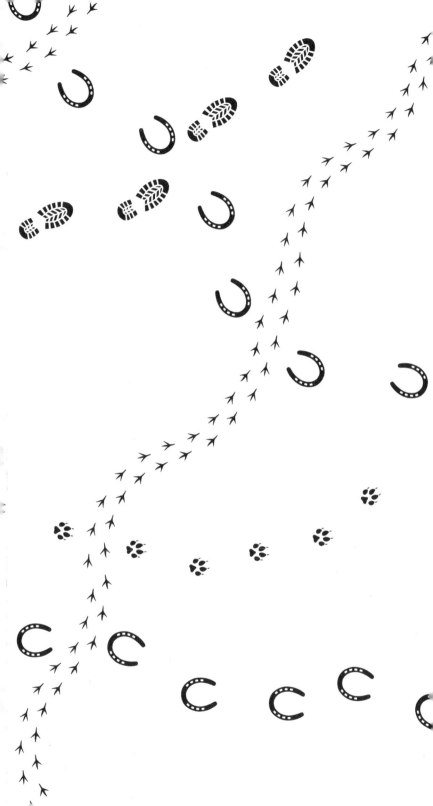